The Little General: Gene Mauch
A Baseball Life

Mel Proctor

Blue River Press
Indianapolis

Published by Blue River Press
Indianapolis, Indiana
www.brpressbooks.com

Distributed by Cardinal Publishers Group
2402 N. Shadeland Avenue, Suite A
Indianapolis, IN 46219
317-352-8200 phone
317-352-8202 fax
www.cardinalpub.com

ISBN: 978-1-935628-53-8

Cover Design: Phil Velikan
Cover Photos Courtesy of the Los Angeles Angels of Anaheim
Proofreader: Charleen Davis
Book Design: Dave Reed

Printed in the United States of America

10 9 8 7 6 5 4 3 2 1

Contents

Acknowledgements

I would like to thank Fate for putting me in Palm Springs, California in 2002 where I met Gene Mauch and I thank him for his kindness and friendship.

Thanks to Tom Doherty and Blue River Press for believing this old sportscaster has talent as a writer.

Jolene Smalley, Gene Mauch's sister and Lee Anne Mauch-Simons, Gene's daughter, were instrumental in making this book a reality. Thank you

Roy Smalley III, Gene Mauch's nephew and former major league shortstop, opened the door to the real Little General.

Thanks to Mauch's former teammates with the Los Angeles Angels of the Pacific Coast League including Gale "Windy" Wade, Eddie Haas, Jim Fanning, Bob Usher, Johnny Goryl, and John Pyecha.

Gene Mauch touched many lives and for their memories, I thank former major league players Jim Bunning, Bobby Wine, Pat Corrales, Clay Dalrymple, Art Mahaffey, Rusty Staub, Bob Boone, Mike Witt, Rod Carew, Eddie Bane, Tim Foli, Geoff Zahn, Frank Robinson, Jim Palmer, Jerry Johnson, Randy Jones, John Lowenstein, Ken Singleton, Ron Darling and Irv Noren.

If you want to read more about Gene Mauch, try the hard-to-find *View from the Dugout* by Ed Richter, published in 1963. Also try *Anaheim Angels: A Complete History*, written by Hall of Famer Ross Newhan and Gaylon H. White's *The Bilko Athletic Club*, a terrific history of the 1956, Los Angeles Angels of the Pacific Coast League, whom Gene Mauch felt was the best minor league team of all time. Both Newhan and White were invaluable contributors as was baseball historian Bill Swank, who wrote *Lane Field*, a history of the San Diego Padres of the PCL. Thank you my friends.

Special thanks to two of the best public relations directors in baseball history, Tim Mead of the Angels and Larry Shenk of the Phillies, who provided insight and put me in touch with the players I interviewed.

For providing photos, thanks also to Matt Brown and Matthew Birch of the Angels, Amanda Rodriguez of the Minnesota Twins and David Crosthwait and Craig Asato of D.C. Video.

SABR, the Society for American Baseball Research, provided a wealth of information, including the vaults of *The Sporting News*. Other invaluable research sources include The Newspaper Archive, UCLA's Special Collections Department and the San Diego Public Library.

I thank my wife Julie and kids Billy and Maile as well as my three dogs: Koa, Lanikai and Camden.

Foreword

In 2002, I was between baseball broadcasting jobs. I had left the San Diego Padres and needed a job. You can read all about it in *I Love the Work but I Hate the Business*. Anyway, I was eventually hired as Sports Director for KPSP-TV, a brand new station in Palm Springs, California.

There, I got to know Gene Mauch. Who's Gene Mauch? If you live in Philadelphia, Montreal, Minneapolis or in Southern California, you know the answer to that question.

Gene Mauch managed in the big leagues for 26 years. He's twelfth on the all-time win list with 1902 victories. He's also third on the all-time list for losses with 2037.

He's remembered for winning more games than any manager who never made it to the World Series.

Many baseball people think Mauch was a genius, a baseball savant, a master strategist, who knew more about the game and thought more deeply about its meaning than anyone, ever.

Others think Gene Mauch was a control freak who over managed and wouldn't allow the natural flow of a baseball game

Three times Mauch was on the doorstep of the World Series and three times he was involved in the greatest collapses in baseball history.

Brilliant, intense, inventive, creative, daring, aggressive, handsome, innovative, stubborn, cocky, introspective, gruff, stern, angry, haunted, unapproachable, arrogant, combative, intimidating, fascinating, complex, sensitive, caring, poised, dignified, regal. All words that writers have used to describe Gene Mauch.

The best sports columnist of all-time Jim Murray said, "He's as intense as a light bulb, as explosive as six sticks of dynamite in a bouncing truck."

I got to know Gene Mauch when he joined me on sportscasts during the 2002 World Series. I became friends with the most complex, fascinating man I'd ever met. When he managed, he was known for his knee buckling-glare and his long silences before answering questions.

But I discovered the other side of Gene Mauch. A sensitive, caring, incredibly intelligent man who actually had a sense of humor and dropped some of the best one liners ever.

Let me introduce you to Gene Mauch.

The Little General: Gene Mauch
A Baseball Life

Chapter One

"Toto, I Have a Feeling We're Not in Kansas Anymore"

– Dorothy in *The Wizard of Oz* (1939)

As the sun set on another hot, dry summer day in Salina, Kansas, a boy and his father played catch in the back yard. They'd been at it for almost an hour and the boy was whipped. His mind wandered to what 12-year old boys think about: supper, comics, or a ball game on the radio. He muffed a few throws. But he knew if he kept dropping balls, his dad would make him stay out longer, so he concentrated, squeezing every throw from the old man.

"He forced me to keep my mind on the games as well as my eye on the ball," recalled Gene Mauch years later. "It was a wonderful lesson because you have to concentrate in baseball, know exactly what the momentary situation is and anticipate that play.[1] This is where Mauch's competitive fire was lit. He loved walking into the house, with his dad's arm around him, telling him he was a ballplayer.

George Mauch lived vicariously through his son's exploits. He loved sports and with a push from Dad, Gene started playing baseball when he was eight. At 11, he was a scrawny 100-pounder playing American Legion ball against older, stronger 15 and 16-year-olds.

Gene Mauch and his Dad, George.
Credit: Mauch Estate

Note: Unless otherwise noted,
all photos were also provided by the Mauch Estate.

Gene William Mauch was born on November 18, 1925. According to his sister Jolene, their dad named him after heavyweight boxer Gene Tunney.

Gene wasn't a pitcher but he should've gotten credit for a save when he was 12. He and Jolene were walking home from school when Gene suggested they try a shortcut their parents had forbidden them to take. "We had to walk across this river that was iced over," remembered Jolene, "but I fell through a hole in the ice. Gene jumped into the water and pushed me up on the bank. I'm still here."

"Gene was a mother hen," Jolene said, "in high school, guys I was interested in wouldn't ask me out because I was Gene's sister."

George Mauch and his wife Mamie owned a bakery in Jetmore, Kansas, until the Depression wiped them out. "Jetmore had 914 people," Gene Mauch said, "and 910 when we left."[2]

Going wherever George found work, the Mauch family moved from town-to-town with stops in Concordia, Hays, Dodge City, Schoenchon, Ellis and Russell. When he was unemployed, George moved his family to Salina, where he found work as "a roustabout," in the oil fields. He helped build oil rigs and progressed to drilling. During a night shift in the frigid winter, George Mauch's hands became frozen to the oil rig and his coworkers had to pry them loose.

George Mauch realized it was time to flee the sand and dirt and wheat fields of Kansas and find a new direction. He also felt young Gene might have exceptional athletic talent and what better place to grow athletically than Southern California? Leaving his family in Salina, George headed west and found work selling cars. Several months later, his family joined him. "What the hell," said Gene, 'I was never in one town long enough to become attached to anything. Besides we weren't moving away from anything but a bunch of dust."[3]

Gene Mauch excelled at sports and was the student body president at Berendo Junior High School, where he met the love of his life, Nina Lee Taylor. Their first date was the junior high graduation dance. Although they attended different schools, they dated throughout their high school years.

Harry "Cap" Trotter was the baseball coach. He later became famous as the founder of UCLA's track program and the Bruins' long-time coach. Trotter saw Mauch's talent in football and basketball and encouraged Gene to go to college but Mauch had his mind set on becoming a major league shortstop.

When Gene found out that the city's best high school baseball program was at Fremont High School, he enrolled, even though he had to take the S streetcar 40 minutes across town.

Gene also starred as a guard on Fremont's basketball team. He wanted to play football but his dad said no. He didn't want Gene to get hurt. Finally, he relented and Gene played one year as a T-formation quarterback.

One of Mauch's prized possessions was a photo showing him returning a kickoff 65 yards for a touchdown against Los Angeles High in 1941. The player who had the last shot at Mauch and missed was Don Paul, later a star defensive back with the Los Angeles Rams.

Although he was the team captain, Mauch said "I didn't really consider myself a good football player although I did have a chance to go to Stanford or Southern Cal on a football scholarship." Football and basketball were just a way to stay in shape until spring arrived.

Gene knew that Fremont was a baseball factory, having produced a number of big leaguers, including one of Gene's idols, Boston Red Sox second baseman Bobby Doerr.

Gene Mauch at Fremont H.S. 1943.

Gene's father George lit the fire but like-minded teenagers ob-sessed with baseball, fanned the flames. With year round sunshine in Southern California, Mauch and his friends played baseball every day. If they weren't playing, they were at the beach, talking baseball. They were also fortunate to get some great coaching.

Les Haserot was the Fremont coach for 28 years. Among the play-ers he sent to the major leagues were Hal Spindel, Dick Conger, Merrill Combs, George "Catfish" Metkovich, Nippy Jones, George McDonald, Larry Barton, Glenn Mickens, Al Grunwald, Vic Mo-rasco and Clint Conatser. Haserot had starred at shortstop for Hollywood High in 1923 and had been a three sport star in base-ball, basketball and football at Occidental College. After graduat-ing, he played for the Portland Beavers and Mission Bells of the Pacific Coast League in 1927-28. Haserot was good defensively but couldn't hit a curveball, called it quits in 1929 and became Fremont's baseball coach.

Haserot ran his program like a major league training camp. He was a stickler for fundamentals and conditioning. "Haserot gave us the knowledge to prepare for pro ball," said Bobby Doerr. Haserot's Fremont teams won L.A. City Baseball Titles in 1932, 1933 and 1939. During Mauch's years, they won in 1942 and 1943 and later took more titles in 1946, 1947 and 1948. Haserot coached at Fremont through 1956. After leukemia began to sap his strength, he died of a self-inflicted gunshot in 1957.

The players also received excellent instruction in the summer from Mike Catron, coach of the Sunrise Post 357 American Legion team. Like Mauch's high school coach, Les Haserot, Catron was also a believer in hard work and fundamentals. Catron was only 5'4" and almost as wide as he was tall. During infield, Catron hit fungoes. If a player muffed a ground ball, he'd hit more balls, harder and harder, until one was caught.

"Mike was a rough, crusty little fella who really was made out of Jell-O," recalled Gene Mauch, "but he loved us."[4]

In 1941, Sunrise lost to San Diego Post 6 in the Southern California championship game. "We had it stolen away from us," said Mauch. "It was the worst umpiring I ever saw in my life. We were up by one run and our pitcher threw pitch after pitch right down the middle of the plate, but the ump kept calling them balls and the tying and winning run walked in."[5] San Diego Post 6 went on to win the national American Legion title that year.

In the summer of '42, Sunrise had not forgotten the loss to San Diego. This club was loaded and determined. Eight players from the Sunrise team played professionally. Besides Gene Mauch, there was Nippy Jones, who played on two World Series winners, the 1946 St. Louis Cardinals and 1957 Milwaukee Braves where he is remembered for the "shoe polish" incident.

Leading off the tenth inning, Jones jumped back from a low pitch that umpire Augie Donatelli called a ball. Jones claimed the ball hit his foot and after showing the ump a shoe polish mark on the ball, he was awarded first base. The play was the turning point in the series as the Braves went on to win in seven games.

The Sunrise team also included slugging first baseman Ralph Atkins, who set a Southern Association record for home runs by a left-handed hitter, with 34 for Little Rock in 1953. Catcher Dick Kinaman spent eleven years in the Cleveland Indians system. Outfielder Jim Muhre had a five-year career in the minors and then spent many years as the visiting clubhouse attendant at Dodgers' Stadium.

Sunrise and San Diego Post 6 met again in 1942. San Diego's star was outfielder Bob Usher, who played six years in the big leagues and was later Mauch's teammate. San Diego won the first game in the best-of-three series 10-6, handing Sunrise their first loss of the year. Sunrise came back to win the next two, 9-5 and 19-5 to win the Southern California Championship.

Then Sunrise hit the road, playing in Stockton, California; Miles City, Montana and Hastings, Nebraska chasing an American Legion Championship. The team usually traveled by train, logging over 11,000 miles. In the sectional playoffs in Hastings, Nebraska, they faced the powerful Stockham Post team from St. Louis. Stockham, coached by Leo Browne, who founded Missouri's Legion program, featured three future pros, Bobby Hoffman at second base, Jack Maguire at shortstop and Lloyd Lowe at third, with Jim Goodwin and Roger Powell, handling the pitching.

Hoffman spent seven years with the New York Giants and was on their 1954 World Championship team. Maguire played with the Giants, Pirates and St. Louis Browns. Goodwin spent six seasons in the minor leagues and had a cup of coffee with the Chicago White Sox and Powell spent ten years in the minors, mostly in the St. Louis Browns system. Another Stockham alum "Ruck" Steger, chose football and was the fullback on Illinois' Rose Bowl Champions.

The team was loaded but the star was squatty leftfielder, Lawrence Berra. Soon to be nicknamed "Yogi" by teammate Bobby Hoffman, for his resemblance to a Hindu yogi, after he saw Berra sitting in the dugout, with his arms and legs crossed, waiting to hit. "I remember Yogi Berra stealing home to help beat us on Sunday afternoon to even the series 1 and 1," said Mauch. Then on Sunday night we had a big seven-run inning to break up the final game."[6] Sunrise won the final two games to advance to the American Legion Finals in Manchester, New Hampshire.

Yogi Berra steals home as Mauch (5) watches.

Sunrise suffered a serious loss in game one of the national finals. Running out a ground ball, Nippy Jones stumbled at first base and broke his ankle. He was finished for the rest of the series.

Montreal manager Gene Mauch and New York Mets manager Yogi Berra
holding up American Legion photo.

Despite the loss of Jones, Sunrise went to New Hampshire, home
of the host team. Sunrise won the first game 6-2 and in the second, Gene Mauch doubled, the only extra base hit in the game,
to drive in the first run in a 5-2 victory. Then, Sunrise blanked
New Hampshire 3-0 to win the National American Legion Championship. Gene Mauch was named the tournament's Most Valuable Player. The team's reward-a trip to the World Series. "What
a great baseball thrill that was," said Gene Mauch, "to watch my
first World Series."[7] The 1942 American Legion Champions were
honored at a banquet at Hollywood's Roosevelt Hotel. "Casey"
Stengel, manager of the Boston Braves and Lou Stringer, a Sunrise alum and second baseman for the Chicago Cubs, handed the
players trophies and wrist watches.

Chapter Two

A Brooklyn Dodger at 18

With war clouds gathering, the U.S. passed the Selective Training and Service Act, signed by President Franklin Roosevelt. Every American male between the ages of 21 and 36 was required to register for 12 months of military service and baseball began to lose players to the draft.

On December 7, 1941, the Japanese attacked Pearl Harbor, shattering peace and further changing baseball. Stars like Hank Greenberg and Bob Feller rushed to enlist. Soon, other big names like Stan Musial, Joe DiMaggio, Jerry Coleman and Ted Williams traded their baseball uniforms for khakis. Eventually, more than 500 major league players took part in World War II.

To fill their rosters, teams went to extremes. The St. Louis Browns had a one-armed centerfielder Pete Gray, the Cincinnati Reds used a deaf player Dick Seipek in the outfield, and the Washington Senators signed combat vet Bert Shepard, who had an artificial leg.

Rules were different then. There was no player draft and players could sign with major league teams before they graduated from high school. Gene Mauch was a hot commodity. After starring for the Sunrise American Legion team, Mauch had offers from eleven major league clubs and after his junior year at Fremont, the Dodgers' Branch Rickey personally signed the 17-year-old Mauch and sent him to their Class D farm club in Durham, North Carolina in the Piedmont League. Rickey told sports writer Red Smith of the *New York Times*, "Look at him and you think he's 16. Talk to him and you think he's 26. Talk baseball with him and you think he's 36."

Gene Mauch—a Dodger at 18.

"Mr. Rickey liked Gene because he had brains and desire," said his 18-year-old roommate at Ma Gregory's Boarding House, pitcher Rex Barney. "He was aggressive and scrappy, an Eddie Stanky type. He'd fight at the drop of a hat."[1]

Barney recalled the first time he met Gene Mauch. "He was a real California hot dog, blond, ducktail haircut, suntanned, a pepper pot, like nobody I'd ever seen." The two teenagers each paid $12.50 a month rent and walked everywhere they needed to go.

In a game against Portsmouth, Mauch crashed into second baseman Ray Hoffman trying to break up a double play. Hoffman charged Mauch, they traded punches and both teams joined in the bench clearing brawl. Order was finally restored and Mauch, minus his shirt, was ejected. It would be the first of many battles for Gene Mauch.

Early on, Durham manager Bruno Betzel took Barney and Mauch aside and said, "You're the only two guys on this club with a chance to go up to the big leagues. If you want to come out early every morning, I think I can help you." Mauch and Barney showed up every day for instruction.

Betzel's full name was Christian Frederick Albert John Henry David "Bruno" Betzel. He was named after his six uncles and nicknamed after the family St. Bernard. Betzel had a brief career as an infielder with the St. Louis Cardinals and roomed with Hall of Famer Rogers Hornsby. Betzel once touched off a brawl in spring training when his errant throw hit Ty Cobb. Betzel had a brief career from 1914-18 hitting only .231 but found more success as a minor league manager.

He won six pennants in a 30-year minor league managing career. In 1944 Betzel piloted the AAA Montreal Royals of the International League and mentored a young second baseman of whom he said, "I don't care if he is polka-dotted, he will play in the major leagues. I would tuck him in at night if necessary to get him to play in the major leagues."[2] That player was Jackie Robinson. Robinson said that Betzel was one of the best people he ever played for and was responsible for rounding him into a major league player.

Gene Mauch and Jackie Robinson.

The 17-year-old Mauch played well at Class B, for the Durham Bulls, hitting .322 in 32 games. He and Rex Barney had only been there for two months, when Betzel told them they were moving up to AA Montreal.

They took a bus from Lynchburg to Durham and then caught a train to Baltimore where Montreal was supposed to be playing. But the manager of the Emerson Hotel wouldn't let them check in because the Montreal club was still in Jersey City and wouldn't get to Baltimore until the next day. Finally, he gave them rooms. "I wondered where we should go to get something to eat," remembered Barney. "So, we walked to "The Block.""[3] The Block was a notorious area filled with strip clubs and bars and they were too young to get in. They finally found a restaurant, ate and played pool.

At Montreal, Barney struggled with his control and Mauch only hit .169 in 31 games. When the season ended, Mauch returned to

California to complete his high school degree.

With soldiers traveling to stateside bases or being shipped overseas and civilians heading to munitions plants away from home, the nation's railroads were jammed. In 1943 Commissioner Kennesaw Mountain Landis decreed that no club would travel south for Spring Training, leaving transportation to those involved in the war effort. "I do not propose" Landis said, "to have athletes lolling about in the sands in some semitropical climate."

The Dodgers, who normally trained in Florida, shifted to the Bear Mountain Inn, a resort in Rockland County, New York. Life was good at the inn. There were pool tables, thick steaks, and fireplaces where Branch Rickey could be found at night, playing checkers with players. The restaurant whipped up specialties like "Stewed Mixed Fruits Fitzsimmons" in honor of Dodger' pitcher, Fat Freddie Fitzsimmons. And despite a government limit on gas usage, Dodger manager Leo Durocher tooled around in his long white Lincoln.

Branch Rickey had several baseball fields built behind the inn and while working out, players could watch ice skaters on Hussein Lake or skiers negotiating nearby slopes. When the "Blizzard of '44" covered the fields with eight inches of snow, the Dodgers moved inside. Rickey cut a deal with West Point, seven miles away, to allow the team to work out inside the huge, steam-heated field house when the Cadets weren't marching there.

When Rickey took over in Brooklyn, he inherited a veteran team with many over-the-hill players Rickey called "anesthetics." With players being drafted or enlisting, he saw a perfect time for a youth movement. Rickey unloaded vets like Joe Medwick, Johnny Allen, Dolph Camilli, Paul Waner and Fred Fitzsimmons, who were either traded or released.

In 1943, Pee Wee Reese, Larry French, Pete Reiser, Johnny Rizzo, Billy Herman and Kirby Higbe all went into the armed services.

With veteran players entering the service and young players called up to replace them, minor league talent was drained. Many teams folded some of their minor league teams and fired scouts. Branch Rickey took the opposite approach, telling Dodgers scouts to sign every young prospect they could find.

In 1944, 200 players passed through the Dodgers spring training. Rickey brought 31 players to big league camp including seven players who were 18 or younger. They included 18-year-olds Gene Mauch and pitchers Ralph Branca and Cal McLish. In D ball at Durham, North Carolina, Mauch had played for manager Christian Frederick Albert John Henry David "Bruno" Betzel. Now, he became friends with Calvin Coolidge Julius Caesar Tuskahoma McLish.

Cal McLish was the son of two Native Americans. His mother was Choctaw and his father Cherokee. Of his name, McLish explained that his dad never got to name his previous six children, "So I guess he got into the firewater and named me."[4]

Over the next 40 years, the lives of Gene Mauch and Cal McLish would be intertwined. Leo Durocher preferred veteran players but with Rickey's kids, he had no choice. Walking into the Dodgers' clubhouse, the teenaged Mauch was in awe of grown men he saw like French Bordagaray, Dixie Walker, Augie Galan and Gil English, all in their thirties. Plus, there was "Big Poison" Paul Waner, who was 41 and his brother "Little Poison," Lloyd Waner who was 38.

Mauch, a scrawny 5-10" 165-pounder, later admitted that he'd been intimidated by the reputation and ability of these players and had compromised his game. Instead of just swinging away, he became a player who choked up on the bat, crowded the plate, worked the count, bunted and hit behind the runner.

Leo Durocher's biggest problem was his infield. With Pee Wee Reese and Billy Herman in the Navy and Arky Vaughn holding out at his California farm, the only returning starter was 6-6" first baseman "Howie" Schultz, who was 4F because he was too tall for the Army. During spring training, Durocher had seven different men playing third base and another half dozen at second.

At shortstop, Gene Mauch was a surprise, a California schoolboy with little experience. With only 50 pro games under his belt, Mauch was brought up just to work out a few days with the big club. But he got some key hits in exhibition games and Durocher loved the kid's quick hands and take-charge attitude. So the Dodgers kept him, with Durocher and Rickey watching his every move. Leo knew Mauch had talent but he was only 18 and needed a calming influence next to him. Billy Herman would have been perfect; but since he was in the Navy, Branch Rickey urged Durocher to play second base.

Leo hadn't played regularly since 1939, but said, "I'm younger than some of my men and my legs are okay. I could get in shape by working hard, but I can't play either shortstop or second base. If Mr. Rickey thinks I ought to play, I'll suggest I hop on a flight to St. Louis and let the Doctor carve these "acorns" out of my right elbow. Maybe then I'd be able to throw in a month or two."[5]

Despite Durocher's bone chips, Rickey asked Leo to play second base. His comeback, though, was cut short after two days. In the third inning of an exhibition game with the Boston Red Sox, Mauch bobbled a ground ball and then hurried his throw to second for a force play. But the ball sailed on him. Durocher tried to bare hand it and the ball hit his right thumb, breaking it in two places. Was Leo mad at his young protégé? Hardly. "Leo gave me a brand new tweed topcoat the next day," said Mauch. "It was out of gratitude. He didn't want to play anymore and I gave him the perfect excuse."[6]

The Dodgers began the 1944 season in Philadelphia with a patchwork infield of incumbent Howie Schultz at first, Louie Olmo at second, Gene Mauch at shortstop and Gil English at third base.

On April 18, 1944, 18-year-old Gene Mauch made his major league debut before 11,910 fans at Shibe Park in Philadelphia." I wouldn't say I was nervous," recalled Mauch, "that wasn't the word really. I was excited."[7]

"Kewpie Dick Barrett was pitching for the Phillies," said Mauch, who batted eighth and knew the scouting report on Barrett, "he doesn't throw hard but paints the corners with pinpoint control and has a great curveball."[8] Columnist Emmet Watson said, "Barrett had a curveball that bowed like a head waiter. You could almost hear it when it broke."

"My first time up, I grounded out to shortstop," said Mauch. "I couldn't wait for my second time up and when it came, I doubled to left center."[9] Mauch led off the third inning and flied to right. He came up again in the fourth, with two outs and a runner and second and hit a comebacker to Barrett who threw him out.

In the sixth, Leo Durocher lifted Mauch for a pinch hitter, 41-year-old Lloyd Waner who walked. Barrett pitched a complete game six-hitter as the Phillies won on opening day 4-1.

Next, the Dodgers faced lefthander Al Gerheauser. Mauch took a called third strike in his first at bat and came up again in the fourth with the Phillies ahead 2-1 with runners at second and third. The first clutch situation for Mauch, with two men in scoring position. Mauch singled, his first major league hit, and drove in two runs to put the Dodgers in front 3-2.

Mauch grounded out in his next two at bats. Scheduled to bat with the score tied 4-4 in the tenth, Leo Durocher called him back, sending up Lloyd Waner as pinch hitter. Waner singled, driving in what proved to be the winning run to put the Dodgers in front 5-4. It was the 3,113th hit of Waner's career.

With the series even at one game apiece, the Dodgers took game three 8-2 as Gene Mauch went 1-4 with a walk. His only hit was a pop fly double in the fourth inning.

The Dodgers returned to Brooklyn for their home opener against the New York Giants. Right-hander Ace Adams, a former pro boxer, started for the Giants. Normally a reliever, he pitched a complete game as the Giants won 3-2 win. Mauch flied to left, grounded to third and walked before being lifted for a pinch hitter.

The Giants won the second game 2-1 as rookie Big Bill Voiselle pitched a complete game. The 6'4" 210-pound Voiselle looked even bigger because he wore number ninety six. Commissioner Kenesaw Mountain Landis okayed the number because Voiselle was honoring his hometown of Ninety Six, South Carolina. 96 was the largest number ever worn by a major leaguer.

Mauch was helpless against Voiselle. He failed to get the ball out of the infield; popping up to Voiselle, grounding out to third and striking out. Voiselle would go on to enjoy a banner rookie year. He led the league in innings pitched, went 21-16 with a 3.02 ERA and was named the first Sporting News National League Pitcher of the Year.

In five major league games, Gene Mauch hit just .133 with two hits in fifteen at bats. As the team left for Boston to face the Braves, Leo Durocher benched the rookie, replacing him with veteran Bill Hart. "Don't think I'm giving up on the kid," said the Lip. "He was trying too hard. His father told me he's a good ballplayer but he thinks he has to make a hit every time he comes to bat. And I agree with the old man. Gene had tightened up. I'm going to keep him on the bench beside me for awhile to build up his confidence."[10]

Although Mauch's primary concern was survival, he also studied Leo Durocher as a manager. He noticed that Leo would make outrageous comments to the press, argue with umpires and do anything needed to shift attention from his players to him. He got other managers to think about beating him rather than his team. This was the first piece he put into the mosaic that became Gene Mauch the manager.

Mauch needed experience and with the Army about to grab him, the Dodgers sent him to AAA Montreal to play for his old manager Bruno Betzel. Mauch only played in 12 games for the Royals, hitting .283 before he was snatched away by the Army-Corps.

Chapter Three

You're in the Army Now

After basic training, Gene was sent to Marana Army Air Field outside of Tucson where his assignment was to play for the base sports teams.

Mauch played for the Marana Hosses in a six team semi-pro league that included the Aztecas, made up of Mexican-Americans; the Elks Club; the American Legion; the Southern Pacific and the Davis-Monthan Air Base.

The teams played before small crowds with a quarter charged for admission but the *Tucson Daily Citizen* promoted the games and sprinkled with pro players like Mauch, the league began to attract crowds and rivalries developed.

An overflow crowd of 3,000 turned out at Randolph Field for a game between bitter rivals, the Davis-Monthan Mustangs and Gene Mauch's Marana Hosses. The game did little to improve relations between the bases. Twice, players from both teams nearly came to blows and both managers bickered with the umpires. By the 11th inning, the fuse was lit. Marana's pitcher Bobby Fontaine, future general manager of the San Diego Padres, fielded a bunt and made a high throw to second for a force play. Gene Mauch, playing shortstop, leaped high in the air to catch the errant throw. Umpire Virgil Spangler ruled that the runner hit the bag before Mauch landed on it. Mauch disagreed and as the two men argued, Mauch shoved the umpire while showering him with abusive language. Mauch was ejected. Marana's manager protested the game but the protest was later dropped and Mauch was suspended for a week. Davis-Monthan won the game 7-6 in 11 innings.

The next day, in the *Tucson Daily Citizen*, Bill Lucas wrote, "It was too bad that so much bad feeling was generated in last night's game between Davis-Monthan and Marana. Some 1,000 youngsters under 10 years of age, who were admitted free under presentation of bundles of newspapers and magazines, were treated to an evening of haggling, shoving and general umpire baiting that can only give those not frequent visitors at Randolph Park a distorted view of the national pastime."[1]

Besides starring on the baseball team, Mauch played point guard and was the leading scorer on the base basketball team. When Marana beat the University of Arizona 51-31, Mauch got rave reviews in the *Tucson Daily Citizen*: "The play of little Gene Mauch, a refugee from the Brooklyn Dodgers, was little short of sensational as time and time again, the gent who plays a lot of shortstop would break loose for a phenomenal dribbling effort or pass play."[2]

Mauch was about to begin flight training when the war ended. Discharged from the service in 1945, Gene Mauch married his sweetheart, Nina Lee in November. They were both 20.

Mr. and Mrs. Gene Mauch.

Chapter Four

The Odyssey Begins

In the spring of 1946, Gene Mauch headed to the Dodgers' spring training camp in Florida. Although Pee Wee Reese was back, Mauch was confident he could make the team. Branch Rickey agreed, "I don't see how Gene Mauch is going to be kept off this club." With Reese sidelined with his annual case of shin splints, Mauch saw plenty of action. But when Reese returned, Mauch was sent to the St. Paul Saints, the Dodgers AAA affiliate in the American Association.

Mauch's wife, Nina Lee, quit her secretarial job to join her husband in Minnesota. They lived in one room in a downtown boarding house where other players and their wives stayed.

St. Paul manager Ray Blades had been an outfielder with the St. Louis Cardinals in the 1920's and 1930's. His playing career was derailed by a collision with an outfield fence and he became a minor league manager with Cardinals' farm teams in Columbus and Rochester. In 1939 he was named manager of the St. Louis Cardinals. After turning the team around in his first year, the team plummeted. Blades was fired, replaced by Billy Southworth.

Branch Rickey, President of the Dodgers, felt that despite a terrible temper, Ray Blades had a great baseball mind and was a leader. He hired Blades to manage the St. Paul Saints, the Dodgers AAA affiliate in the American Association. A teacher, Blades found a willing student in Gene Mauch, who'd realized he couldn't survive on talent alone. He sat next to Blades in the dugout, peppering him with questions. Blades patiently explained why he had called for a bunt, why he sent up a certain pinch hitter or why he made a pitching change.

When St. Paul played Toledo, Blades was worried about the Mud Hens' red-hot first baseman Jerry Witte, a right handed hitter. The night before St. Paul had lost 13-0. So Blades shifted his defense to the left side for Witte, a dead left field hitter. The left fielder played near the foul line, the centerfielder moved to deep left center and the right fielder to straight away center field. The infield played deep. The third baseman was just a step off the foul line, the shortstop halfway between second and third and the second baseman was directly behind the second base bag. The first baseman, the only fielder on the right side, was stationed halfway between first and second.

Witte popped out to the first baseman, singled, flied to deep left and walked twice. While Witte was held in check, the Mud Hens won again 9-5.

Mauch listened to Blades explain his unorthodox theories. In an era when pitchers completed what they started, Blades said, "My idea is never to save anybody for tomorrow. Let's win today's game today. Save a man for tomorrow and you may lose two games. I'll relieve with anyone who can relieve. There won't be any regular rotation necessarily. In a short series, I believe in trying to beat the other club's best pitcher with my best pitcher, and with all my pitchers, if necessary."[1] Mauch made notes about Blades' defensive shifts and his "let's win today" philosophy of pitching as two more mosaic pieces slipped into place.

Like future manager Gene Mauch, Ray Blades was often his own worst enemy. He detested losing and after a defeat he'd sit for hours, brooding and analyzing the game and his decisions.

In 1946, Mauch played in 149 games, hitting .248 with 6 homers, fifty five RBI and 9 stolen bases but committed an outrageous 66 errors. The Saints finished the season in third place in the American Association, with an 80-71 record.

In 1947, players returned from the service to join Branch Rickey's kiddie corps. The Mahatma had a surplus of players. In May, he sold five of them to the Pittsburgh Pirates. Brooklyn fans howled as popular pitcher Kirby Higbe, Cal McLish, Hank Behrman, catcher Dixie Howell and Gene Mauch went in the trade that brought outfielder Al Gionfriddo to Pitt along with a reported $250,000. Commenting on the trade, a New York writer said, "The deal originally was for five Dodgers for cash. But at the last minute, Branch Rickey asked the Pirates to throw in outfielder Al Gionfriddo to carry the dough from Pittsburgh to Brooklyn.

Former Dodgers try on their new Pirate uniforms. Left to Right: Cal McLish, Kirby Higbe, Dixie Howell, Hank Behrman and Gene Mauch.

Roy Hamey was Pittsburgh's General Manager when Mauch arrived. As American Association President, Hamey had fined Mauch several times and threatened to suspend him for arguing with umpires but Hamey also recognized Mauch's talent and leadership qualities.

Mauch hit .300 in 16 games with Pittsburgh. Although he played little, he got his name into print in a 3-2 loss to Boston. With first baseman Hank Greenberg sidelined by a chipped bone in his elbow, Pirates' manager Billy Herman put himself in Greenberg's spot. In the eighth inning with the score tied 2-2, Braves rookie first baseman Earl Torgeson was batting with the count two balls and two strikes. As Pirates pitcher Hank Behrman threw his next pitch, Torgeson checked his swing. Herman argued that Torgeson had swung but plate umpire Art Gore called it a ball. Torgeson hit the next pitch into the visitor's bullpen for a game winning home run and the Pirates went wild.

Herman, followed by Mauch, charged out of the dugout to protest the call. Gore threw them both out of the game. For the fiery Mauch, getting tossed was no big thing but it was the first time in 16 years that Billy Herman had been ejected.

Herman and Haney decided that Gene Mauch's future was at second base so the Pirates sent him to their AAA Indianapolis farm club to learn the position. Paired with 25-year-old shortstop Pete Castiglione, the two got rave reviews. Indianapolis manager Jimmy Brown rated both as "definite major leaguers". "They're both practically finished products right now," Brown said, "and playing the rest of the season should give them all the seasoning they need."

In 58 games with the Indians, Mauch hit .300 with no homers and sixteen RBI and committed only 12 errors.

Although Mauch thought he had a future with the Pirates, he was traded back to the Dodgers along with pitcher Preacher Roe and infielder Bobby Cox for Dixie Walker, Hal Gregg and Vic Lombardozzi. Mauch began the 1948 season with the Dodgers, went 2 for 13, was placed on waivers and claimed by the Chicago Cubs. Mauch hit just .203 in 53 games with the Cubs but did belt his first major league home run off Cardinals' right hander Jim Hearn.

Although he didn't play much, Mauch enjoyed his time with the Cubs. "Phil Cavarretta, Peanuts Lowery, and Bill Nicholson-we played cards on the train and we'd shoot craps," he remembered.[2]

Chapter Five

Welcome to Wrigleyville

The Cubs held spring training on Catalina Island, owned by William Wrigley Jr., who also owned the Los Angeles Angels of the Pacific Coast League. Wrigley developed the island as a resort destination and in 1921, brought his team to Catalina for spring training. The players stayed at St. Catherine's Hotel in Descanso Bay. They played in Avalon, on a field built by Wrigley, which had the same dimensions as the Cubs' home, Wrigley Field, in Chicago.

Cowboy movie star Tom Mix lived on Catalina. Gene Autry met Ronald Reagan there when Autry's band was performing. Radio stars Fibber McGee & Molly visited spring training. Tarzan, Johnny Weissmuller golfed and swam on the island. Comedian Joe E. Brown brought teams of movie stars to play the Cubs in exhibition games. Big band leaders including Benny Goodman, Jimmy Dorsey, Rudy Vallee, Stan Kenton and Count Basie took batting practice with the team.

In 1949, Cubs shortstop Roy Smalley reported early to Catalina so he could roam the island's back country, chasing goats and buffalo to get in shape. He roomed with pitcher Don Carlsen, his teammate at Pepperdine University and also became friends with Gene Mauch.

Gene with Chicago Cubs.

"Roy Smalley hit 12 home runs that spring," Mauch said. "He and I had a deal-we'd put up a buck for each homer. I'd only hit one all spring. I had to buy him two pairs of Argyle socks. They cost about $12. I told him, 'that's $6 a foot.'"[1]

Mauch and Smalley were roommates on road trips. "Even though I had beaten Gene out for a regular job," said Smalley, "Gene was my biggest booster. He kept on telling me that I could be the greatest shortstop in the game, fielding and hitting. He told me I COULD hit, I COULD field, and Gene kept on day-after-day to the point where I began to believe him."[2]

Mauch also introduced Smalley to his sister Jolene. "I went to Chicago to visit Gene and Nina Lee," Jolene said. "I was promised to another man at the time but I was smitten by Roy who was playing shortstop with my brother at second base." They married and Mauch's road-roomie became his brother-in-law. "The wedding took place after a 13 inning game in Boston. Gene and Nina Lee stood up with Roy and me at a Baptist Church in Brookline, Massachusetts. It lasted for 61 years."

Roy Smalley had a canon for an arm, although not always accurate. A Chicago announcer wrote a poem called "Miksis to Smalley to Addison Street." His new wife attended many Cubs' games but boos that rained down on her husband made her cry. "I wasn't always a lady," Jolene said, explaining her retorts to the crowd. "To me, he was the best shortstop in the world. Those fans were brutal."

Chapter Six

Second Base is Wide Open

In December 1949, the Cubs traded Gene Mauch and cash to the Boston Braves for pitcher Bill Voiselle. In 1950 Mauch joined the Braves at their training camp in Bradenton, Florida. "Second base is wide open," said manager Billy Southworth, "It's going to be a fight right down to the wire."[1] Mauch was one of four candidates for the job along with veterans Sibby Sisti, Connie Ryan and rookie Roy Hartsfield.

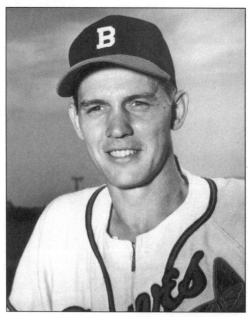

Gene Mauch with Boston Braves.

The 24-year-old Hartsfield had been the MVP in the American Association. Playing for the Braves' AAA team in Milwaukee, he hit .317 with 203 hits, 27 doubles, eight triples and 12 home runs. He drove in 86 runs and stole 33 bases. In the field, he had 471 put-outs, most in the American Association since 1927. "This kid can really fly," said Southworth. "He gets a good jump on the ball and covers plenty of ground."[2] Southworth thought Hartsfield resembled two former Braves, Eddie Stanky and Alvin Dark, who were traded to the New York Giants the previous season.

Billy Southworth also loved Sibby Sisti, who could play any position. In 1948, when Eddie Stanky broke his ankle, Sisti stepped in and helped lead the Braves to their first pennant in 34 years.

30-year-old Connie Ryan had been trying to break into a regular spot for three seasons. Although third base was his best position, Ryan had played everywhere in the infield. In spring training, with first baseman Earl Torgeson injured, Ryan saw most of his action there.

"This is the kind of ball team I can play for," said Gene Mauch, who'd filled in at shortstop for Roy Smalley in 1949 with the Cubs and had also played second base.[3] Mauch was only 25 but it seemed like he'd been around forever. This was his 7th season in pro ball after breaking in with the Dodgers at 18.

As opening day approached, all four were playing well so as the team left Bradenton, Billy Southworth alternated them. Mauch started one game, Sisti the next and then Ryan, but in an exhibition game in Columbia, S.C. Roy Hartsfield seemed to take the lead with two doubles and a single.

Surprisingly, Connie Ryan was the opening day second baseman when the Braves began the 1950 season against the New York Giants at the Polo Grounds in New York. "Ryan won the job by the way he played in spring training," said Billy Southworth. "He'll stay there as long as he shows me he can keep it up."[4]

Leading off, Ryan went two for five with two RBI, including a 6th inning home run off the Giants Sal "The Barber" Maglie in the

Braves 11-4 win. Ryan had two more hits in the Braves' 10-6 win in the second game as Hartsfield and Mauch watched from the dugout.

Mauch didn't make his first appearance until the 15th game of the season when he came in as a late inning defensive replacement.

Ryan began to slump. He hit three home runs but his batting average dropped to .196 and after 20 games was traded to the Cincinnati Reds for Walker Cooper.

Hartsfield was nearly as invisible as Mauch. Through the Braves first 24 games, he made three pinch-hitting appearances with two hits but never played in the field.

"I'm going to give Sibby Sisti the first crack at the job," explained Southworth, "But don't overlook Mauch and Hartsfield who are ready to jump in."[5]

Sisti was steady in the field but struggled at the plate. In the 30th game of the season, Mauch finally made his first start for the Braves in Boston. Batting seventh, Mauch went 0-4 and committed an error in a 6-2 loss to the Cincinnati Reds. He stayed at second base for the next eight games and hit .250 with eight hits in 32 at bats. In a loss to the Pittsburgh Pirates at Forbes Field, Mauch hit his first home run of the season, a three run shot off rookie right hander Bill MacDonald.

In June, Southworth put Roy Hartsfield at second base and in the leadoff spot. Hartsfield hit .277 with seven homers and 24 RBI but while in the field, he struggled. In AAA, Hartsfield was regarded as a second baseman with range and the ability to turn the double play but with the Braves his play was spotty. In 96 games he committed 26 errors, the most among N.L. second baseman and had the league's lowest fielding percentage .946.

Although Mauch was benched, he was in the middle of the action at Braves Field when Pirates lefthander Cliff Chambers threw a four hit shutout beating the Braves 1-0.

Chambers was the previous day's starter but didn't survive the first inning. He had also hit Braves first baseman Earl Torgeson in the back and two weeks earlier, had drilled Sid Gordon on the wrist. Torgeson and Chambers were old rivals, dating back to their days as American Legion foes in the state of Washington. Despite Chambers' ineffectiveness, Pirates Manager Bill Meyer brought him back the next day and Chambers was brilliant. In the third inning, after Torgeson ripped a pitch foul into the right field stands, Chambers low-bridged him with a pitch at his head. Torgeson fell flat on his face to avoid being hit. After Torgeson fouled out to end the inning, the two yelled at each other as Chambers walked off the mound. Torgeson then ripped off his glasses and went after Chambers. The two exchanged punches and grappled on the ground until they were separated by players from both teams. Gene Mauch ran onto the field to help his teammate in the melee and both Torgeson and Mauch were ejected.

Chambers was allowed to stay in the game and pitched a brilliant four hit shutout. The Pirates scored an unearned run in the second and won 1-0 handing Warren Spahn the loss.

At Braves Field, against Brooklyn, Mauch got tossed out of another game in which he didn't play. With the Dodgers' Gil Hodges up, plate umpire Lou Jorda called Johnny Sain's pitch a ball. Braves reserves, led by Mauch, barked at Jordan. After Hodges homered, the bench jockeys turned up the volume and one of them called the umpire "an old goat."

Jorda ripped off his mask, approached the Braves dugout and yelled, "Mauch, I know your voice. You're out." Manager Billy Southworth protested that it hadn't been Mauch who yelled and Jorda ejected him too. Then Jorda ordered all the Braves out of the dugout except the coaches, trainer and batboy. Mauch and Southworth were forbidden to return but the others were allowed to play if needed. Brooklyn won the game 4-3.

Mauch was thrown out again in Cincinnati. In the fifth inning, Braves third baseman Bob Elliott protested a called third strike by umpire Frank Dascoli. When Elliott kicked dirt on home plate, Dascoli gave him the thumb and when Manager Billy Southworth charged out of the dugout, he was ejected. Dascoli wasn't finished.

Hearing Mauch screaming at him from the dugout, Dascoli also gave him the heave-ho.

Nobody was more critical of Gene Mauch than Gene Mauch. He was harder on himself than any manager could be. Del Crandall, his teammate with the Braves, remembered that after a game in which Mauch stranded several baserunners, he was so furious that he grabbed a razor. "I didn't know what he was going to do," said Crandall. "Well, he didn't cut his throat but he did dry-shave. Blood was coming down his cheek but he kept right on going, mumbling to himself."[6]

Gene Mauch realized he would never be a superstar but he loved the game and someday hoped to be a manager. In 57-year-old Billy Southworth, Mauch found a kindred spirit. A future Hall-of-Famer, in three years as the St. Louis Cardinals manager, his teams won 106, 105 and 105 games, three pennants and two World Series. Since Mauch wasn't playing much, he studied Southworth's every move and wrote them down in a notebook.

Watching the fiery Mauch, Billy Southworth could see a future big league manager. "He said to me 'one day you're gonna' be a manager and I'm gonna' give you one piece of advice. Don't fall in love with your players.' It's the first piece of advice I got," said Mauch "and maybe the best, but I've never been able to abide by it. Incidentally, neither could he.'"[7] Perhaps the most important part of the Gene Mauch mosaic was put in place.

In his career as a manager, Billy Southworth was 1,044-704, a winning percentage of .597, second only to Joe McCarthy's .615. Mauch was learning from a master.

Mauch wound up playing in 48 games, hitting .231-1-15 as the Braves finished fourth.

As the Braves reported to spring training in 1951, second base was still a problem. Southworth said he'd mishandled Roy Hartsfield the previous year, trying to change his style of play. Tired of reading about his inability to turn double plays, Hartsfield admitted that he'd played most of his rookie season with a broken finger on his right hand. The injury occurred in a collision at second base with the Giants' Eddie Stanky. Hartsfield said his finger was healed after a winter of rest.

Southworth then paired Hartsfield with veteran shortstop Buddy Kerr on one squad and put Sibby Sisti at second with rookie Johnny Logan at short on another team. "That way, I'll have a veteran alongside a youngster all the time," reasoned Southworth. "And then, of course, I'll also have Gene Mauch around to work with the kids."[8]

Southworth had just labeled Mauch as a utility man, although he was only 25. Baseball is a game of labels. He can't hit lefthanders. He can't hit a breaking ball. He's a poor fielder. Once a player gets labeled, it's tough to shake. His manager might as well have stamped "utility man" on Mauch's forehead.

Did Southworth know that at 25, Mauch was the same age as Hartsfield and Logan? By opening day, Sibby Sisti was the oldest at 31 and Buddy Kerr 28. But in baseball's mind, Mauch was the old vet.

As the 1951 season began, Logan was at shortstop and Hartsfield at second. Hartsfield was hitting and turning double plays. Although Hartsfield was much improved, Johnny Logan went 2 for 17 to start the season and was soon benched in favor of Buddy Kerr. The competition for a job stimulated Kerr. He hit .360 into May. When Kerr missed a few games with a leg injury, Mauch filled in but didn't hit. From then on, Southworth used Sibby Sisti at shortstop.

Through the Braves first seven games, Mauch's only appearance was as a pinch-runner. On April 23 at Ebbets Field in Brooklyn, Braves ace Warren Spahn was celebrating his twenty-ninth birthday until Mauch sat on the cake. Mauch entered the game as a pinch-runner in the twelfth and stayed in to play third base. With the score tied 1-1 in the bottom of the sixteenth inning, the Dodgers' Billy Cox led off with a single and Clyde King's sacrifice bunt moved him to second. Eddie Miksis pinch hit for leftfielder Don Thompson. Miksis hit a ground ball to Mauch which he bobbled for an error, putting runners at first and third. Then Carl Furillo delivered a game winning single to give the Dodgers a 2-1 victory and hand Spahn a heartbreaking loss. Spahn had pitched 15 2/3 innings, allowing 2 runs but only one earned. He scattered ten hits walked two, one intentionally and struck out 8. In the newspaper accounts the next day, Mauch's error was referred to as "school-boyish." Whatever it was, it cost Warren Spahn a victory in one of the greatest performances of his Hall of Fame career.

In June, Billy Southworth stepped down as manager and was replaced by Tommy Holmes. With the Braves struggling, at the All-Star break they recalled Johnny Logan and sent Mauch to Milwaukee.

It seemed like a bad break, but led to one of Mauch's best seasons. Thirsting for a chance to play, Mauch had two hits in his first two plate appearances with the Brewers.

Mauch played in 37 games at second base and shortstop and hit .303 with one homer and sixteen RBI. He was the central figure in leading the Brewers to the American Association pennant with a 94-57 record.

In the American Association playoffs, Milwaukee beat Kansas City four games to one and in the championship finals, polished off St. Paul 4-2 to advance to the Junior World Series to face the International League Champion Montreal Expos.

After the Royals won the opener in Montreal 6-3, Gene Mauch singled in a 4-3 Milwaukee win that evened the series at one game apiece.

Montreal's George "Shotgun" Shuba's second two-run homer of the game in the 11th inning gave Montreal a 5-3 win in game three and put the Royals up 2-1 in the series.

In game four in Milwaukee, before an overflow crowd of 11,595, Milwaukee combined the six hit pitching of Dick Donovan with Buzz Clarkson's three run homer to win 4-2 and even the series at two games apiece.

Gene Mauch sat out game five and watched Ernie Johnson blank Montreal on 4 hits to win 6-0. The Brewers led the series 3-2. One more win would do it.

In game six, the home team, Montreal jumped out to a 10-2 lead after two and a half innings, Milwaukee staged a spectacular comeback, scoring five runs in the sixth, one in the seventh and three in the eighth to win 13-10 and take the Junior World Series.

Chapter Seven

New York, St. Louis, Boston, Milwaukee... All Aboard!

Gene Mauch in Cuba.
Mauch (L), Ray Dandridge (C) Billy Herman (R)

In the major league draft in November of 1951, the New York Yankees selected Gene Mauch. "That's the dream of every player-to become a member of the Yankees," Mauch said while playing winter baseball in Cuba for the Cienfuegos Elephants.[1] When Mauch knew he'd be wearing pinstripes, he decided to go home to rest before reporting to the Yankees spring training. Just before he left, Mauch received news that his father George had died of a heart attack in California. He was only 52.

Mauch played in five spring training games for the Yankees and went one for thirteen. He was placed on waivers and every American League club passed on him. But the St. Louis Cardinals' Eddie Stanky knew Mauch from their Dodgers' days and suggested the Cards take him. Since the Yankees and Cardinals both trained in St. Petersburg, Mauch didn't have to go far. He left the Yankees' Soreno Hotel and walked a few blocks to the Cards' spring training home, the Bainbridge.

Mauch played in only seven games with the Cardinals, going 0-3. The Cardinals released him but he was quickly snapped up by his old team, the Boston Braves, who sent him back to the Milwaukee Brewers who were in first place in the American Association.

The Boston Braves had fired manager Tommy Holmes, replacing him with Brewers' manager, Charley Grimm. "Jolly Cholly" wasted no time making moves, recalling shortstop Johnny Logan and sending pitcher Gene Conley and infielder Buzz Clarkson to the Brewers.

Brewers' G.M. Richard "Red" Smith replaced Grimm as interim manager and the team went 7-0. Then, pitching coach Bucky Walters became the manager.

After joining the Brewers, Gene Mauch pinch hit twice and then replaced Logan at shortstop. In Toledo, with Mauch in the middle, the Brewers turned six double plays to tie a league record in a 6-3 win. Mauch was involved in five of the twin killings. The next night, the Brewers turned four more, with Mauch starting three of them. With Mauch at shortstop, the Brewers caught fire. Mauch went four-for-four in a win over Kansas City and homered in a victory over Columbus as the team went 15-2 to start the month of June.

In mid-June, the Braves recalled second baseman Jack Dittmer, the Brewer's top RBI man and ace reliever Virgil Jester. In return, the big club sent infielder Roy Hartsfield and pitcher Dick Donovan to Milwaukee. The loss of Dittmer and Jester weakened the team temporarily. As the Brewers went into a slump, Kansas City got hot, winning 12 out of 13 in late June to move into first place.

But the Brewers had too much pitching, defense and speed to lie dormant for long. In a series in Indianapolis, Gene Mauch went ten-for-eighteen with ten RBI. By the end of August, Milwaukee was 82-48 and back in first place.

With superb pitching by Don Liddle, Gene Conley, Billy Allen, Murray Wall and Dick Hoover, the Brewers were tough to beat.

Then, the Brewers got some unexpected help. With the parent Boston Braves in sixth place and headed nowhere, Braves management decided to help their AAA team win a pennant. They sent first baseman George Crowe to Milwaukee. With a .258 average, Crowe was the Braves' third leading hitter, behind Sid Gordon and Johnny Logan. In 1951 Crowe had a huge year with the Brewers, hitting .339 with 24 homers and 119 RBI. Management knew that Crowe could help the Brewers pull away from the pack.

Pull away they did. In 27 games, Crowe hit .351 with six homers and 29 RBI. Milwaukee won nine of their last eleven games while Kansas City faded. Milwaukee clinched the pennant with a 2-0 win over the Blues as Gene Conley won his eleventh game.

The Brewers finished the season at 101-53, twelve games ahead of Kansas City. Luis Marquez finished second in the batting race with a .346 average, Bill Bruton hit .325 and stole 29 bases and Gene Mauch was ninth in the American Association with a .324 average.

Diminutive lefthander Don Liddle went 17-4, Murray Wall 16-10 and Gene Conley 11-4. An amazing stat-the Brewers won seventeen doubleheaders while losing just 5.

Gene Mauch was presented with a 20-inch TV set for being named by the fans as the most popular Brewer.

In the first round of the playoffs at Borchert Field in Milwaukee, Buzz Clarkson hit two homers and Gene Conley hit a three run blast in the Brewers 12-11 win over St. Paul.

Milwaukee won the second game 9-7 as Gene Mauch had one of the shortest doubles in history. In the eighth, after Bill Bruton's two run triple tied the score, Mauch drove in the decisive run with a perfectly executed squeeze bunt. But as Mauch ran to first, he noticed nobody covering second base and slid in with a double.

In St. Paul, George Crowe got the Brewers started with a first inning home run and ace Don Liddle pitched Milwaukee to a 3-2 win and a three-games-to-none lead in the series. One more to go.

Milwaukee's Murray Wall took a shutout into the ninth but gave up a three run homer to St. Paul's Danny Ozark. But Gene Mauch had two hits and two RBI in a 6-3 Brewers win as they swept the Saints.

In the opening game of the playoff finals in Milwaukee, Kansas City won 4-3 and the next night, Don Liddle, backed by a 15 hit attack, breezed to a 7-2 victory as Milwaukee evened the series

At Blues Stadium in Kansas City, Milwaukee's Pete Whisenant hit two home runs and drove in six runs as the Brewers outslugged the Blues 10-8 to take a 2-1 lead in the series.

In the third inning, Gene Mauch was on first with the hit-and-run on. As Mauch took off, the hitter, George Crowe, swung and missed. Mauch stopped running between first and second as Blues' catcher Roy Partee, one of Mauch's boyhood friends, faked a throw and ran toward Mauch. Mauch gave Partee a forearm shot, trying to knock the ball loose but was tagged out, completing a double play.

In Mauch's next at bat, he and Partee exchanged words. Mauch dropped his bat. Partee took off his mask. They tore into each other at home plate. Both were ejected but Mauch insisted Partee meet him under the grandstand for round two. In a wild duel, Mauch pummeled Partee with right hands until they were separated. "I didn't lose that one," said Mauch.[2]

The Mauch-Partee rumble pumped up the attendance as 7,160 fans watched Kansas City score seven runs in the seventh to win 7-4 and even the series at two games apiece. The big blow was a grand slam home run by the Blues' rookie Bill "Moose" Skowron, who led the American Association with 134 runs batted in.

Another big crowd of 7,000 saw the Brewers Gene Conley pitch a four-hitter with ten strike outs and his teammates had 19 hits in a 12-1 Milwaukee win, to take a 3-2 lead in the series.

Back in Milwaukee, Kansas City pounded starter Don Liddle and five others for 13 hits, winning 10-4 to even the series at three games apiece and set up the deciding seventh game.

6,427 attended the final game at Borchert Field, the Brewers home since 1888. The city of Milwaukee had taken over the field and would convert it into a playground while the team would move to their new home, County Stadium.

The home crowd had little to cheer about with the Brewers trailing Kansas City 8-2 going to the ninth inning. But their heroes rallied for five runs in the ninth, falling a run short as Kansas City won 8-7 to take the series. Bill Renna, Don Bollweg and Moose Skowron all homered for the Blues who advanced to the Junior World Series.

In the Junior World Series, Kansas City took a 3-1 lead but then Rochester won three straight to take the series four-games-to-three. Gene Mauch had enjoyed Milwaukee and was looking forward to another season, when his baseball odyssey took another turn.

Chapter Eight

The Crackers Come Calling

Gene Mauch was home in bed in Los Angeles when he got a phone call from Earl Mann, owner and president of the Atlanta Crackers of the Southern Association. "I had never met him and was plenty surprised when he offered me the job," Mauch said.[1]

When the 1952 season ended, Mann made it clear he wanted a young player-manager with big league experience to manage his club. His team's greatest success had come with Eddie Moore, a second baseman and then Paul Richards, a catcher, managing the team.

When Mann showed interest in Mauch, Braves G.M. John Quinn made Mauch available. He signed a contract in New Orleans and Mann announced he had hired 27-year-old Gene Mauch as a player-manager, succeeding Dixie Walker. "He's got the ability to be a major league manager," said Mann, "and a good one. It's just a matter time."[2]

Mauch also received an endorsement from Walker, his former Dodger teammate. "Gene Mauch is the fiery type and I believe he will make a good man for them," Walker said. "The Braves wanted Mauch as a player and knowing that he would not take the assignment unless the leadership went with it, Quinn and Mann made a good decision when they signed Gene. Whitlow Wyatt, who is returning as coach, will be a fine balance wheel for Mauch."[3]

One columnist described Gene Mauch as, "the loose-lipped, slick fielding, light-hitting shortstop who patterns himself after Eddie Stanky, a fresh little guy with a lot of fight. Southern Association umpires are in for a lot of guff. Always a top bench jockey, there is no reason to believe the little blond guy is going to change merely because he's taken to managing. "[4]

Spring Training with Atlanta 1953.

Although only 27, Mauch had collected pieces of knowledge from experienced big league managers like Leo Durocher, Ray Blades and Billy Southworth and had cemented them into his mosaic. Nearing completion, it was still missing a few tiles. One of them was hands-on experience.

Mauch was greeted by 23 players at the initial drill in Miami Beach. Earl Mann called the workout "the toughest first day practice since Paul Richards was in charge of the Crackers."[5]

With impressive wins over Milwaukee, Pittsburgh and the World Champion New York Yankees, the Crackers created a following.

In Atlanta, before a crowd of 9,238 the Crackers beat the Yankees 4-3 as Art Fowler, the projected opening day starter, went the distance, scattering 10 hits. Yankee Lefthander Whitey Ford allowed seven hits, walked four and threw four wild pitches and ran out of gas after seven innings. One of the hits off Ford was a home run by Mauch.

The Crackers broke camp with a veteran team with a few kids sprinkled in. Mauch played second base and was surrounded by players from Atlanta's 1952 team, including first baseman Junior Wooten who hit.347 and third baseman Vernon Petty, a .311 hitter. Both were 29-years-old, career minor leaguers who would never see an ounce of big league action.

Player-Manager Gene Mauch leads Crackers onto field 1953.

Mauch was concerned with the shortstop position until Earl Mann acquired 24-year-old Bob Mainzer from Toledo. Mainzer was in the worst slump of his career and hit just .137 in his first two weeks with Atlanta but then caught fire, going 3 for 3 with two home runs in a victory over New Orleans.

The catcher was 24-year-old Jack Parks, who played 18 years in the minors without a day in the big leagues. His backup was LeRoy Jarvis, Mauch's teammate with the 1944 Dodgers.

Career minor leaguer, Dick Sinovic was in the outfield along with two young flyers, Pete Whisenant and Chuck Tanner.

30-year-old right hander Art Fowler was the ace of the pitching staff. Fowler had originally signed with the New York Giants in 1944 and then began a long journey through the minor leagues. In four previous seasons with Atlanta he had gone 48-33 including a 16 win season in 1952. Another vet pitcher was 26-year-old right-hander Leo Cristante, a 14 game winner for the Crackers in 1952.

With experience as a member of Branch Rickey's kiddie corps, Mauch had an eye for young talent and fell in love with 19-year-old right hander Bob Giggie and 20 year old southpaw Taylor Phillips. "We'll win twenty games," the two said confidently[6]. They meant twenty games each.

Taylor Phillips had a sizzling fastball and what Atlanta pitching coach Whit Wyatt called, "The best curveball in the league. "He's got control of his curve," Wyatt said. "I've never seen a kid as young as he is with as much stuff as he's got who can control it like he can."[7]

Phillips lived at home with his parents in Douglasville, a few miles west of Atlanta, close enough that they hosted a barbecue for the entire team. Signed out of Douglasville High School, Phillips had moved up to Atlanta after two years in Class D ball with Waycross in the Georgia-Florida League. He was 10-8 in 1951 but blossomed the next year with a 21-10 record, 265 strikeouts, a 1.40 ERA and he pitched a no-hitter.

Bob Giggie, an Italian kid from Milton, Massachusetts, had signed out of high school despite an 0-7 record as a senior. After a 2-2 year in the Mississippi Ohio Valley League, he went 18-7 with Hagerstown in 1952. He had spent a few days working out at the Boston Braves camp in spring training and Braves coach Bucky Walters saw him as something special. One day, Giggie was fooling around throwing sidearm and his manager, Dutch Dotterer, a former catcher, saw the tremendous movement on his pitches. "From now on, you are a sidearmer," Dotterer told him.[8]

Phillips and Giggie were the two brightest pitching prospects the Southern Association had seen in years. "And you can say I'm awful happy to have them on my side," said their manager Gene Mauch.[9]

For the first time in franchise history, Atlanta's season opener was a twilight game. The start was originally set for 8:00 p.m. but conflicted with the telecast of the heavyweight bout between Rocky Marciano and Jersey Joe Walcott. 11,590 packed Ponce de Leon Park in Atlanta to watch the young manager and his charges. Crackers catcher Jack Parks homered and doubled, driving in two runs in a 10-5 victory over Mobile[10]. Mauch played second base, hit second and went 1 for 3. Art Fowler got the win, scattering 11 hits in 8 2/3 innings.

In the second game of a doubleheader against Mobile, Crackers' owner Earl Mann filed a protest with league President Charles Hurth accusing the Bears of stalling, charging that Mobile players made no effort to retire the Crackers, hoping that darkness would halt play before the game became official. Atlanta eventually won in five frames 5-4, after dropping the opener 9-2 in a twin bill which began at 2 p.m. and ended at 7 p.m. "Baseball fans will not be treated the way they were if I can do anything about it," Mann said.[11]

Mobile president John Toomey of Mobile fired back that Gene Mauch was to blame for the slow play. "It would suffice to say that the first game took three hours to play."[12]

With the offense struggling, Gene Mauch asked his old Dodgers' teammate Paul "Big Poison" Waner to come in for special batting instruction. That night Atlanta pounded out a season high 13 hits but still lost to Birmingham 14-4.

Mauch was certainly having no trouble getting on base as he walked 19 times in the first 15 games and reached base safely in all of those games.

Mauch was also encouraged by the early success of his two whiz kids, Taylor Phillips and Bob Giggie.

Phillips got away to a faster start. In his first 37 2/3 innings, the young lefty allowed just 23 hits and nine runs while winning four straight. His first two starts were five-hitters and his third was a two-hitter.

Gene gets to know the umpires in the Southern Association.

Giggie beat four different teams: Nashville, Little Rock, Mobile and Memphis. He hit his peak against the hard hitting Chicks on May 19 with a two hitter. He had a no-hitter into the seventh until Ken Landenberger singled with two out.

The pitching staff got a boost in May when Gene Mauch made a phone call to former teammate Dick Donovan. Mauch knew the pitcher was unhappy, bouncing back and forth from the parent Boston Braves to the minors. When the Braves told him he'd been sold to their Toledo farm club, he'd had enough. He asked to be traded to another organization but the Braves said no.

"I was just about ready to chuck the whole thing when I got a call from Gene Mauch, my old roommate in Boston and Milwaukee," Donovan said. "He and Earl Mann begged me to come to Atlanta. It brought me together with Mr. Mann, one of the finest gentlemen I've ever known and with Whitlow Wyatt."[13]

Wyatt showed Donovan how to throw a slider, taught him mound savvy and got him started in a lucrative career in the insurance business.

After a poor first start, Donovan threw 15 2/3 innings without yielding an earned run and won twice. Donovan finished the season 11-8 and also hit .282 with five home runs.

Gene Mauch was cocky and aggressive and irritated rivals like Chattanooga pitcher Gerry Lane. When Mauch stepped into the batter's box and crowded the plate, Lane glared in, wound up and planted a fastball in the middle of Mauch's back. Normally, Mauch would have charged the mound but as the team's manager, he knew his only utility player was sidelined with a sprained wrist. Later, Lane drilled him again, this time on the thumb. Mauch seethed as he again ran to first base.

The next night, Mauch arrived early, dressed and headed for centerfield where Gerry Lane was catching fly balls. "They tell me you've never thrown at anybody over 160 pounds," shouted Mauch.[14] "Well, let's see if you've got any guts now," he added as he slammed his right fist into the side of Lane's face. Mauch landed another punch, staggering the 6'2" 230-pounder but Lane recovered and wrestled Mauch to the ground with a crushing headlock. "He twisted the devil out of me," Mauch said. "I couldn't turn my head for a week."[15]

Mauch played second, short and third; providing versatility, toughness and leadership. For the most part, his strategy was sound. He frequently called for a bunt or a hit-and-run and always seemed to make the right move. Well, almost always.

In a game against Memphis, Mauch's Crackers ran into trouble in the bottom of the 11th when the Chicks had runners on second and third with two outs and the score tied 2-2. Mauch told Art Fowler to walk left handed hitter Paul Lehner, loading the bases and setting up a force at any base, a percentage play with right handed hitting Bill Wilson coming up. Wilson pounded Fowler's third pitch over the 475 foot barrier in centerfield, a grand slam that gave Memphis a 6-2 win, dropping Atlanta into fourth place. Wilson finished the year with a league high 34 home runs and 111 RBI.

27-year-old outfielder Dick Sinovic was the team's most consistent hitter. By the end of June, Sinovic had driven in 50 runs and the Crackers were in fourth place. But in the next 29 games, Sinovic drove in 33 runs, had a 14-game hitting streak, lifted his average to .330 and was named to the midseason All-Star game.

Atlanta entered July with a 13-26 road record but Mauch said boldly, "If we can play .500 ball on the road, we can win the pennant."[16]

Mauch personally led the charge with two doubles and two singles in an 8-2 win at Little Rock, the team's ninth win in their last 10 road games as they improved their record to 59-47.

Mauch also decided to start Art Fowler every third day in an effort to catch first place Memphis. The Crackers promptly reeled off seven straight wins. By July 30, Atlanta had won ten of its last 11 on the road to move into second place, just a half a game back of Nashville.

But in mid-August, the team went into a tailspin. Nashville lefthander Jack Harshman set Atlanta down on five hits for his 20th win, as the Crackers losing streak extended to six straight.

But all of a sudden, the team jelled. With consistent pitching, solid offense and enough defense, Gene Mauch's team took off, winning seven straight games. Buoyed by a Car Night promotion, where fans could win a free car, 10,597 turned out at Ponce de Leon Park to see Pete Whisenant hit a two run homer in the ninth to beat New Orleans.

The Crackers drew their two largest crowds in the last three years in the final two home games. An estimated 15,000 including 13,008 paid, overflowed Ponce de Leon Park They saw Don Carlsen pitch the Pelicans to a 3-2 victory. It ended Atlanta's longest winning streak of the year.

On Ladies Night, 15,668 watched the Crackers final home game against New Orleans. Despite a 4-for-4 performance by Dick Sinovic with two homers and two singles, Atlanta lost 8-5.

The two huge crowds ballooned the Crackers home attendance to 290,510, the club's best gate since 1950.

The Crackers finished the season on the road with a schedule designed by the Marquis de Baseball. They played their last 15 games on the road in nine days including five doubleheaders in the final 6 days of the season.

While Gene Mauch wondered if his pitching staff could hold up, 43-year-old pitching coach Whit Wyatt volunteered to come out of retirement. Mauch said no thanks and went with the nine pitchers he had.

In the opener of a doubleheader in Mobile, Leo Cristante whipped the Bears 10-2 as the Crackers took over first place with an 80-64 record compared to 81-65 for Memphis and Nashville. Then, three straight one-run losses crushed the team's pennant hopes.

Atlanta lost the nightcap 3-2 when Art Fowler wild-pitched home the tying and winning runs in the ninth.

Unbelievably, the very next day, Mauch started the rubber-armed Fowler again, in the first game of another doubleheader. With the score tied 2-2, the tiring Fowler gave up a single and two walks to load the bases in the overtime 8th inning. Finally, Mauch made a pitching change but his successor Bill George walked in the winning run to give Mobile another 3-2 victory.

Mobile pulled the second game out of the fire with two runs in the ninth to win 6-5 as Ashton Heckel stole home on reliever Leo Cristante for the winning run. Atlanta won the final game of the series 11-2 as Jack Parks hit two home runs but the three straight, one run, extra inning losses were too much for the Crackers. While Nashville lost and was eliminated from contention, Atlanta still had a chance to tie for the pennant on the final day of the regular season.

When Atlanta lost the first game of a doubleheader 2-1 to New Orleans, the Crackers were eliminated, giving the pennant to Memphis. Atlanta also lost the nightcap 7-4 to the Pelicans in the final game of the year.

Under their first year manager's guidance, the Crackers finished third, just 2 ½ games out of first place.

Dick Sinovic led the Southern Association with 201 hits, 126 RBI and finished second in the batting race with a .342 average. Chuck Tanner finished 8th in hitting with a .318 mark.

Art Fowler was 18-10, his win total second only to Pitcher of the Year, Nashville's Jack Harshman who was 23-7. Fowler didn't hit the big leagues until he was 31. In addition to a nine-year major league career, he also pitched 19 years in the minors until he was 47. Fowler is best known as Billy Martin's drinking buddy and pitching coach for five different teams that Martin managed.

Little Rock's Ralph Atkins, Gene Mauch's old Fremont High teammate, hit 34 home runs to tie Nashville's Bill Taylor for the league lead.

Gene Mauch was a perfectionist. Nothing he did was good enough. Earl Mann loved Mauch's work, wanted him back and knew that his 27-year-old find would only get better. Mauch didn't agree. "I didn't think I measured up to the standard I had set for myself as a manager," he said, "even though we finished third," Mauch said.[17] He felt he'd put too much pressure on his young players, expecting them to have the same intensity he did. Mauch asked Mann for a few days to think about his future and flew to Chicago to talk with his brother-in-law Roy Smalley and his sister Jolene about his future.

They listened as Mauch explained what a challenging, sometimes frustrating experience his first season as manager had been. He'd always been angry at someone-himself, his players and the umpires. He stressed, he didn't eat right. His weight dropped from 173 to 153 pounds and by the end of the season he was exhausted. He'd been hard on his players, often berating them for not playing like major leaguers. Although he recalled Billy Southworth's advice that a manager shouldn't fall in love with his players, Mauch loved his players.

Only 27, he still wanted to play. He'd had a good year and felt he still had a few seasons left as a player. .

When Earl Mann offered him the job, Mauch declined. "The job is for guys like Lou Boudreau and Joe Gordon who can concentrate on two jobs at once," Mauch said "Maybe I'll manage again when I'm too old to play." So, Mauch was sold to the Los Angeles Angels.[18]

Chapter Nine

Angels in the Infield

The Pacific Coast League was a ballplayers' Shangri La. Many players made more money in the PCL than they could have earned in the big leagues and loved the schedule. Teams traveled mostly by plane, arrived on Monday and spent a week in cities like Los Angeles, San Diego, San Francisco, Seattle and Portland, playing a seven game series, including doubleheaders on Sunday.

Gene Mauch looked forward to going home to L.A. and playing for the Angels, the team he'd watched as a kid.

Insiders figured it was only a matter of time before Angels' manager Stan Hack would move up to the major leagues to manage the Angels' parent club, the Chicago Cubs. That time came more quickly than anyone imagined. Hack had signed a contract for another year with the Angels and was busy with spring training in Fullerton when a bombshell hit.

Chicago owner P.K. Wrigley fired Phil Cavarreta, the first time a big league manager had been canned during spring training. Wrigley had met with Cavaretta a few days earlier to assess the 1954 Cubs. The manager was brutally honest, pointing out the team's weaknesses and told his boss that the club would not be a contender and might very well finish last, not what Wrigley wanted to hear.

Accusing Cavarretta of "defeatism," Wrigley fired him, replacing him with Stan Hack. In a bizarre twist, Wrigley asked Cavarretta to switch jobs with Hack and go manage the Los Angeles Angels with the same salary. Cavarretta said no and left the Cubs. In 17 years as a Cubs' player and two full seasons as the team's manager Cavarretta was unable to win. Since the Cubs had already lost 15 of their first 20 spring exhibition games, it looked like more of the same.

Angels' President Don Stewart said that the new skipper would not come from their ranks, ending media speculation that Gene Mauch would be named manager.

With opening day just a week away, Bill Sweeney was named the Angels new skipper. Sweeney had managed the Angels from 1943-1946, had won two pennants and guided Seattle to a second place finish in 1953. Known as "Ole' Tomato Face," because his face reddened when he got angry, the fast-living, hard-drinking Sweeney had always been popular with Angels' fans and media.

Wrigley Field was a Los Angeles treasure. Named after William K. Wrigley Jr., the chewing gum magnate who owned both the Chicago Cubs and the Angels, the ballpark was located in the South Central section of L.A. at the intersection of 42nd Street and Avalon Boulevard. Built in 1925, the park was designed to look like the Chicago Cubs home, Wrigley Field in Chicago, only with a Southern California feel. It was classic art deco, a white façade with a red roof, resembling many homes in the neighborhood. There was a nine story office tower at the park's entrance, with two large Spanish style clocks, visible from the field. The clocks were fifteen feet in diameter. Instead of numbers, the clock's capital letters spelled out "Wrigley Field." Unlike Chicago's Wrigley Field, the L.A. version had stadium lights, installed in 1931.

It was small ballpark, seating 20,500 with a covered, double deck grandstand that wrapped around from one foul pole to another. It was a hitter's paradise, a mere 340 feet down the left and right field lines and 427 to center. But the power alleys were only 345 feet away. There was a fifteen foot brick wall in left, which was later covered with ivy to resemble the Cubs' home in Chicago.

Since Wrigley Field looked like a major league park, movie studios used it frequently for films including *Damn Yankees, The Pride of St. Louis, Pride of the Yankees*, and *The Kid from Left Field*. Gene Mauch appeared in *The Stratton Story, It Happened One Spring, The Winning Team*, and *The Jackie Robinson Story*, along with his friends Peanuts Lowery and Bob Lemon. "It used to be a good deal for a ballplayer," said Mauch. "You could pick up $200 a week for just sitting around in the mob scenes. I've been doing it since I was 16. I think I still have my union card."[1] Wrigley Field was later the sight of the classic TV program, *The Gillette Home Run Derby*.

Wrigley Field had been a teenaged stop for Gene Mauch. When he wasn't playing baseball, Gene Mauch was in the stands watching the Angels. Mauch's favorite player was centerfielder Arnold "Jigger" Statz, who played for the Angels for 17 years, the longest any player ever performed for one team in the minor leagues. Just 5'7" and 150 pounds, Statz hit over .300 eleven times, once stole 61 bases in a season and played until he was 44. Statz also played in 681 games over eight years in the big leagues with the Giants, Red Sox, Cubs and Dodgers.

Statz had carved the palm out of his glove to get a better feel. It must have worked. He was an acrobat in the outfielder and Duke Snider, a great fly chaser himself, called Statz the best centerfielder he ever saw.

Gene Mauch skipped school in 1942, Statz's final year, to watch his idol hit two homers on opening day, the only two he hit all year. Little did Mauch know that someday he would be a Los Angeles Angel.

After the 1953 season ended, the Pacific Coast League rescinded the edict that prohibited clubs from receiving players on option from the big league teams. The Cubs ended their agreement with their other AAA team, Springfield in the International League, freeing up more players for the Angels. Pitchers Sheldon Jones and Tom Simpson, catcher John Pramesa, outfielder Herb Adams and infielders Gene Hooks and Tommy Brown were sent from Springfield to L.A. The Angels would also get players sent down by the Cubs.

The Angels were set at first and second with returnee Fred Richards and Gene Mauch. But center field, shortstop and third base were wide open.

Back in action with the Angels.

With Gene Baker promoted to Chicago, Bud Hardin had first shot at shortstop. Hardin was a good fielder although he was a light hitter. Mauch's former Dodgers teammate Tommy Brown played third for a while but it wasn't until the Cubs sent down Bruce Edwards, that they had an everyday third sacker. Edwards, a former catcher, didn't have the arm for the position and he was no great shakes defensively but he could hit and played third base the rest of the year.

Bill Sweeney's starting outfield consisted of Dixie Upright, Herb Adams and Bob Usher, Gene Mauch's old American Legion foe, from San Diego. Upright was a defensive liability and Adams was sent to Columbus with Usher taking over in center and Tommy Brown moving to left. The Angels hoped that veteran Max West could play right field but he hadn't fully recovered from knee surgery. Rookie Jacques Monette, Don Roberts, sent down by the Cubs and Vic Marasco, acquired from the Dodgers, all played right field.

The catchers were Al Evans and Johnny Parmesa. With veterans Cal McLish, Joe Hatten, Bob Spicer and Sheldon Jones and rookie Lorenzo Hinchman, the pitching rotation seemed sound.

In the final spring training game, the Angels and arch rival Hollywood Stars met at Recreation Park in Long Beach. This wasn't just *any* exhibition game. The rivalry had become a bitter feud, that one writer said, "Makes the Hatfield and McCoys look like amateur debaters." Former Stars player Chuck Stevens said, "I'd rather beat the Angels than eat."[2] Extra bleachers were installed to accommodate the expected crowd of over 3,000. Fans knew that anything could happen–and it did.

Gene Mauch set the tone in the fourth inning, engaging in a rhubarb with Umpire John Luksig over what Mauch saw as a bad call. Mauch was just about to get thrown out, when he cooled off and walked away.

Then, with Hollywood leading 6-2 in the ninth inning, Stars' rookie pitchers Dick Smith and Solon Shaw walked Max West and Dave Cunningham with nobody out.

After Gene Hooks fouled out to the catcher for the first out, Bob Usher, enjoying a perfect game with a triple, double and two singles, walked to the plate as the pro-Angel crowd cheered for a rally. One of Shaw's pitches came in high and tight, sending Usher sprawling in the dirt. Umpire Emmett Ashford, the first black umpire in organized ball, indicated Usher had been hit by a pitch and sent him to first, loading the bases.

Stars' manager Bobby Bragan shot out of the dugout, claiming the ball hit the bat, not Usher. Arguing with Ashford, Bragan took off his cap and threw it 30 feet in the air. It landed on the screen behind home plate and Ashford immediately threw Bragan out of the game. But Bragan continued to argue and was joined by his players Larry Dorton, Jack Phillips and Chuck Stevens, who surrounded Ashford at home plate. Finally, Bragan sat down in front of Ashford and crossed his legs. Ashford again told Bragan to leave the field and walked away. Bragan lay down flat on his back.

Then, umpire Al Mustact raced in from his position near second base and ordered Bragan to end his sit down-lie down strike as the crowd went wild. Finally, he stood up, talked briefly with his players and headed for the clubhouse, accompanied by the booing crowd.

Bragan left and rookie lefthander Don Corella came in to pitch. Fred Richards popped up to Mauch on an infield fly rule. Dixie Upright stepped in, worked the count to two and two, and then tapped a comebacker to the pitcher who threw him out, ending the game. Hollywood won the game 6-4.

The Angels began the 1954 season in San Diego with a twin opener, one game in the afternoon and another in the evening. 3672 turned out for the first game and 5,690 for the nightcap. San Diego Mayor John Butler threw out the first ball and then the teams traded shutouts. In the first game the Padres' Eddie Erautt held the Angels to three hits, winning 5-0. In the evening, lefty Joe Hatten and reliever Cliff Fannin combined for a seven hitter as the Angels won 4-0. Gene Mauch went 1-7 for the day.

Back at Wrigley Field for the home opener, the weather was uncommonly cold for Los Angeles, 49 degrees, and only 3,667 fans turned out in freezing rain and fog. Seals pitcher Elmer Singleton handcuffed the Angels on three hits and no runs until the ninth inning when Fred Richards and Dixie Upright homered but San Francisco held on to win 4-3.

Disturbed by his team's anemic offense, Bill Sweeney posted a note announcing mandatory team batting practice. But when the Angels pounded out 18 hits in a 12-2 win over the Seals that night, he cancelled the session.

For most of April, the Angels played .500 ball and Mauch's hitting was one of the few bright spots. The Angels hit 28 home runs in their first 29 games but with only six coming with men on base.

With hitters generating little offense besides an occasional solo homer, Bill Sweeney was constantly changing his lineup. Fred Richards, who'd had a good year in 1953 batting second, couldn't hit and when moved to the cleanup spot he still couldn't hit. His batting average was below .200 with eight home runs, all solos, and only nine RBI. Both Bob Usher and Dixie Upright were struggling, hard pressed to match their 1953 numbers. As if this wasn't enough for Sweeney to bear, his son Mike fell over a bicycle at a little league game and broke his arm.

In late April, the Angels prepared for their first series with the Hollywood Stars. The seeds of hatred were planted deep. "There were some historic, legendary battles," remembered Gene Mauch. "We were never too far away from fighting."[3]

A little history here-on August 2, 1953 the teams met in a Sunday doubleheader. The rivalry began to heat up on Friday night when the Angels' Fred Richards slid hard into Gene Handley at third on a triple. Both dugouts emptied and the two were ejected. The Stars won in the ninth on Frank Kelleher's two-out pinch-hit single.

The next day, Kelleher started and singled in a run in the first inning, off Joe Hatten. In Kelleher's second at bat in the fourth, Hatten threw two pitches at his head. Kelleher's answered with a triple off the center field fence and scored on a squeeze bunt as the Angels took a 2-0 lead.

As Kelleher came up in the sixth, he knew he had a target painted on his back. Hatten planted a fastball between his shoulder blades. Kelleher charged the mound and began punching Hatten. Fred Richards ran over from first base to join in the fray. Within moments, players from both teams dashed onto the field.

Kelleher was ejected. Ted Beard pinch ran for him. Later in the inning, Beard slid into third base with his spikes high. Angels' third baseman Murray Franklin went after Beard and soon six different fights broke out like California wildfires. Los Angeles Chief of Police William Parker, watching the game on TV, ordered every available police unit to Gilmore Field.

The combatants slugged it out for thirty minutes with the helpless umpires looking on. When the police arrived, they got things under control. Beard and Franklin were ejected and every player not in the lineup was sent to the clubhouses where police were stationed. Many baseball historians believe this was the worst brawl in the history of the game.

Now it was 1954 and the teams met again at the Stars' home, Gilmore Field. Angels' manager Bill Sweeney offered a new cashmere suit to the first player who started a fight with the Stars.

Gene Mauch was first in line. He hated Carlos Bernier, the Stars showboating outfielder who often stole bases with his team enjoying a big lead, violating "The Code." Known as "The Comet," the Puerto Rican-born Bernier did everything with a flair and twice led the PCL in stolen bases. He spent just one full season in the big leagues with the Pittsburgh Pirates in 1953 but flourished in the minors for 17 years.

He became a cult hero in Hollywood. When the Pirates wanted to recall Bernier, Grouch Marx led a protest to keep him in Hollywood saying it would be a demotion if he went to Pittsburgh.

When his 65-year-old mother Rosario visited from Puerto Rico, Bernier had a present waiting for her: a box of cigars. "My mamma, sure, she smokes cigars," said Bernier, "maybe two, three a day. I have to watch her or mamma will raid my supply."[4]

Bernier was cocky, flamboyant and irritating. He liked to hit down on the ball, chopping it into the ground, a swinging bunt that frequently resulted in a hit followed by a stolen base. Angels' pitcher John Pyecha hated Bernier. "I tried seriously, seriously, one of the few guys I seriously tried to hit," said the pitcher "and I seriously tried to hit him in the damn shins. He was fast. He'd chop that ball on the ground and take off. I said I'll stop that bastard. I'll hit him and he won't be able to run. In one game, I threw twice trying to get his shin but I missed him."

The Stars won two of the first three games as Mauch waited for his chance to get Bernier. He told his teammates to let him be the only Angel who would tag Bernier. Finally, in the fourth game, Bernier reached first base, ready to run. As Bernier led off from first base, Mauch grabbed a handful of dirt. As Bernier came in, spikes high, trying to break up a double play, Mauch threw the dirt in his face and it was on. The two scuffled and Mauch said "I sort of walked all over Bernier," but Sweeney reneged on his cashmere suit offer, saying it took too long, four days, to incite a brawl.

Fun and Games with the Angels.

Confrontations with Bernier and Angels' wins meant more to Mauch than a new suit and whenever these teams met, you could count on fireworks. Still, the Stars won two more games 1-0 and 4-1.

The Angels finally broke out of their hitting doldrums with 20 hits in a Sunday doubleheader sweep of the Stars. Gene Mauch had a home run, three walks, three RBI and two runs scored in the first game. Afterwards, Angels manager Bill Sweeney breathed a sigh of relief saying, "it had been the worst hitting slump he'd seen in thirty years in baseball."[5] But the Hollywood Stars won the first series between the two clubs, four games to three.

The Angels got good pitching for the first six weeks but eventually an anemic offense and poor defense dropped them into the cellar.

By early June, the Angels and Stars were headed in opposite directions. With the Angels in last place, the Stars, after a slow start, caught fire and were in first place, threatening to pull away from the pack.

Just before the intra city series renewed at Wrigley Field, manager Bobby Bragan predicted a massacre, calling his 1954 Hollywood Stars, "the greatest team I've ever managed, and the greatest minor league team I've ever seen."[6]

The Stars had been floundering in early May when shortstop Dick Smith was sent down by the parent Pittsburgh Pirates. The 5'8" 150 pound Smith was a top leadoff man, base stealer and ignited the offense. The Stars also had great pitching: Mel Queen was 11-1 and Lino Dinoso and Red Munger were both 7-1. And third baseman Jack Phillips was second in the league in hitting at .352.

The first two games of the Angels-Stars series in June at Wrigley Field produced some statistical oddities. In the first game won by Hollywood 7-4, each team had 22 hits and 22 strikeouts.

In the next game, a 7-1 Stars' victory, each team had eight hits, the Angels lost their eighth straight and Stars ace Red Munger won his eighth straight game.

The Angels broke the losing streak the next night, before a Ladies Night crowd of 15,350, the biggest Wrigley Field turnout of the season. The uncommonly large crowd was aided by a Chamber of Commerce promotion and the appearance of movie star Kim Novak. Gene Mauch was three-for-four with a home run as Los Angeles won 4-2. Hollywood took the next two games 4-2 and 8-5 setting up a Sunday doubleheader.

So far, it had been a tame series but 13,576 showed up for a Sunday doubleheader, many hoping for the usual fireworks between the rivals. Lino Donoso pitched a four-hitter and struck out thirteen as the Stars won 9-0 but the Angels took the nightcap 2-1 as Cal McLish pitched a two-hitter and the fans got what they'd hoped for.

In the fifth inning, the Stars' Carlos Bernier tried to steal second. Bernier slid in hard and leg-whipped shortstop Bud Hardin who tagged him out. When Bernier jumped up to argue the call, Hardin thought he was going to hit him and swung first. Within moments, the dugouts emptied. Gene Mauch, of course, jumped in, nailing Bernier with several punches as other fights broke out around the field. Hollywood's Dale Long and Los Angeles' Bob Usher squared off and Dixie Upright charged the Stars' dugout, met by the Stars' Jack Phillips, waving a baseball bat.

Finally the umpires, with help from the police, restored peace. Bernier and Hardin were ejected and Hollywood took the series five games to two.

PCL President Clarence "Pants" Rowland fined Hardin and Bernier $50 each and suspended Bernier for five days because he had started the fight which Rowland said, "could have caused a riot."

The rivalry between the Angels and Stars was so heated that even the team broadcasters hated each other. On KMPC radio, Bob Kelley voice of the Angels, ripped Carlos Bernier for starting the brawl. Stars' voice Mark Scott on a KFWB sportscast accused Bill Sweeney of being "a rabble rouser."

Sweeney said, "After the free-for-all, I told Bernier he had better not start any more fights and Bernier told me where I could go. Then I 'read' him off, the same as I would have any other player."[7]

The hot-headed Bernier didn't heed the message. In a game against San Diego in August, Bernier got into an argument with plate umpire Chris Valenti about a strike call, bumped the umpire with his stomach and then slapped him in the face. "Pants" Rowland was sitting 30 feet away in a box seat. Bernier was ejected and suspended for the rest of the season.

Hollywood manager Bobby Bragan said, "I don't see why so much fuss was centered around Carlos, anyway. Gene Mauch was worse than Bernier when it came to arguing and starting trouble. I'll admit he didn't strike an umpire, though."[8] The total attendance for the Stars-Angels series was 65,120, the biggest week's gate in the league all year.

Two near fights enlivened a game between the Angels and San Diego Padres in July. First, Gene Mauch charged the Padre dugout searching for a heckler and couldn't find him. Later, Padres manager Lefty O'Doul invited a taunting fan to come on down and they slugged it out until the cops broke it up.

When Mauch was ejected from a game against Oakland, newspapers reported that Mauch "turned the air blue" and "his salty words could be heard by each of the 1380 fans in the stands."

Chicago Cubs director of player personnel Wid Mathews was among the small crowd of 1864 on August 3 at Wrigley Field, when the Angels' 28-year-old right-hander Bubba Church threw a no-hitter, beating Portland 3-0. It was the first no-hitter of his career and the Angels' first nine inning no-hitter since Warren Hacker threw one in 1951.

Although impressed by Church, Mathews watched the impotent Angels offense and said he was not optimistic about finding players to help the sinking team. By August 5, the Angels were in last place with a 50-72 record, twenty six and a half games back of first place Hollywood.

Although PCL President Rowland said fans didn't come to the ballpark to see fights, 11, 946 showed up at Wrigley Field when the teams met again. Veteran Max West come out of the dugout with two on and one out in the ninth and Hollywood leading 4-3. West got ahold of George O'Donnell's pitch and pulled it over the right field screen to give the Angels a 5-4 win.

The next day 6438 saw a 15 inning thriller that lasted 3 hours and 38 minutes, Los Angeles won 2-1 on a home run by catcher Al Evans. Cal McLish pitched all 15 innings for the win.

The Angels played the game under protest from the 12th inning on. They had the bases loaded and the count was 3-1 on Vic Marasco when Stars' pitcher Jim Walsh threw a pitch wide of the plate. As Marasco headed to first with an apparent walk, third base umpire Al Mustart called him back, saying that Hollywood manager

Bobby Bragan had requested and had been granted a time out to make a pitching change.

Manager Bill Sweeney, coach Jackie Warner and several Angels' players rushed Mustart, ranting and raving at the call. Sweeney and Warner were both thrown out of the game.

The crowd was howling at the call when suddenly thousands of seat cushions rained down on the field. The umpires threatened to forfeit the game unless order was restored. They needed a peacemaker and believe it or not, asked Angels' captain Gene Mauch to come out and quiet the crowd.

An even bigger crowd of 9319 turned out the next night to see Hollywood win 5-4 on a twelfth inning squeeze bunt by Tom Saffell.

Then, 14,416 showed up for a Sunday doubleheader. The Angels took the opener 4-0 as Bubba Church pitched a two-hitter but the fireworks came in the nightcap, won by Hollywood 2-1.

In the fourth inning, Hollywood's Tom Saffell complained about a close pitch and was ejected. For some reason, he ran out to his post in center field and had to be tossed for a second time

Then, plate umpire Jerry Van Keuren walked out to the mound and asked to inspect the baseball. Hollywood's pitcher George O'Donnell threw the ball to the plate but catcher Jim Mangan let it sail past him to the screen. An irate Van Keuren threw Mangan out of the game and then pushed him. The Stars stormed the field in protest and fans began to sail seat cushions down onto the field.

Finally, order was restored, temporarily. In the Hollywood half of the seventh with the score tied 1-1 with two men on and one out, the Stars Eddie Malone hit a foul pop up near the box seats. Angels' catcher Al Evans was all set to catch the ball when a fan deflected it.

The beleaguered Van Keuren called Malone out and then had to deal with an angry Bobby Bragan. Bragan got the thumb as fans hooted and hollered, but put on his usual vaudeville skit before exiting. He doffed his cap and bowed to Van Keuren before leaving. The fans went crazy again throwing seat cushions and even a chair sailed onto the field. The police had to be summoned to quiet things down. Finally, pinch hitter Jack Lohrke singled in the winning run in the Stars 2-1 victory. The Angels won three of the five games in the series which drew a total of 42,119 fans to Wrigley Field.

A four-game winning streak against Seattle, pulled the Angels out of last place and into sixth. A major reason for their improvement was pitching. Bubba Church won six games over the last five weeks of the season and Turk Lown, a disappointing starter with the Cubs, found new life as a reliever in Los Angeles. In 30 games, he was 5-3 with a 2.48 ERA with no home runs allowed, a remarkable accomplishment for a pitcher who often toiled at Wrigley Field.

The offense was terrible. The Angels were shut out 19 times. They did not have a .300 hitter. Bruce Edwards led the team at .298 and Mauch was second, hitting .287 with 11 home runs, 58 RBI and a club leading 12 stolen bases. The baseball writers named Mauch the Angels MVP for 1954.

The Angels finished in sixth place with a 73-92 record, twenty-seven games back of first place San Diego. Total home attendance at Wrigley Field was a mere 238, 567, lowest of the Post War period.

To make matters worse the Angels franchise suffered a tragic blow when team president Don Stewart died of a heart attack on September 6. In accordance with his widow's wishes, all of the Angels games were played as scheduled but the flag atop Wrigley Field Tower was lowered to half-staff. He was replaced by John Holland, son of a long-time minor league owner and general manager at Des Moines.

Despite Bobby Bragan's boast that the Hollywood Stars were the best team ever, they wound up tied with San Diego as the regular season ended. In a one game playoff, the Padres Bob Elliott homered twice to give San Diego a 7-2 win and the PCL title.

P.K. "Phil" Wrigley, who owned the Chicago Cubs and the Los

Angeles Angels was tired of seeing his team finish behind the Hollywood Stars. In the past, the Angels, like most PCL teams, were a collection of the too-old and the never-good-enough. Wrigley was determined to stock his AAA team with talent. Coming off the poor 1954 season, the parent Cubs and Angels knew they had to make changes. Only eight players remained from the previous year.

One holdover was third baseman Jim "Buzz" Clarkson, a Negro league vet who had toiled for many years with the Pittsburgh Crawfords, Newark Eagles and Philadelphia Stars. In 1952, with the Boston Braves, he hit just .200 in 14 games but also helped lead their AAA farm team in Milwaukee to a second straight American Association title. Clarkson said he was 37, although he was really 40. No matter. The man could rake. In 1954 in the Texas League, he hit .324 with 42 home runs and 135 RBI.

Just before the 1955 PCL season began, the Chicago Cubs trimmed their roster, optioning seven players to Los Angeles. They were pitchers Jim Brosnan, Bob Zick, Don Elston and Bill Tremel, outfielders Don Robertson and Bob Talbot and first baseman Steve Bilko. Four days later, the Cubs sent infielder Eddie Winceniak, catcher Joe Hannah and pitcher Joe Stanka to Los Angeles.

The Angels were an older, veteran club with an average age of 27.4 years. During the season, they used 39 players. Buzz Clarkson was the lone 40-year-old, but they had eight players in their thirties and nineteen players, twenty-five or older. Every member of the opening day lineup had major league experience.

As the 1955 season began, a poll of league managers tabbed the Hollywood Stars as the favorite to win the PCL. Stocked with players sent down by the Cubs, Manager Bill Sweeney boldly predicted his Angels would be neck-in-neck with the Stars at the finish line. On April 6, the Angels and the other PCL teams began the 1955 season.

The Angels opening day lineup consisted of Steve Bilko at first, Gene Mauch at second, Bud Hardin at shortstop and Buzz Clarkson at third. Don Robertson, Bob Talbot and Bob Usher manned the outfield spots and John Pramesa was the catcher. Jim Brosnan was the opening day pitcher against Portland and lost 3-2.

Portland took the second game 7-2 but then, in game three, rookie lefthander George Piktuzis made an auspicious debut, throwing a two hit shutout to beat Portland 5-0. Piktuzis had gone 24-6 with an 0.67 ERA in two years in the Army and looked like a star on the rise. Buzz Clarkson blasted a 400-foot home run to support him.

Then, the bottom fell out. Portland swept a doubleheader 4-2 and 2-0. Steve Bilko was 0/8, committed three errors and was booed by the crowd. Former PCL president and now Chicago Cubs executive, Clarence "Pants" Rowland, watched the series and promised to send help.

In the last week of April, the PCL announced that between games of a doubleheader, Angels' second baseman Gene Mauch would be presented with the Don Stewart Memorial Award as the team's most valuable player in 1954. After accepting a trophy and the crowd's adulation, Mauch, riding an 11-game hitting streak, went 0 for 6 and was ejected from the second game. In the fifth inning, pitcher Bob Murphy's first pitch was over Mauch's head. Mauch shouted at Murphy. When the next pitch was high and inside, Mauch charged the mound. Murphy backpedaled, shedding his hat and glasses and the two wrestled to the ground. Both teams ran onto the field and the brawl was on. Umpire Emmet Ashford waded into the fray trying to separate the two and Mauch was ejected.

Trying to speed up games, new league President Claire Goodwin had originated monthly Pacific Coast League Hustle Program awards. The first place Seattle Rainiers were awarded the Team Hustle Award and Gene Mauch won $200 as the most colorful player of the month.

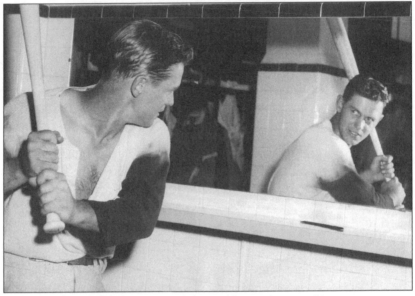

Practice Makes Perfect. Credit: Gaylon H. White

Before a game between the Los Angeles and Oakland, the Oaks' Bill Serena was in a playful mood as he waited to take his swings in batting practice. He decided he'd have a little fun with the Angels' Gene Mauch, so he started a rumor that Mauch and Bob Usher were going to be traded to Oakland. As things often do in baseball, information spread like a California wildfire. When Mauch and Usher heard they were being traded, they went to manager Bill Sweeney who assured them they weren't going anywhere.

The Angels' manager was furious. When Serena walked past Sweeney on his way to the Oakland dugout, Sweeney yelled, "And who are you trading off next?"[9]

Thinking that Sweeney believed the phony trade was in the works, Serena, replied, "Oh, several of your guys."[10] He then began to name off players.

Now furious, Sweeney countered with, "Why don't you wait until you get in a few games before you pop off? You aren't even playing regular, yet you're busy trading away my players."

"If you pitch a couple of lefthanders Sunday, I'll be in there," said Serena. "I hit against lefties."

"Yeah," Sweeney said, "and I might just have one of them bury a fastball in your ear!"[11]

Sure enough, the next day, Sweeney started Johnny Pyecha who threw a fastball at Serena's head and sent him sprawling in the dirt. Serena jumped up, raged at Sweeney and had to be restrained by Umpire Emmett Ashford and Oakland coach Eddie Taylor.

It's getting so that I don't know whether I'm an umpire or a referee," said Ashford[12].

In the Angels batting order, Bob Talbot led off. Gene Mauch, a great bunter and hit-and-run artist batted second. The 3-4-5 hitters were Bob Usher, Buzz Clarkson and Steve Bilko.

With Buzz Clarkson batting fourth and Bilko fifth, the Angels were dangerous. Clarkson got good pitches to hit because teams didn't want to walk him with Bilko up next. Clarkson hit five homers and Bilko eight as the Angels improved to 16-10, within one game of first place.

Steve Bilko didn't just hit home runs, he often hit tape measure blasts. In an 9-6 11 inning win in Oakland, Bilko connected off lefty Adrian Zabala and hit a ball over the centerfield fence that struck a building 552 feet away. He also hit one over Gilmore Field's high centerfield fence, a rare feat.

As the Angels and Hollywood Stars prepared for another series, Carlos Bernier retuned after serving a suspension for slapping an umpire "I learn my lesson," Bernier said. "I'm a good boy now."[13]

According to a spokesman for the Angels, the Stars offered to sell Bernier to them for $50,000 plus Gene Mauch and Bobby Usher. No thank you.

In the first game of a doubleheader at Wrigley Field with Steve Bilko batting in the seventh inning, Hollywood Stars pitcher Lino Donoso threw what he was sure was strike three. When umpire Don Flecky called it a ball, Stars manager Bobby Bragan was enraged.

Bragan held in his anger until the ninth. With the Angels leading 7-3, Bragan sent up eight consecutive pinch hitters to the plate
for Donoso who was due to lead off. He replaced most of the hitters before they faced a pitch. A ninth pinch hitter was about
to go to the plate but Clarence Bubeller, the eighth, checked his
swing when he heard Bragan yell from the dugout and hit a weak
ground ball for an out. "All those batters were used to show up
the umpires," admitted Bragan "because they had already made
a big farce of the game."[14] Bragan was later fined $30 by league
President Claire Goodwin.

The game was costly because Buzz Clarkson, fielding a bunt,
slipped on the wet grass and broke his foot. He missed the next
seven weeks. Piper Davis, acquired from Oakland, replaced him.

With Clarkson sidelined, the team and Bilko began to sink. With
little protection in the batting order, pitchers attacked Bilko. With
Clarkson out, Bilko's average dropped seventeen points and the
Angels fell to fifth place.

In early May the Cubs sent outfielder Hal Rice, catcher Jim Fan-
ning and pitchers Bubba Church and Hy Cohen to Los Angeles.
But Angel's manager Bill Sweeney, who'd been ill, resigned on
May 23 on the advice of his doctor.

39-year-old Bob Scheffing replaced Sweeney. Scheffing had been a
Cubs coach under Stan Hack and he and Mauch had been teammates with the Cubs.

Mauch said Bob Scheffing was the best manager he'd ever played
for. He knew how to handle players and get inside their heads to
motivate them. "He'd say things quietly, like I wasn't supposed to
hear," recalled Mauch. "He'd stand by the batting cage and whis-
per loudly, 'That Mauch sure is a great hitter' to somebody."

When Scheffing went to Los Angeles, he knew only three players
on the club so Mauch, with his photographic memory, filled his
skipper in with a scouting report on every player.

Remembered catcher Jim Fanning, "Mauch was the smartest guy on the club. He knew more baseball than the managers." Mauch would position infielders and outfielders and sometimes even call pitches for his hurlers. "I went to the mound in Los Angeles many times," said Fanning, "and when I got there, he and Scheffing had already determined what we were going to do and they didn't make any bones about it."

The Angels were in fifth place, 25-25 when Bob Scheffing took over as manager. After being blitzed by the Stars, the team lost 14 of 21 games under their new manager, with nine games decided by one run and five going to extra innings.

Bob Cobb owned the Stars as well as the Brown Derby Restaurants and invented the Cobb Salad. He was married to actress Gail Patrick and the Stars' Gilmore Field, was a haven for celebrities.

Irv Noren, who played for Hollywood in 1949 recalled meeting, "George Raft, Bing Crosby, Bob Hope, the Marx Brothers, they all came to the games."

Jayne Mansfield was "Miss Hollywood Star" of 1955 and drove fans to a frenzy when she came onto the field and a teenaged Elizabeth Taylor was a bat girl.

The Hollywood Stars started the year slowly and fell into last place. But, by the time the Angels visited Gilmore Field in early June, the Stars had caught fire. They whipped the Angels six out of seven games and within a six-day span, moved into third place, improving their record to 19-8 at home.

After watching the Stars devastation of his team, Angels' President John Holland predicted Hollywood would win it all. As the Angels fell to within two percentage points of last place, Holland and Wid Mathews went to work. The Cubs recalled pitcher Dave Hillman and sent another hurler, Hy Cohen, to the Angels. Slick-fielding infielder Casey Wise was acquired from Des Moines, pitcher Al Lary was snared from Macon and pitcher Ray Bauer reported to the Angels from North Carolina University, where he'd been working on a master's degree. The most important addition was centerfielder Gale "Windy" Wade, obtained from Toledo.

Like Gene Mauch, Wade was tough as an old leather glove and they became good friends. Wade loved to break up double plays and was fearless in challenging outfield walls to make catches.

"Gene was the leadoff hitter and I batted second," explained Wade. "If I got on base, Gene would give me a sign. I would break for second base and Gene would pull the ball to the left side of the infield. I wouldn't even slow down at second. I'd keep running to third. We wound up with a runner at third and one out. We scored many, many runs that way. That play was the talk of the league."

One time, though, Mauch thought he gave Wade the sign but Wade didn't see it. "Gene swung at a horrible pitch but I didn't run and he was so mad," said Wade.

When the inning ended, Wade headed for the outfield and Mauch for second base. Suddenly, Mauch started yelling at Wade. "He was cussing' and when he got mad the blood vessels in his neck would stand out," said Wade. "He was giving me hell because I didn't pick up the sign. I said, 'Gene, you didn't give me the signal.'"

"Yes I did, by God," yelled Mauch. "You screwed up the sign."

The story has grown into saying the two came to blows. Wade insisted that never happened, saying that they were friends and besides, "Gene was smaller than me. My God, we never would have done anything like that."

Mauch and Wade both knew Chuck Connors with whom they'd played in the Brooklyn Dodgers system. After playing for the Los Angeles Angels in 1952, Connors retired to pursue an acting career. "Chuck was trying to get started in Hollywood," recalled Gale Wade. "He had a little house in the northern part of L.A. and bought him a little ole horse. He'd have cookouts and me and Gene and Steve Bilko would always be there."

Connors career blossomed. He appeared in over 40 movies and

television shows but was best known for playing Lucas McCain in "The Rifleman," which aired on network TV from 1958-63.

Wade also introduced Mauch to his friend "Gorgeous George," the most popular pro wrestler in the world in the 1940's and 50's. GG was estranged from his wife and had left his home on a turkey ranch he owned, to stay in the same apartment complex as Wade. At a bar, they became friends and Wade invited GG to Wrigley Field.

"He came to the ballpark one time and he stopped the game," said Wade. He had his bleached blonde hair all done up with gold plated bobby pins and all that crap and when he came up a ramp, with his two guys, the crowd sent crazy and they stopped the game."

Buzz Clarkson's returned, with two pinch hits and then went two-for-four in a loss to San Francisco. Clarkson's return energized Bilko who went four-for-four with a homer in the same game, the start of an incredible hot streak for Stout Steve.

Two games later, Bilko went five-for-five with two home runs, including a two run shot with two outs in the ninth to give the Angels a 9-8 win over the Seals. For the week against San Francisco, Bilko went 13 for 24, hitting .542 to raise his average to .303 with 21 home runs.

Gene Mauch also got hot, with an 11-game hitting streak. In the opener of a doubleheader, Mauch went 5-for-5 in a 9-5 win over Sacramento and had seven straight hits that day before the streak ended in the second game.

In a game against Oakland, Mauch stole home on rookie southpaw Tom Borland to give the Angels a 4-3 12 inning win. Mauch and Hal Rice homered on successive pitches against Gene Bearden of San Francisco in the fourth inning and Jim Fanning's single won the game in 12 innings 3-2.

In addition to playing well Gene Mauch showed qualities that would make him a big league manager. Mauch was intense, ultra- competitive and a student of the game. "He was the type of guy that, if there was anyone around that wasn't with it, focused or whatever, they're going to hear from Gene," said pitcher Red Adams. "That took enormous pressure of Bob Scheffing."[15]

The Angels were 49-55, in fifth place, thirteen games back of first place San Diego when a rash of no-hitters broke out. Angels' rookie lefthander George Piktuzis no-hit the Seals, winning 2-1 in San Francisco. The often erratic southpaw walked three and struck out nine, improving his record to 7-10. The only run came on a wild pitch.

Two days later, Seattle's Elmer Singleton pitched the first no-hitter of his sixteen-year career, beating San Diego 2-0.

Then in Oakland, 28-year-old Oaks forkballer Chris Van Cuyk pitched a seven inning no-hitter against the Angels in the first game of a doubleheader in Oakland.

More excitement came when Sammy Davis Jr. was a featured entertainer at a Goodwill Baseball Party at Wrigley Field, but his appearance was costly to him. Davis had offered his services free to the Angels but his union, the American Guild of Variety Artists ruled that appearing gratis was a violation of union rules and fined Davis $1,000.

Steve Bilko passed out cigars July 20 after getting word from home in Nanticoke, Pa. that his wife had given birth to a daughter, Sharon Ann. Bilko also lit up the offense in August. At Gilmore Field, he homered over the high center field fence and had three doubles and five RBI in a 7-3 win over Hollywood.

Bilko's bat carried the Angels to a four game sweep of Seattle. He had 7 hits in 14 at bats and drove in the winning runs in the first three straight games, then he hit two homers in the fourth win raising his league leading total to 34.

The addition of Gale Wade strengthened the Angels outfield and with Mauch and Bilko leading an improved offense, for the rest of the year, the Angels may have been the best team in the league.

They went over the .500 mark in early August and came home to win six of seven from Hollywood as the crowds returned; 18,007 on Sept. 1 and 15,217 for a doubleheader two days later. They won seven straight and finished 91-81, tied with Hollywood.

With the teams sharing third place, Angels' President John Holland and Stars' owner Bob Cobb agreed on a playoff to decide the city champion. Hollywood vs Los Angeles. The teams had split the regular season series, with each winning fourteen games. All of the best of five series was played at Wrigley Field.

The Stars won the first two, the Angels the next two. In the fifth and deciding game, the Stars led 7-6 with two outs in the ninth, the tying run at third and Steve Bilko hitting. Bilko had three hits in the game and was hitting .450 (9/20) in the series. Stars manager Bobby Bragan brought in righthander Joe Trimble to face Bilko. He threw four straight curveballs, striking out Bilko as Hollywood won 7-6 to win the city title.

Gene Mauch presents 1955 MVP award to Steve Bilko.
Credit: Stephen R. Bilko.

After a dismal previous year, 1955 had been the Angels most exciting season in years. After a slow start, they drew 335,491.

Jim Brosnan and Don Elston won 17 games. Turk Lown was 12-5 with ten saves and Bubba Church and Joe Hatten each won 11.

Gene Mauch finished with a .296 batting average with 8 homers, 49 RBI and 22 stolen bases. Steve Bilko won league MVP honors, finishing third in hitting with a .328 average, first in homers with 37 and second with 124 RBI. Gale Wade hit .301, played great defense in center field and led the club with 23 stolen bases.

After improving in 1955, the Angels' next goal was a Pacific Coast League Championship. The surprising '55 team had supplied the Chicago Cubs with pitchers Jim Brosnan, Don Elston and Turk Lown along with outfielder Gale Wade. The Angels also parted ways with pitchers Bubba Church and Joe Hatten, outfielder Hal Rice and Buzz Clarkson. But the cupboard certainly wasn't bare.

Chapter Ten

The Best Minor League Team of All Time?

Going into spring training in 1956, the Angels still had Gene Mauch and Steve Bilko as their core. They added a key piece, drafting power hitting third baseman George Freese from New Orleans.

Manager Bob Scheffing's team was set in the infield and had plenty of hitting but he wasn't sure about his outfield, catching and particularly the pitching.

"We need some help on the mound ourselves," Scheffing said. "You can't lose three pitchers like Jim Brosnan, Don Elston and Turk Lown without it hurting. We hope the Cubs can provide the help."[1]

The Angels had two potentially great arms but 19-year-old Dick Drott and 20-year-old Bob Anderson were young and unproven.

George Piktuzis, the early season phenom in 1955 was back but had not fully recovered from arm problems. They also had veteran lefthander Harry Perkowski and Dave Hillman, a 16-game winner in the Texas League.

"We should get off to a good start," Scheffing said. "The outlook is better than it was last year. But so is the competition. We've got a better bench this time and if we get the help we need, we'll be right up there."[2]

Despite Bob Scheffing's optimism, the team didn't play well in spring training, losing 16 of 21 games, although Bilko hit 11 home runs. Gene Mauch hit well and paired with rookie shortstop Casey Wise to give the Angels a solid double play combo.

Gene Mauch was responsible for Wise becoming a pro. In 1952, while Mauch was playing for Milwaukee in the American Association, Wise was a semi-pro in Nebraska. The White Sox invited Wise to Chicago for a tryout but three days of rain ended that. Wise's father Hughie was a Brewers scout and arranged for his son to drive to Milwaukee to work out. He was assigned to Gene Mauch. Casey impressed Mauch, who told General Manager Red Smith that the club should sign him. When Wise and the Brewers couldn't agree on compensation, Mauch phoned Wid Mathews, the Chicago Cubs player personnel director, who signed Wise.

Wise had graduated from the University of Florida and after three years in the minors was now an Angel and was moved to shortstop. In spring training Mauch tutored the youngster.

A new IBM electronic brain, the Electronic Data Processing Machine, sifted through a pile of statistics and predicted Seattle would repeat as champion. The machine picked San Diego to finish second, followed by Portland, Sacramento, Los Angeles, Vancouver, Hollywood and San Francisco.

Steve Bilko set some lofty goals. "I'd like to hit 40-50 home runs, bat .360 and drive in more than 200 runs," he said. "I think I can do better than last season. I've got a whole season behind me. When I came here last spring, it was like starting all over again since I'd sat around the previous season."[3]

Besides Bilko at first base, the opening day lineup had Gene Mauch at second, Casey Wise at shortstop, George Freese at third and Joe Hannah catching. The outfield consisted of Bob Coates in left, Jim Bolger in center and rookie Eddie Haas in right.

The Angels opened the 1956 season with a split doubleheader in San Diego, wearing new uniforms designed by former Angel Max West, who'd retired and entered the sporting goods business.

Steve Bilko and Eddie Haas homered as the Angels won the first game 9-2 and Haas' second homer of the day prevented a shutout in the evening game which San Diego won 3-1.

Rookie Eddie Haas was a sweet-swinging, left-handed hitter from Paducah, Kentucky who learned a lot from Gene Mauch. "He was the second baseman and I was the right fielder," Haas recalled, "and Bob Scheffing made Gene my coach. I dressed beside him before and after the game. He was pouring stuff on top of my head and it was too much. I couldn't absorb it all."

If Haas misplayed a ball in the outfield or threw to the wrong base, Mauch explained the right way to do it. Mauch waved to Haas to position him in the outfield, depending on the hitter and the situation. "Hitting wise, he'd tell me, 'if this pitcher gets ahead of you, he's gonna throw you a slider.' He was brilliant and one of the better minds that's ever been in baseball."

In a guest column in the Long Beach Press-Telegram, Bob Scheffing wrote: "If I was a fellow who wrote cowboy pieces for the movies, I'd make a star out of Gene Mauch. Some way, somehow, with or without the benefit of scenario writers, this fellow would find a way to eliminate the villains and woo the leading lady, if she appealed to him, that is. I say IF she appealed to him because Gene has a very beautiful wife at home and to beat them it would take a great combination, the likes of which I cannot conjure in my head."[4]

Scheffing had envisioned a Murderer's Row with Gene Mauch, Steve Bilko, George Freese and Jim Bolger. Jim Bolger had hit just .206 in 64 games with the Cubs in 1955, but was just 24. The Cubs figured a full year at Triple A would help him improve. Bolger was an RBI machine but despite good hitting, the team's pitching was inconsistent and the team was playing .500 ball midway through April.

The outfield got more help when Bob Speake was sent down by the Cubs. In 1955 Speake was all the rage in Chicago hitting ten homers in May, then cooling off when big league pitchers figured out he would chase high fastballs. At 25, he was still regarded as a top prospect.

The Pacific Coast League made several changes before the 1956 season. Seven of the eight teams now had major league affiliations and San Francisco and Los Angeles, the two largest cities in the league, would play mostly day games with only one night game per week. Attendance suffered but the ball seemed to carry better on hot L.A. summer afternoons. The Angels won 22 of their first 29 games at Wrigley Field.

Steve Bilko hit six home runs in the Angels' first fourteen games, including a 500-foot bomb over the right field bleachers in San Francisco's Seals Stadium. Eddie Haas told Bilko, "If I had them muscles, I wouldn't take nothin' off nobody."

Bilko wasn't the only player flexing his muscles. The Angels blasted 23 home runs in their first nineteen games. At Wrigley Field, they swept a four-game series with the Hollywood Stars. 9592, the largest crowd of the young season, watched the Angels take a Sunday doubleheader as Jim Fanning had a grand slam, while Steve Bilko had two singles, a double and a homer in the second game.

Gene Mauch put together a 16-game hitting streak as the Angels moved into first place in mid-May and in a 15-1 rout of Sacramento, Mauch went 3-for-5 with two three-run homers and 6 RBI.

On May 15, the major league cut-down date, the Cubs sent outfielder Gale Wade and catcher Elvin "El" Tappe to L.A. Also going down were pitchers Bob Thorpe and Johnny Briggs and infielder Richie Myers.

Wade had played for the Angels in 1955 and was reunited with his friend Gene Mauch. Besides being hard-nosed players, they were both students of the game. "I've said it many times," remembered Wade, "Gene Mauch was the smartest player I ever played with or against."

Gene Mauch makes a play for the PCL Champs, 1956.

Wade was certainly no slouch when it came to baseball knowledge. He studied every hitter and catalogued them in a notebook. "I knew what they would do when they were behind in the count or ahead in the count," said Wade.

Wade would position himself and the other two outfielders depending on the count and what pitch was about to thrown. He got that information from Gene Mauch.

"I couldn't see the catcher's signs from centerfield," explained Wade, "so Gene would use hand signals, behind his back, telling me whether the pitch was going to be a fastball or curveball."

Based on the count and the type of pitch, Wade would position himself and the other outfielders. "If a hitter is behind in the count and a fastball is coming," said Wade, "you may shift thirty or forty feet from where he normally pulls the ball to the opposite field because that's the kind of hitter he is when he's behind in the count."

"With Speake in left and Bolger in right, I had two rabbits on either side of me. Each of them could have played centerfield. You couldn't hardly drill a hit between us. That 1956 outfield was the best I've ever been involved with, bar none."

To make room for the new players, the Angels sent Eddie Haas to Des Moines and Buzz Clarkson and pitcher Hy Cohen to Tulsa. The demotion of Cohen was surprising because he led the staff with five wins but he had a high ERA of 5.70 and was winning because the Angels were just outslugging their opponents.

The young pitchers were coming through. In a 6-5 win over San Francisco, the Angels tied the Pacific Coast League record with 19 strikeouts. Rookie Dick Drott fanned 14 and two relievers tacked on five more. Three days later, Drott tied the Angels record with 15 strikeouts in a 6-2 win over Sacramento.

In May, at Wrigley Field, before 20,000, Sugar Ray Robinson knocked out Bobo Olson in a middleweight title fight. The same night at Gilmore Field, 6961 fans watched the Hollywood Stars K.O. the Angels 6-0 to start a four-game series sweep, returning the favor after the Angels had swept the Stars in April at Wrigley Field. An overflow crowd of 10,224 saw Hollywood take a Sunday doubleheader.

The Angels ended a five-game losing streak, beating San Diego before only 689 fans at Wrigley Field. Despite the team's success, playing day games during the week looked like a mistake. Only 550 turned out to see the Angels win the second game and just 583 saw Dave Hillman pitch a four-hitter, shutting out Seattle 6-0.

The crowds increased on weekends. 3,101 saw Gene Mauch homer in a win over Seattle and for a Sunday doubleheader 9914, the largest Memorial Day crowd of the season, viewed a sweep of Vancouver.

In late May the Angels exploded, hitting 21 home runs in seven games, putting together a nine-game winning streak which ended in a wild 18-13 loss to Vancouver. Steve Bilko hit seven homers in a seven-game stretch.

Mauch was hitting over .400 and topped off a ten-game hitting streak with a five-for-five night at San Francisco. Mauch was hitless the next day but during the streak had 21 hits in 36 at bats, hitting .583. As great a hitter as Steve Bilko was, Gene Mauch may have been more valuable to the Angels because of his effect on teammates.

Johnny Goryl had a unique perspective on Mauch. As a 22-year-old, he was Mauch's teammate on the 1956 Angels, played for Mauch with the Minneapolis Millers in 1959, was a Twins' coach when Mauch managed the team and succeeded him as manager in 1975.

"As a player in Los Angeles, I was so young but the wonderful thing about Gene is he could teach the game of baseball to anybody who wanted to listen," said Goryl. Playing with him in L.A., I was in awe of everything he did."

Mauch and Steve Bilko were enjoying career years. Bilko hit his 23rd homer the first week of June and had a 24-game hitting streak. Mauch was hitting for average and power. Bilko and Mauch were one and two in the PCL batting race.

Gene Mauch and Steve Bilko complemented each other. Often hitting in the leadoff spot, Mauch would take pitches, working deep in the count which allowed teammates to see what a pitcher was throwing. Mauch also got good pitches to hit because opposing pitchers didn't want the hitters ahead of Bilko to get on, because he was such a home run threat.

Mauch also helped Bilko by telling him what pitches to look for. If Mauch was on first, he led off, peered in and often saw the catcher's sign. He did the same thing when he was at second, often signaling to tip Bilko off. Some hitters didn't want to know what's coming but Bilko did.

"Steve Bilko was a great athlete, very loose with a great pair of hands," Mauch said. "He loved to eat. If you left icing on the table-cloth, he'd eat it-and he loved to drink beer."[5] Oh, did he love his beer. After games Bilko and George Freese would take off their shoes, their uniform and sit in the clubhouse and drink beer.

"Freese could stay with Hump for a while but no one could stay with Bilko," remembered Gale Wade. "He could drink a six pack and you'd never know he'd had a drink. I never saw Hump act like he was drunk."

After Bilko had taken a sledgehammer to his Portland club, manager Tommy Holmes said, "That guy should go back to the majors again. Steve's a much better hitter now than when I first saw him with the Cardinals. He's no longer a swinger, he's thinking when he's up there."[6]

By June 7, the Angels had taken over first place with a 33-19 record and were getting rave reviews. Manager Bob Scheffing said his Angels were the best minor league team he'd ever seen. Comparing them to his 1940 pennant-winning Rochester team, he said, "We had a great club. There were players on that team who ultimately made the grade in the majors-Preacher Roe, Mike Ryba, Whitey Kurowski, Johnny Grodzicki, Hank Gornicki, Hal Epps, Frank Crespi, George Fallon, Buster Adams, Ray Mueller and myself-yet this Angel club has more power and speed and better pitching."

Gene Mauch also thought the 1956 Angels were the best minor league team of all-time. "I managed three clubs in the big leagues that weren't as good as the '56 Angels."[7]

During a trip to L.A., Cincinnati Reds G.M. Gabe Paul watched the team and said, "The Angels have the greatest bunch of major league prospects I've seen on one team in many a year."[8]

Having a record-setting season, Steve Bilko was a hot commodity. Unable to get a power hitter from the parent Boston Red Sox, the San Francisco Seals offered $25,000 cash for Bilko and asked that shortstop Richie Myers and pitcher Marino Pieretti be included in the deal. Angels president John Holland said, "If we had been offered $75,000, I would still say no."[9]

Bilko had 45 home runs entering August and Bilkomania was

rampant in L.A. "More people know Bilko than Marilyn Monroe," said Bob Scheffing.[10]

San Francisco Seals pitcher Jerry Casale said, "Steve looked like King Kong up there."[11]

Bilko was pictured in the newspaper with actor Phil Silvers, who played Master Sergeant Ernest G. Bilko on TV's "The Phil Silvers Show." Bilko was wearing an army sergeant's hat and Silvers an Angel's hat. Silvers had adopted the slugger's name for his character. "I could have just as well have been Corporal Hodges or Private Musial but I gave the pub to a guy who needed it."[12]

Despite Steve Bilko's amazing season, many felt that Gene Mauch was the Angels' Most Valuable Player. Among them was scout Dutch Reuther, "He should be in the big leagues right now."[13]

Mauch's first big league manager Leo Durocher said, "Pittsburgh is a definite pennant threat...what the Pirates need most is a second baseman. If they had Mauch I'd pick them to go all the way. Mauch is one of the finest team players I ever saw. He likes to win, he's a born leader. Right now he's worth at least $50,000 to the Angels which means he's worth three times as much to Pittsburgh. If I had the say, I'd pay $200,000 for Mauch and he'd win the pennant for the Bucs."[14]

In July, Angels' president John Holland made sure his two stars weren't going anywhere, giving Gene Mauch and Steve Bilko new contracts through 1957. Both agreed to waive their major league draft rights and were given raises that boosted Mauch's contract to a reported $12,000 and Bilko's to $14,000.

Things were going so well for Gene Mauch that during a trip to Portland, he had a hole-in-one at Tualatin Country Club.

When Portland fired manager Tommy Holmes in July, one Hollywood Stars exec said, "I know who I'd get for manager if I was running the Portland club-Gene Mauch."[15] Since the Angels weren't going to release Mauch, Portland hired former L.A. skipper Bill Sweeney.

The Angels ruined Sweeney's debut as Beaver's manager, exploding for 12 runs in the first inning in a 13-4 romp in Portland. George Freese had a single, double and home run and tied the club record with 8 RBI. Winning pitcher Dick Drott had four hits including a home run.

Gene Mauch had more than his share of arguments with umpires but said he was never so angry as when umpire Chris Pelekoudas ejected him for growling. When he was called out on strikes, Mauch muttered under his breath. "The ump couldn't have heard what I said, because I didn't say anything," Mauch said. "All I did was make a growling sound. Which probably makes me the first ballplayer to get the boot for clearing his throat. But what I said to that guy AFTER he kicked me out wouldn't have made good reading in a Sunday School class."[16]

On September 4, the Angels clinched the 1956 PCL pennant, beating the defending champion Rainiers 8-2 in Seattle. "This is the greatest bunch of guys I've ever been associated with," said skipper Bob Scheffing. "We had our ups and downs and our share of injuries, but the Angels never quit."[17]

Los Angeles had held first place since July 13 and clinched the pennant with 13 games to play. It was the team's fifteenth championship since the league began in 1903 and the first since 1947.

In September, with five games left in the season, Mauch was sold to the Boston Red Sox for a reported $100,000. Gene Mauch played his final game as a Los Angeles Angel on "Gene Mauch Night" at Wrigley Field. 5,976 showed up to honor the hustling second baseman. Mauch went out with his bat blazing, with a triple, two singles and two RBI in four at bats to lead the Angels to an 11-7 win over Hollywood.

As Mauch was packing his bags for Boston, Lorenzo "Piper" Davis came up to say goodbye. Mauch loved the 39-year-old veteran of the Negro Leagues, who could play every position and was a pinch hitter extraordinaire. Davis handed his infielders' mitt to Mauch and said, "Take that glove with you. That's the only way it's getting to the big leagues."[18]

"These were the best three years of my life," recalled Mauch. "I had played in the big leagues six or seven years before I was an Angel and no one in Los Angeles knew who the hell I was. As soon as I came to L.A. I made a lot of friends."[19]

"Gene Mauch Night," was the first of four nights honoring the 1956 Angels and their stars.

Next, was "Angels and Bob Scheffing Night" as the manager received presents including a brand new Oldsmobile and a rifle from his players.

Then, on "Bob Anderson Night" the Angels honored their amazing 20-year-old reliever who had been named league Rookie of the Year with a league record 70 appearances and a 12-4 record.

On the final day of the season, Sunday, September 16, 7032 turned out for "Stout Steve Bilko Day" as the big man was presented with the league and Angels MVP awards and the Tony Lazzeri Memorial Award for winning the league's home run crown.

Bilko also received a check from team president John Holland, a color TV set and other gifts. Not that it mattered but the Angels split a doubleheader with San Diego losing the first 7-6 and winning the second 2-1 to finish with an incredible 107-81 record, sixteen games ahead of second place Seattle.

Bilko led the PCL with 55 home runs but fell short of Tony Lazzeri's record of 60. Stout Steve also led the league in hitting (.360) and RBI (164) and topped the loop in eight offensive categories.

Gene Mauch had the best year of his career, finishing third in the league with a .348 batting average and career highs with 20 homers and 84 RBI.

Mauch called the 1956 Angels the best minor league team of all-time. They were certainly the best PCL team in recent history. They led the Pacific Coast League with a .297 team batting average and scored 1,000 runs in 168 games, nearly six runs per game. Six Angels also hit 20 or more home runs and batted over .300.

Chapter Eleven

Back to the Bigs in Boston

Boston Red Sox, 1956.

Upon acquiring Mauch, Red Sox General Manager Joe Cronin said, "He hit .348 in Los Angeles and our scouts called him the best player in the Pacific Coast League. He was a big reason why they won out there."[1]

After joining the Red Sox in Cleveland, Gene Mauch pinch hit twice and was hitless. In his first start, Mauch played second base and went 0-4 as the leadoff hitter. In a Boston win the next day, he was 0-for-5. Hitless in nine at bats was not the way Mauch envisioned his Boston debut.

Finally, in his fourth game in Detroit, Mauch went four-for-four in a 5-4 loss in Detroit in the first game of a doubleheader. In the nightcap, won by Detroit 8-4 Mauch went 1-5 but injured his back and missed the next four games.

Mauch made his Fenway Park debut against the New York Yankees. In his second at bat he drilled a single off the Green Monster in left field and went one-for-three in a 7-4 loss.

In a 10-4 win over Washington, Mauch was two-for-three with an RBI and two runs scored but committed two errors.

With his back acting up, Mauch sat out the final four games of the season. In seven games with the Bosox, Mauch hit .320 in 25 plate appearances.

During the winter in Los Angeles, Mauch was visiting with former player Roy Partee, now managing Stockton in the California league. Yes, the same Roy Partee that Mauch had once given a black eye. Mauch showed Partee his prized bat. Partee took the bat, ran his finger over the grain and complimented Mauch's choice. "How do you rate this kind of bat, Gene?" Partee asked.[2]

"Well, when I got my contract from Joe Cronin, general manager of the Red Sox," Mauch explained, "I signed it and sent it back with a postscript. I told Cronin that this was the first time I ever signed my first contract; that I generally hold out for a while. I also asked Cronin to order me two dozen bats and to have the manufacturer stamp them with Ted Williams' name."[3]

Puzzled, Partee asked "What has that had to do with getting such a fine bat?"

"Well, you know darn good and well if the manufacturers thought Ted Williams was going to use their bats, they would go first class all the way," Mauch answered.[4]

Mauch took his new bats to Sarasota, Florida for spring training in 1957. After finishing fourth two years in a row, Red Sox manager Pinky Higgins knew he had to make changes. Second base had been a sore spot since Bobby Doerr retired in 1951. Encouraged by Mauch's play at the end of 1956, Higgins said "I want to see more of Gene Mauch at second base."[5]

Mauch's competition came from lifetime .300 hitter Billy Goodman, in good health after recovering from mononucleosis, utility man Ted Lepcio, who hit 15 home runs in 1956 and rookie Ken Aspromonte.

Mauch wasted no time impressing his manger and winning the second base job. "He's shown he can make the plays," said Higgins. "He doesn't have a great arm and he is not too fast. But he does the job. He knows how to play the hitters. He'll do for me."[6]

With Mauch in the middle, the Red Sox turned 15 double plays in 11 spring training games, winning seven of them. The biggest surprise was Mauch's hitting. In 11 spring training games he hit .356.

It was thirteen years ago to the month that 18-year-old Gene Mauch tried to replace Pee Wee Reese as the Dodgers' shortstop. Now, at 31, he was finally getting the opportunity to be an everyday player.

"I have to prove to myself that I can do it," said Mauch. "This is the best chance I ever had and I'm going to make the most of it. There were opportunities before but I wasn't ready. If I had been a good ballplayer then, I would have made it. I just didn't hit at all, period."[7]

Mauch's former competitors weren't surprised when they heard he'd won the second base job. Pirate's manager Bobby Bragan said, "He's a valuable man. Gene seldom gets spectacular but he's had a lot of experience and he fights you all the way. His fiery spirit is contagious and he'll keep the infield on its toes. He's at his best when things are toughest."[8]

Yankee Manager Casey Stengel said, "That fellow Mauch knows the position, he knows how to make the right play and gives you a lot of trouble at bat."[9]

Red Sox star Ted Williams said, "I saw Leo Durocher one day this winter. He had seen Gene Mauch in Los Angeles last summer as well as during a few National League seasons while he was managing. I asked him about Mauch."

"Leo told me, 'You can forget about second base. Mauch will make it. He hasn't got a lot of range or speed but if he gets the ball, he'll make the play for you."[10]

The Red Sox opened the 1957 season at Baltimore's Memorial Stadium as Mauch, batting seventh, went two-for-four with an RBI and run scored in a 4-2 Bosox win.

Mauch made a big splash in the Red Sox homer opener against the Yankees. He led off the fifth with a triple and then faked out Yankee Starter Johnny Kucks and scored on a suicide squeeze bunt by pitcher Frank Sullivan. Mauch went two-for-three but the Yankees won 3-2. New York took the second game 10-7 as Mauch went one-for-six.

In the final game of the series, on the verge of a sweep, New York led 4-1 going into the eighth inning. After Boston scored twice to cut the Yankee lead to 4-3, with two outs, the Red Sox had the tying run with Dick Gernert at second and Mauch due up. As he stood in the on-deck-circle, Mauch figured with a righthander Bob Grim on the mound, Red Sox manager Mike Higgins would send up a left-handed hitting pinch hitter. He had two of the best, former batting champs Billy Goodman and Mickey Vernon.

"I thought Mike would take me out but when he didn't, it was just like giving me a pat on the back. I was determined to come through for him."[11] As Mauch walked to the plate, he recalled the scouting report on Grim, a former 20-game winner who'd become the Yankee closer: good fastball which he likes to keep low, plus curveball and a changeup he'll throw at any time.

Mauch ripped a single to left and wanting to make sure Gernert would score, exposed himself on the bases, rounding first and trying to draw a throw at second. Not only did Gernert score to tie the game, but Mauch reached second, representing the winning run. Then Sammy White popped the ball up, it caught in the swirling winds and dropped for a base hit near the mound as Mauch raced home with the game winner in a 5-4 victory, the Red Sox only win in the series against the defending world champions.

Five days later the teams met again in a three-game series at Yankee Stadium. The Bosox beat New York twice, turning eight electrifying double plays, with Mauch in the middle of six of them. Although he took a few hits from Yankee baserunners, Mauch said, "I'll take a few every time," said Mauch, "If we can beat the Yankees two out of three."[12] With one hit in the first game of the series and two in the second, Mauch extended his hitting streak to ten straight games, hitting .381 during the streak.

Mauch's streak ended the next day as he went 0-3 against Whitey Ford and the Yankees who won 3-2.

Mauch was also second to Chicago's Nellie Fox in early voting for the second base spot on the American League team in the All-Star Game

Finally, his opportunity had come. After years of bouncing from Brooklyn to Montreal to Pittsburgh, Indianapolis, Chicago, Boston, Milwaukee, Atlanta and Los Angeles, Gene Mauch had made it. The starting second baseman for the Boston Red Sox. "Unless a ballplayer is a Mickey Mantle, Willie Mays or Al Kaline, blessed with extraordinary talent," Mauch said, "he has to play a lot of games to know what's going on in the majors."[13]

Box scores couldn't measure Gene Mauch's contributions. He

didn't hit home runs or put up a monster batting average but he was the "take charge" guy the Red Sox so dearly needed. He'd tell pitchers how to work a particular batter and position the defense based on his knowledge of the hitter, pitcher and the count. When leading off at first base, he'd peek in, steal the catcher's signs, then signal a Red Sox hitter what pitch to look for. He was constantly on alert. He came to the ballpark early and noticed everything. He studied opposing hitters during batting practice. Did they adjust their feet on certain pitches? What did they try to do with certain situations? He would watch everyone. Did the catcher have a strong arm? How about the outfield arms? Who was hurt? Who could steal a base and who couldn't?

There were no computers then except for Mauch's mind. When a situation arose during a game, in a split second, he knew what to do, where to play, where to throw the ball. He envisioned every possible situation before it happened.

Mauch's hitting was the big surprise. He studied pitchers and took notes about how they pitched. What did they throw when behind in the count? What was their out pitch? He crowded the plate and worked the count in his favor until he got a pitch to hit. If he got a fast ball away, he would slap it into right field. He knew when to look away and when to look inside for a pitch he could jerk down the left field line. His PCL experience had shown him that he had enough power to hit an occasional home run.

One of his moves backfired. In the 7th inning of a game against Baltimore with the Orioles leading 7-5, the Sox had runners at first and third with one out. Mauch hit a ground ball to first baseman George Kell who stepped on the bag to retire Mauch and then as Kell fired to the plate to nail Gernert, Mauch threw up his hands and the ball struck his right wrist. But Mauch didn't get away with it. Umpire Ed Rommel ruled interference. Mauch was out and Rommel declared Gernert was also out, resulting in an unusual double play. But the Red Sox fans loved Gene Mauch because he would do anything to win.

In May, injuries and illness hit the Red Sox. Mauch, leading the team in RBI's, injured his knee, limped for two weeks and then had to miss four games. Infielder Billy Klaus was hit in his right eye by a bad-hop ground ball and outfielder Jimmy Piersall was sidelined with a sore arm. And Red Sox star Ted Williams, leading the league in hitting, was forced to the sidelines with a heavy chest cold and missed four games.

Mauch and Williams developed a mutual admiration society. The Splinter appreciated Mauch's leadership and gutsy play and Mauch said, "I had the locker next to Ted's. I developed a tremendous respect for him, not only as a player, but also as a man. There were a few fellows on the club who were jealous of Ted, fellows who tried to drag him down to their level because they aren't his equal on the field. They tried to needle him with sarcasm but Ted was too big to even notice. I had to admire him for that."[14]

On May 22 at Fenway Park, the Red Sox broke out of a long hitting drought in the final game of a home stand. In the sixth inning, Gene Mauch connected on a 2-0 changeup from his old friend and former teammate Cal McLish, sending it into the left field net near the foul pole for a home run.

Then, Ted Williams jumped on a low fastball and hit a towering fly ball over the visitor's bullpen in right field.

After Jackie Jensen walked, Dick Gernert pounded a low curve over the left field wall and screen and then Frank Malzone lifted a hanging curveball over the left field wall.

The four home runs in one inning tied the American League record set by the Red Sox in 1940 and tied by Detroit in 1950.

After losing 11-0, McLish said, "I'd say I threw them a variety of pitches but all of them turned out badly, didn't they?"[15]

After playing well in April and May, back and leg injuries knocked Mauch out of the lineup. He tried to play through the injuries but missed games in June, all of July and played little upon his return in August. By then, the Red Sox were looking to the future and Ted Lepcio, Billy Consolo and Ken Aspromonte played the remainder of the games at second base.

© DON WINGFIELD

Gene Mauch part of history 1957.

In Cleveland, Mauch was involved in a bizarre situation. With one out in the top of ninth, Mauch was the runner at second base and Pete Daley at first, when the batter, Mike Fornieles, hit a sinking liner to center. It looked like a base hit and the runners took off at the crack of the bat. But suddenly, a strong wind kicked up in center field, holding the ball up just enough to allow Indians' shortstop Chico Carrasquel to make a spectacular running catch.

When he turned around after the catch, Carrasquel saw Daley at second, trying to scramble back to first. Mauch had kept on running and had crossed home plate.

The shortstop now had a choice. He could walk over to second base and tag it, doubling up Mauch or he could throw to first to double Daley. But Carrasquel apparently didn't see Mauch, so he threw to first, doubling Daley for the third out.

The Indians headed to the dugout and the Red Sox took the field. The moment Boston pitcher Mike Fornieles made the first pitch in the bottom of the ninth, plate umpire Hank Soar turned toward the press box and shouted to the official scorer, "The run counts." The scoreboard blinked in answer making the score 11-0 Boston. Since the Indians were out of the game, they didn't argue the call.

After the game, Soar explained what happened. "Mauch crossed the plate before the appeal was made on Daley at first base for the third out. I couldn't count the run at that moment though because Mauch had left his base too soon and therefore had scored illegally, you might say. The Indians had the right to appeal Mauch's run but their time of appeal ran out at the next pitch, according to the rules."[16]

Even though there were three outs, any time before the next pitch, the Indians could have touched second base, appealing that Mauch had left too soon and the umpires would have called him out. "The fourth out, in this case," explained crew chief Charley Berry, "takes precedence over the third out. The scoreboard wouldn't show the extra out because the original third out would be ignored and the new one substituted for it."[17]

The Indians claimed the umpires should have indicated in some way that Mauch had scored. "We couldn't," said Soar, "without tipping off that he left the base too soon. On an appeal, it's up to the teams to call our attention to the play, not for us to call their attention to it. In fact, after the inning, the Red Sox coaches came to me and asked, 'Didn't Mauch score before the third out?' I told them, 'We'll handle it. Just go away.' I guess they understood because they said okay and walked away."[18]

In 65 games, Mauch hit .270 with two homers and twenty-eight RBI. An anonymous Red Sox teammate said, "If we had had Gene Mauch in action for a full season, instead of 65 games, we would have finished second and might have pressed the Yankees for the flag. That guy's one of the inspirational leaders that all winning clubs need. The Yanks have such a leader in Casey Stengel and the White Sox have a pair in Nellie Fox and Al Lopez."

Boston finished 1957 in third place with an 82-72 record, sixteen games back of the New York Yankees. Ted Williams was second to the Yankees Mickey Mantle in voting for the American League MVP award. Williams led the league with a .388 average with 38 home runs and 119 RBI. Mantle was second in hitting and had 34 homers with a league leading 146 RBI.

Gene Mauch was among those who thought Williams should have won. Addressing the San Diego Hot Stove League in November, Mauch said, "The Yankees would have finished no worse than second without Mantle but the Red Sox, without Ted Williams, might have wound up in the American Association."[19] Little did Gene Mauch know but he was about to wind up in the American Association.

Chapter Twelve

It's Miller Time

Gene Mauch's career as an active player ended after the 1957 season, when the Red Sox asked him to manage the Minneapolis Millers, their AAA team in the American Association. He had played parts of nine seasons with the Brooklyn Dodgers, Pittsburgh Pirates, Chicago Cubs, Boston Braves, St. Louis Cardinals and Boston Red Sox. He played in 304 games, with a lifetime average of .239 with 5 home runs and 62 RBI.

Mauch felt he could have hung around as a utility man but as he aged, injuries took their toll. "Maybe all the sports I'd played and sliding into bases head first were beginning to take effect," Mauch said.[1]

Millers' General Manager Tommy Thomas said, "We consider Mauch to have a bright future in the managerial field. He has played in the American Association with three clubs—St. Paul, Indianapolis and Milwaukee, so he has an idea about the league."[2]

"Ever since I was a young boy it has been my ambition to play in the big leagues and to be a manager," said Mauch. "About all any manager can do is try to get along with his players, stay on the top step and make the right moves. I know you can always learn. Even Casey Stengel is still learning something new."[3]

As his playing days counted down, Mauch was ready to move into the next phase of his career. He understood that many new managers began in the low minors and he knew he was fortunate to begin at AAA.

Mauch had enjoyed playing in St. Paul and the Millers' job excited him. Both teams' winter baseball dinners were held on the same night. Ed Doherty, the American Association President needed to be at both rubber chicken dinners. So, did Mauch, who'd played for both clubs. The doubleheader came about because the Minnesota Boosters were told that it was the only date on which Red Sox star Ted Williams could appear. Ironically, Williams thought the Millers dinner was the day before. So he came in a day too soon and with time to kill, he went ice fishing.

So, Doherty addressed the Saints' crowd at the St. Paul hotel while Mauch spoke to Millers' fans at the Radisson Hotel. When both were finished with their speeches, Doherty and Mauch were driven to a halfway point, where they switched limos. Before you could say twin cities, Mauch was reminiscing about his days as a St. Paul Saint and Doherty was entertaining Millers fans.

The Saints and Millers had more in common than dueling speakers. As Mauch began his first year as Minneapolis' manager, his friend and former roommate Max Macon was in his fourth season as St. Paul's skipper. In 1943, with Montreal, the veteran Macon, a pitcher-first baseman who hit .347, had a new roommate, a 17-year-old kid just out of a California high school.

"Gene Mauch may have just been a kid but he had more guts than any of us," Macon remembered. "He took charge right away."[4]

Regarding Mauch's hiring as the Millers' manager, Macon said, "He's a fine addition to the league. He's a great little hustler."

Mauch answered with, "Max is a first class gentleman and a fine representative of baseball," but then added, "Sure, we're good friends but we'll still try to beat each other's brains out."[5]

Macon even offered Mauch a $50 bet as to who would be ejected more often in the coming season. With a laugh, Mauch said no thanks.

The San Francisco Giants had swapped their Pacific Coast League farm team, the San Francisco Seals, to the Boston Red Sox for the rights to the San Francisco territory, then acquired the Phoenix franchise and set up their Pacific Coast League farm team there.

So, some players from Minneapolis' 1957 PCL championship team were now playing for Phoenix and some Giants' prospects, who'd played with the Seals were now Millers. They included veterans Harry Malmberg, a good field-no hit infielder; first baseman Frank Kellert, catcher Ed Sadowski and outfielder Tom Umphlett.

Gene Mauch couldn't wait to get started so Minneapolis became the first team to begin spring training March 5 at their new home in Deland, Florida.

Mauch had learned from his year of managing in Atlanta, tempered by four more years of playing. He knew he couldn't berate his players or expect them to play like big leaguers. He softened his approach slightly and tried to be more of a teacher as more mosaic pieces slid into place.

Among his young players, 23-year-old, switch-hitting infielder Elijah "Pumpsie" Green, from Oakland, California impressed Mauch. "He's the best looking youngster I've seen this spring," said Mauch. "He is just a helluva athlete."[6] In the final two weeks of spring training, Green hit .414 with 12 hits in 29 at bats.

Green was the regular second baseman for most of spring training and displayed great hands, range and a strong arm. But just before the Millers broke camp, Mauch put Green at shortstop and Harry Malmberg at second.

By the end of the spring, Mauch also realized that Joe Tanner was not the answer at third base so he put himself there.

Most of the good pitchers from the PCL champs had been elevated to the parent Boston Red Sox so Mauch's ace appeared to be 28-year-old lefty Dean Stone, who'd pitched in the big leagues with Washington and Boston. Stone was joined by rookies, right-hander Bill Monboquette and lefty Ted Bowsfield.

Despite the inexperienced young pitchers, the American Association baseball writer's picked Gene Mauch's Minneapolis Millers as the favorite to win the pennant, with St. Paul second and

Omaha third.

A crowd of 6,030, the largest opening day crowd in the league that day, turned out at Louisville's Fairgrounds Stadium as the Millers exploded for seven runs in the third inning to beat the Colonels 9-5 as right fielder Faye Throneberry had three hits. The Millers swept the remaining two games to open the season 3-0.

Then, it was on to Charleston. After losing the first game, Millers starter Dean Stone was working on a no-hitter in the sixth inning when Gene Mauch took him out of the game. Although Stone had not allowed a hit, he was extremely wild, had walked four and was in constant trouble. The Millers led 5-1 into the bottom of the sixth, when Stone walked the first two batters, threw a wild pitch to advance the runners and then went 2-0 on Stan Palys. Gene Mauch took him out, bringing in Tom Hurd. An error and a sacrifice fly brought in two runs but Hurd continued the no-hitter until Dick Camilli doubled in the seventh. The Senators got only one more hit as Minneapolis won 8-3. The Millers closed out the road trip, splitting a doubleheader with the Sens and came home 5-2 and in first place.

In the Millers' home opener against Louisville. 8,513 fans turned out at Metropolitan Stadium on a 52 degree day with sunshine. Pumpsie Green's grand slam in the third tied the score at 4-4 and then Harry Malmberg led off the fourth with a solo shot to put the Millers ahead to stay. They won 11-6.

Pumpsie Green got off to a great start, hitting safely in his first ten games. "Pumpsie's like Henry Aaron when he broke in," said Gene Mauch. "He can play any position. The kid is just an athlete; that's all there is to it."[7]

The team's lack of offense became apparent early in the season. Mauch had been playing third base but with a .051 average and hitless in his last 31 at bats, Mauch benched himself. "I've found you've got to concentrate in order to hit," he said. "I guess I had too much on my mind. For the time being, I'll be a utility man."[8] So, Mauch concentrated on managing, put Joe Tanner back at third base and Harry Malmberg at second.

After the Millers suffered through a five-game stretch with only 22 hits, Mauch called for a special hitting session on an open date. The next night, the club pounded out 11 hits in an 8-3 win at Indianapolis.

Brutally cold weather in the Twin Cities in late April cut into the team's attendance. A total of only 975 turned out at Metropolitan Stadium for a three-game series with Louisville with only 196 at one game.

Some good things were happening though. 20-year-old Lou Clinton impressed Mauch early in the season. The year before, Clinton hit only .253 in Class A ball with Albany of the Eastern League, but had five consecutive hits including a three-run homer in a 10-3 win over the Denver Bears and raised his average to .315 by late May.

Aside from Clinton and Pumpsie Green who was hitting .294, the Millers had little offense. Two veteran sluggers that Mauch counted on, Art Schult and Frank Kellert, were hitting in the .200's.

The Millers suffered their first setback in May when outfielder Faye Throneberry, the team's only left-handed power hitter, was called up the Washington Senators, who owned his rights. It was the first of many blows Mauch would have to deal with.

To add to Mauch's headaches, he injured his knee and missed the next two months after Denver's Zeke Bella bowled him over in a collision at second base. With only three outfielders and five infielders, Mauch was left without an extra player except for pitchers and a backup catcher.

The Millers were a strange team. They couldn't win at home but won on the road. By mid-May Gene Mauch's guys were 10-4 on the road and 7-7 at home. And although they couldn't hit for average and had little power, the Millers had an uncanny ability to hit grand slam home runs. When Art Schult and Spencer "Red" Robbins hit bases loaded homers in consecutive innings in a 14-3 rout of Indianapolis, that brought the grand slam total to five in 22 games.

In another attempt to snap his team out of the offensive doldrums, Mauch benched first baseman Frank Kellert, hitting .211, replacing him with outfielder Art Schult. Schult was only hitting .250 but had shown some power. In the game that day Schult blasted a two-run homer in the first inning, boosting his RBI total to a league leading 27. Aided by Schult's bat, lefty Ted Bowsfield hurled a complete game 3-2 win over Wichita.

The 23-year-old Bowsfield and 21-year-old righthander Bill Monboquette were the Millers' best pitchers. Both rookies, both ex-hockey players. Bowsfield was the goalie on his high school team in Penticon, British Columbia while Monboquette was a defenseman in Medford, Massachusetts.

Bowsfield lived in a small town without little league baseball. He started pitching in semi pro ball and after striking out 17 in a 1-0 loss to a team of Cuban All-Stars, the Red Sox signed him.

Even more impressive was Bill Monboquette. Red Sox scout Jack Onslow saw Monboquette throwing sidearm in American Legion ball and told his coach, "No need for a boy with an arm like that to throw sidearm. Have him throw overhanded."[9]

"Monbo" was quickly becoming one of the league's top young pitchers. He had a good fastball, pinpoint control and quickly learned to change speeds. He pitched a two-hit shutout, beating Louisville 3-0, threw his second two-hitter and second shutout in beating Wichita 2-0 and then pitched a seven-hit 4-0 shutout against St. Paul. Then he stopped Omaha 4-1, becoming the Millers' first five-game winner. Gene Mauch knew he wouldn't have Monbouquette and Bowsfield much longer.

12,659 fans turned out at Metropolitan Stadium for an exhibition game between the San Francisco Giants and Chicago White Sox, followed by a regular season tilt between Minneapolis and Omaha. Millers' fans welcomed back some of the team's former stars including Willie Mays, Orlando Cepeda and Willie Kirkland who led the Giants to a 10-1 win. Then in the second game, Omaha lefthander Bill Smith shutout the Millers on five hits in a 2-0 Cardinals win.

Without Faye Throneberry, the Millers had one left-handed bat, Pumpsie Green, a switch hitter. After playing 59 games at short-stop, Green was moved to second base to make room for slick fielding veteran José Valdivielso, acquired from Phoenix.

Then, Art Schult was hit on the right hand by a pitch and the team's only power hitter was out temporarily.

The league's least productive offense had gotten worse. It was time for the mad scientist to go to work. With Mauch's team tied 2-2 with Wichita in the fifteenth inning, Red Robbins stole home on the front end of a triple steal and Minneapolis scored four runs to win 6-2.

There were no pitching coaches or roving pitching instructors in the minor leagues in the 1950's, just the manager who controlled everything and that's the way Mauch liked it. Mauch had some talented pitchers but big league call-ups and injuries disrupted the staff's stability. Mauch did an amazing job getting the most out of his pitching staff. In Indianapolis, Mauch befuddled the Indians and their fans with a pitcher-juggling act unequalled in the history of the American Association.

Protecting an 8-6 lead, Mauch called in righthander Harry Dorish to get the last out of the eighth inning. In the ninth with left hand-ed hitting Joe Altobelli leading off for the Indians, Mauch sent Dorish to third base and brought in lefthander Jack Spring.

After Spring retired Altobelli, Dorish returned to the hill to face right-handed hitting slugger Harmon Killebrew as Spring moved to first base and José Valdivieso took over at third. After Killebrew was retired Spring returned to the mound and retired left-handed hitting Al Facchini to end the game as the Millers won 8-6.

Indianapolis manger Walker Cooper protested the game contend-ing that league rules prohibited moving a player from the infield to the mound unless he is certified as an "infielder-pitcher." A phone call to League President Ed Doherty cleared up Cooper's reasoning.

The next day, Mauch employed similar strategy in the ninth inning of a doubleheader opener. Again Dorish and Spring alternated on the mound with Spring going to first base when not pitching, Dorish to third and then first as the situation demanded and Valdivieso shuttling between the hot corner and first base. The Millers won again, 5-2.

Gene Mauch felt the Millers had the best pitching staff in team history but was worried about their anemic offense. After being shutout four times within a week, Mauch knew the Millers would have a difficult time staying in the first division with pitching and defense alone. His pitching staff was about to take some major hits.

Although Charleston had been in first place for most of the season, the Denver Bears made a push into the top spot in early July and thus would host the All-Star game.

Pumpsie Green, Ed Sadowski and Ted Bowsfield were selected for the team and Bill Monboquette replaced an injured player.

15,240 fans turned out at Bears Stadium and saw the All-Stars whip Denver 10-2. Ted Bowsfield and Bill Monboquette of the Millers combined with Charleston's Jerry Davie, Wichita's Red Murff and St. Paul's Bob Darnell to hold the Bears to four hits.

The Millers good mood was spoiled the same day when the Boston Red Sox recalled Monbouquette, Bowsfield and veteran reliever Bud Byerly. Bowsfield was 8-4 with a 2.62 ERA. Monboquette was the staff's hard luck pitcher with an 8-9 record but had three shutouts and a 3.02 era. To make room for them, Sox G.M. Joe Cronin placed sore-armed pitcher Willard Nixon on the disabled list and sent lefthanders Duane Wilson and Bob "Riverboat" Smith to Minneapolis. A successful minor league manager learns to play the hand he's dealt and Mauch was still holding some face cards.

He sent 25-year-old lefthander Tom Borland to the mound against Indianapolis. A star at Oklahoma State, Borland had been used primarily in relief but without Bowsfield and Monboquette, he became a starter. Borland pitched a 2 hitter, struck out 13 and blanked the Indians 3-0.

Mauch found another starter in righthander Al Schroll who'd been sent down by Boston earlier in the year. He blanked Indy 3-0 on six hits.

In a June exhibition game, the Millers beat the parent Boston Red Sox 14-10 before 18,638 paying fans at Metropolitan Stadium. Red Sox star Ted Williams signed autographs for kids, gave interviews and put on a show in batting practice. He also homered his first time up, to the delight of the crowd.

There were undoubtedly times when Mauch wished he could turn back the clock and activate first base coach Jimmy Foxx. The Red Sox had signed the 50-year-old Hall of Famer as a hitting instructor and good will ambassador, after hearing that Foxx was jobless and destitute.

"Jimmy's a great guy and is doing a marvelous job," said Mauch. "All the players like him and his tips about hitting have helped. Just having Jimmy Foxx in the clubhouse means a lot to a club."[10]

Badly in need of some left-handed punch, the Millers traded slumping first baseman Frank Kellert to Portland for first baseman-outfielder Paul Smith. In Smith's first 31 at bats with the Millers, he had 12 hits, a .387 average and helped spark the team to six victories in nine games.

With Smith hitting third and Art Schult batting cleanup, the Millers began to roll. Smith had three hits, Schult went four-for-four, including a homer and two doubles and the Millers had a season high 19 hits in pounding Louisville 12-1.

Art Schult wanted to get back to the bigs. The 6'3" 210-pounder had signed with the New York Yankees out of Georgetown University, where he'd gone on a football scholarship. After breaking in with the Yankees, he'd played for Cincinnati and Washington in 1957, hitting .263 with four homers and thirty-nine RBI. At 30, Schult knew this might be his last chance. Schult again went four-for-four as the Millers beat Charleston 5-4 and continued with a late July stretch; going 18 for 47, with four home runs.

One of those was a three-run blast in the tenth inning to break up a scoreless duel between Al Schroll and Omaha's Billy Muffett to give the Millers a 3-0 victory. The game-winner highlighted a great night of baseball as 15,900 fans at the Met also watched the Philadelphia Phillies beat the Washington Senators 8-6 in an exhibition game preceding the Millers win.

After returning to the lineup, Gene Mauch played sparingly and his batting average hovered around .200. But in a doubleheader sweep against Louisville, Mauch had his best day, going three-for-three in the first game and added two more hits in the nightcap.

The Millers chances for pennant contention seemed to be dashed in a span of eight games against Wichita. Gene Mauch's team lost seven of the games with their only win coming 1-0 on Dean Stone's three-hit shutout and a ninth inning homer by Paul Smith. The Millers were now in fourth place, a distant eight games back.

But by Labor Day, the Millers finally had a set lineup and began to win. The Millers swept a doubleheader at St. Paul and took three out of four from the Saints. In the final game, a 14-4 Millers win, Pumpsie Green went four-for-five with a homer and two RBI and Gene Mauch was three-for-five with four RBI.

In Denver, against the second place Bears, Mauch had two doubles and three RBI in a 7-5 win in the first game of a doubleheader and the Millers had 19 hits in a 13-5 rout in the second game.

With two more hits, Mauch led the Millers to a 2-1 win over the Bears and then Mauch and Art Schult homered in an 8-7 victory. Denver managed to win the final game of the regular season 11-2.

Gene Mauch went 14-for-29 in the Denver series and Stu Locklin was 12 for 18.

Mauch gets hot against Denver.

The Millers won seven of their final nine games to finish 82-71, third, behind Charleston and Wichita.

Minneapolis qualified for the playoffs despite a .248 team batting average and an average of 4.05 runs per game: both the lowest figures in the league. There was not a single .300 hitter on the team.

Art Schult led the team in just about every offensive category with a .287 average, twenty homers and ninety-one runs batted in.

The Millers won with superb pitching. The team ERA was 3.65 and they had five pitchers with ERA's under 3.00.

In the American Association, the top four teams met in the play-offs. First place Charleston faced Denver and Minneapolis played second place Wichita.

In pro sports, champions are often the clubs with momentum rather than the best teams. The Millers had the momentum and took it into the playoffs.

In the opener in Wichita, the Braves scored three runs in the seventh to win 4-2 and take a 1-0 lead in the series.

Minneapolis took the second game 5-4 as Art Schult's home run in the fourth tied the game. Then the Millers scored two in the fifth to win.

In Game Three, Wichita pounded five home runs, including two each by Ray Shearer and Ed Charles to win 9-2 and take a 2-1 lead in the series.

Al Schroll then hooked up with Wichita's Dave Jolly in a pitcher's duel. The game was scoreless until the eighth. With one out, Pumpsie Green bunted and reached on Joe Morgan's bad throw. Jolly retired the next batter but then Schult hit a 430-foot homer over the left field fence to again tie the series.

In Game Five in Minneapolis, reliever Tommy Hurd blanked the Braves over the final five innings and singled in the deciding run in the ninth as the Millers won 4-3 to go up three games to two. Gene Mauch got into a heated argument with umpire Bill Baker in the eighth, bumped the ump and was ejected. Incredibly, it was the first time Mauch had been ejected all year.

Needing one more win to take the series, Dean Stone allowed just six hits, struck out 11 and singled in the decisive run in the seventh as Minneapolis won 3-2. Taking the series four games to two, the Millers readied for the finals against Denver.

In Minneapolis, the Millers combined a 12-hit attack with the pitching of Al Schroll and won the first game 10-1. Gene Mauch went three-for-five with two runs scored.

In Game Two, Minneapolis was hitless until the fifth, when singles by Red Robbins and Mauch, plus a sac fly brought in the tying run. In the eighth, Art Schult singled in two runs and Robbins one in a 4-1 victory.

Leading the series 2-0, the Millers moved to Bears Stadium in Denver for Game Three. The Bears knocked starter Dean Stone out in the first and reliever Harry Dorish in the second; scoring twice in each frame; then raked Tom Borland for 8 hits and 8 runs; climaxed by George Wilson's two-run homer. Denver led 12-2, but the Millers amazingly came back.

In the sixth Paul Smith singled home two runs and Red Robbins homered for three more. The Millers scored single runs in the 7th and 8th and tied it 12-12 in the ninth as Pumpsie Green doubled, his fourth hit of the game and Art Schult homered. Singles by Stu Locklin, Robbins and Tom Umphlett along with an intentional walk to Schult gave Millers their winning pair off John Kucab in the tenth led them to an amazing, improbable come-from-behind 14-13 victory.

In that game the juggler, Mauch, went wild. He switched Tom Umphlett between center and third; used Red Robbins at second and third; Stu Locklin in right field and first base; Ed Sadowski at third and catcher and Lou Clinton in center and right.

Looking for a sweep, the Millers struck quickly in Game Four. Art Schult belted a two-run homer in the first inning and the Millers took a 3-0 lead. After Denver tied the score at 4-4, Tom Umphlett and Gene Mauch singled in runs in the ninth in a 6-4 win.

A .243 hitting team in the regular season, the Millers hit .300 against Denver. Art Schult had 18 hits in 42 at bats, hit five homers and drove in fifteen runs. Stu Locklin, who'd joined the team in August went 6-for-10 against Denver.

Gene Mauch said, "I've seen a lot of inspirational clubs and been on some, but never one like this."[11]

Minneapolis won seven straight and 15 of 19 since Labor Day and would try to keep the train on the tracks as they headed to Montreal for the Junior World Series.

The Montreal Royals had won the International League pennant with the league's best hitting team. The series began in Montreal with righthander Al Schroll facing the Royals' 30-year-old lefthander Tom LaSorda, the International League's best pitcher with an 18-6 record and 2.50 ERA. The Millers jumped on LaSorda for two runs in the first and two more in the third to knock him out of the game. Gene Mauch had two doubles and a single to pace the offense in a 6-2 win.

In Game Two, the Millers' Stu Locklin led off the game with a home run and pitcher Dean Stone drove in two runs with a homer and double. Stone's pitching was erratic as he allowed seven hits with seven strikeouts but nine walks. Harry Dorish relieved him with the bases loaded in the seventh and got them out of the jam as Minneapolis won 7-2.

Up two games to none over the International League champion, in the third game, in the fourth inning Gene Mauch singled in what proved to be the game winner in a 3-2 Millers victory.

Minneapolis returned to Metropolitan Stadium and was greeted by 8,000 cheering fans. Tom Borland had been a workhorse all year, both starting and relieving. Gene Mauch handed the young lefty the game ball and he pitched a five-hitter, retiring 20 consecutive batters between the second and ninth. Lou Clinton drove in four runs with a triple and homer and the Millers completed a four-game sweep with a 7-1 victory to win the Junior World Series title.

The Minneapolis Millers set what was believed to be an all-time American Association record by winning 11 consecutive games en route to the crown. They took the last three games against Wichita, then swept eight straight from Denver and Montreal.

In *The Sporting News*, Halsey Hall wrote, "With the triumph, Manager Gene Mauch doubtless built himself into leading candidacy as the minor league manager of the year and almost certainly will win "best managing" honors in the American Association.

Mauch received a deluxe Ford, the gift of friends and admirers among Minnesota fans. Jerry Moore of the Metropolitan Sports Arena Commission made the presentation. Each member of the team received a transistor radio.

League President Ed Doherty said, "You can't beat pitching such as the Millers have and have had."[12] Each Miller also received $740 as his share of the series pot.

There were many heroes in the Millers' incredible run. In the Junior World Series, the team's leading hitters were Gene Mauch, who hit .444 with four hits in nine at bats and Art Schult at .375, who went six-for-sixteen with a homer and five RBI.

There were also a couple of unexpected contributors, Jerry Zimmerman and Stu Locklin. When All-Star catcher Ed Sadowski jammed his thumb in the third game of the Wichita series, Zimmerman, his backup, went behind the plate and caught eleven straight games and hit .357 with five hits in fourteen at bats in the Junior World Series.

Locklin was the good luck charm. He had been on the 1956 Indianapolis team that beat Minneapolis in the first round, then won four straight over Denver and four in a row against International League champ Rochester. He was on two of the three sweeps in Junior World Series history.

As expected, Gene Mauch was selected as the American Association's Manager of the Year for 1958.

Gene Mauch's performance as manager of the Minneapolis Millers caught the attention of major league clubs. After losing his best pitchers and with the worst hitting team in the league, Mauch somehow guided his team into the playoffs and with an incredible eleven game postseason win streak, they captured the Junior World Series.

Columnist Dick Young wrote, "Gene Mauch, a Dodger in his infancy, is considered the best young managerial prospect for the Big Time. His baby face is holding him back."[13]

In 1959 Mauch welcomed back several players from the championship team of 1958 including pitchers Tom Borland, Tom Hurd, and Bud Byerly; catcher Ed Sadowski; outfielder Tom Umphlett; and infielders Art Schult, Red Robbins, and Pumpsie Green.

Green was expected to be the first black player in Boston Red Sox history and when he was sent back to Minneapolis during spring training there was an uproar.

The NAACP leveled discrimination charges against the Red Sox. Team business Manager Dick O'Connell responded, "I deny categorically that the Red Sox have a discrimination policy. We have no discrimination against race, color or creed. We think these charges have been unfair."[14]

At first, Green didn't respond but finally, he said, "I figured I just didn't make the club. I was disappointed when I didn't stick with the Red Sox. I'd rather be playing every day in Minneapolis than riding the bench in Boston."[15]

Red Sox star Ted Williams said, "The newspapers built that up. Get it straight. I'm for Green. He's a good prospect. But he's not ready. Let him get that extra experience. He wouldn't play around here, would he?"[16]

Green hit well early in spring training but tailed off. Still, his .327 batting average was the team's fifth best and he added four homers and 10 RBI.

The Red Sox also moved Green to second base where he joined shortstop Jim Mahoney, who'd just completed two years in the service. Rookie Shep Frazier, a former star at the University of Alabama, was at third base with Gabe Gabler, a 28-year-old vet, at first.

Catcher Ed Sadowski was back. Sadowski was the other brother of Ted and Bob Sadowski and the uncle of Jim Sadowski, all three of whom pitched in the big leagues.

Art Schult and Tom Umphlett both returned in the outfield and were joined by rookie Lou Clinton and major league vet Chuck Tanner, who had played for Gene Mauch in AA ball in Atlanta in 1953.

Pitching had been the strength of the 1958 champs but this staff had some new arms including former Boston Braves' lefthander Chet Nichols, who'd missed the 1957 season with arm injuries; Nelson Chittum, who'd gone 12-8 with Omaha; and 6'3" 215-pound Earl Wilson, a hard throwing righthander. They were soon joined by vet Willard Nixon, released by the Bosox.

On April 12, the Millers opened the 58th American Assocication season on the road against the Houston Buffs, added to the league along with the Dallas Rangers and Ft. Worth Cats. 7,482 turned out in Houston to see their new team lose to the Millers 9-5. Art Schult blasted a homer, double, and single, but his debut at first base was marred by two throwing errors.

After opening the season on the road, the Millers finally returned to Minneapolis for their home opener against Ft. Worth. A crowd of 7280 at Metropolitan Stadium saw Chet Nichols pitch a complete game four-hitter in a 4-0 win over Ft. Worth.

In the second game of the series, Duane Wilson shutout the Cats 1-0. It became obvious to Gene Mauch that pitching again would be the strength of his ball club.

23-year-old righthander Earl Wilson was back from two years in the Marines. The 6'3" 215-pounder had originally signed as a catcher. In his first year at Bisbee-Davis in the Arizona-Texas League, Wilson suffered a severe spike wound on his left hand. Because of the soreness from the constant pounding of fast balls on his gloved hand, Wilson could no longer catch. With his team short on pitching, his manager sent him to the mound. Wilson found that pitching didn't put undue strain on his hand and discovered that he could throw real hard. After Wilson went 49-2 in 1957 and 1958 with the San Diego Marines, his catching days were over.

Wildness ruined his AAA debut in Ft. Worth as he walked seven in six innings and lost 6-2, but Gene Mauch saw future greatness in the fireballer.

Pumpsie Green got off to a great start as the Millers swept a doubleheader at Ft. Worth. Pumpsie went 3-for-3 in the opener and got another hit to drive in a run in the nightcap. He also handled 18 chances without an error and took part in four double plays as the Millers won 6-3 and 3-1.

Art Schult who hit .287 with 20 homers and 89 RBI for the 1958 champs, hit for the cycle and drove in five runs in a 9-5 win over Houston.

The pitching staff turned in another gem when Ted Wills blanked Louisville 1-0. Wills extended his string of consecutive innings without a walk to 19 2/3. Wills, who had gone 15-10 the year before with Chattanooga in the Southern Association, was rapidly became the ace of this talented pitching staff.

Top heavy with five lefthanders, the pitching rich team got richer as the Red Sox sent veteran Herb Moford down and the Phillies returned Al Schroll, giving the team the solid right-handed starters Mauch needed.

With his size, 95-mile-per-hour fastball and gold front tooth which showed when he smiled at hitters, Earl Wilson became a force, getting stronger with each start. Against Denver, he pitched a four hitter and struck out eleven. He followed that by pitching three hit ball for six innings, striking out nine and belting two home runs to beat the Bears again.

By June 4, Minneapolis was 33-17 and in first place in the Eastern Division.

Besides great pitching and defense, the Millers had just enough hitting with Art Schult and Chuck Tanner leading the way. Tanner, 30-years-old, with four major league seasons under his belt, needed one more year to qualify for a major league pension. Tanner had been so depressed by being sent back to the minors that he thought about quitting and concentrating on his photography business in New Castle, Pennsylvania.

But when Minneapolis offered him a contract, he decided the only way he could get back to the big leagues was to have a good year with the Millers. Tanner had previously played for Mauch in Atlanta in the Southern Association in 1953 where he hit .318. Before the season began, Mauch told him he could lead the American Association in hitting. Previously a left-handed hitter, Tanner decided to swing from both sides of the plate and was among the top five in hitting all year.

The Millers added more firepower, signing, adding catcher Haywood Sullivan, sent down by the Red Sox, activating Willard Nixon who had been on the disabled list, and signing Gene Mauch's brother-in-law Roy Smalley. Mauch knew there would be plenty of chances for Smalley to help the club and immediately started writing his name in the lineup at third base.

In early July, the Millers extended their winning streak to eight in a row as they battered Denver 13-2. Ed Sadowski, who had 1 hit in his last 27 at bats, broke loose with a single, triple, and home run; and Lou Clinton extended his hitting streak to 19 straight games.

By July 4, Minneapolis was 56-28 with an eight-game lead and threatening to leave the pack in the distance. They celebrated Independence Day with the traditional battle against cross town rival, the St. Paul Saints. In St. Paul, a regular Saints' rooter, a used car salesman began taunting Gene Mauch.

The loud mouth continued to ride Mauch throughout the game but when he got personal, the Little General had had enough. He left the third base coaching box and went into the stands. Grabbing his tormentor by the collar, Mauch said, "I'll give you $100 if you'll punch me. And then I'll knock your____head off."[17] The guy shut up and sat down in his seat.

Just before the All-Star break, the Millers lost six out of nine to Denver and Omaha and led by just three and a half games. "We're alright," said Gene Mauch. "The club hasn't been playing bad ball. Things will get clicking again."[18]

With the American Association's best record at the All-Star break, Minneapolis became the host team for the All-Star game. 11,316 turned out at Metropolitan Stadium.

Charleston manager Bill Adair had a powerful lineup, composed of future major leaguers like Bob Will, Lee Maye, Jim Gentile and Ozzie Virgil. Collectively, the All-Star roster had a .300 batting average. Gene Mauch's pitching staff threw a blanket over the All-Stars. Chet Nichols, Willard Nixon and Duane Wilson held the All-Stars to four singles in a 2-0 win, the first time a league's host team had shutout the All-Stars.

But then the air raid sirens began to screech. As they did in 1958, the parent Boston Red Sox raided the Millers, recalling pitcher Earl Wilson, second baseman Pumpsie Green and shortstop Jim Mahoney. Art Schult, the team's best hitter was sold to the Chicago Cubs, and reliable reliever Bud Byerly was sent to San Francisco. After the player raids, the Millers lost 19 of 36.

On July 24, 22-year-old Indianapolis lefthander Gary Peters no-hit the Millers at Victory Field in Indy, the first no hitter by an Indians pitcher since 1945.

On July 29, Minneapolis fell into second place behind Louisville.

Gene Mauch tried to plug the holes. 31 year-old-Herbie Plews, who spent four years with the Washington Senators, took over at second base, Roy Smalley at shortstop, minor league vet Gabe Gabler at first with Red Robbins filling in where necessary.

As the Millers tried to right the ship, Roy Smalley was their hottest hitter. In a ten-game home stand, he had 13 hits in 36 at bats, a .361 average and drove in nine runs. In the first game of a doubleheader sweep against Houston, he hit two 400-foot home runs: the first a three run shot to spark a 5-2 win, and another in a 13-4 victory.

Outfielder Stu Locklin, a major contributor in the 1958 playoff run, was acquired from San Diego. Locklin had just switched to contact lenses and used his improved vision to bang out three hits to break up a three hour-35 minute marathon and give the Millers a 10-9 twelve inning win over Houston.

While the pitching remained solid, the offense needed an injection of power. Joe Macko was acquired from Ft. Worth in a trade for Gabe Gabler. In his first 20 games with the Millers, Macko had 18 hits in 54 at bats, a .333 average with five homers and 13 RBI. "Macko has been a life saver for us," said Mauch.

With Pumpsie Green and Art Schult gone, the Millers gun rack was empty. By the end of August, the team had scored only 34 runs in 12 games. Desperate times call for desperate measures. Gene Mauch activated himself. In his first appearance, he had a pinch hit single in a loss to Louisville.

In 18 games against Louisville, Gene Mauch had started a lefthander 17 times, trying to negate the Colonels left-handed hitters: Lee Maye, Al Spangler, Earl Hersh, Charlie Lau, Joe Morgan and Dave Roberts. But Mauch played a hunch. He'd been so impressed by young righthander Tracy Stallard, called up from AA Allentown, that he gave him a start in the first game of a series against Louisville. Stallard mowed down the Colonels, allowing just two hits and striking out nine before retiring for a pinch hitter in the eighth but the Millers still lost 4-3.

Stallard then equaled the league's second highest strikeout total of the season when he fanned 14 Omaha hitters in nine innings. Stallard is best remembered for giving up Roger Maris' 61st home run in 1961.

After their brilliant first half season, the player raids took their toll on the Millers. In first place with a 59-35 record on July 12, they went just 34-31 thereafter. Besides the loss of key players, a month-long slump by Lou Clinton also contributed to the team's downfall. Earlier in the season, Mauch said he wouldn't trade Clinton for any player in the league. Hitting over .300 in mid-July, Clinton's average plummeted to .251.

While the Millers struggled, Louisville went 19-5 to win the American Association title, the first team in the 58-year history of the league, to go from last place to first in one season.

The Millers finished with a 95-67 record, good for second place, and two games back of Louisville.

When the regular season ended, the league's fourth-best hitter Chuck Tanner took his .319 average to Cleveland as part of a deal made previously. Tanner returned to the big leagues and played four more years. Then, he managed four major league teams, including the 1979 World Champion Pittsburgh Pirates.

Minneapolis began the first round of the playoffs in Omaha. Lefthander Ted Wills pitched a five-hitter and struck out 13 in a 3-1 win as the Millers took a 1-0 lead in the best of seven series.

In Game Two, another southpaw Tom Borland held Omaha to six hits and had the game winning homer with two outs in the ninth as the Millers won 2-1.

In Game Three, Mauch sent still another lefty to the mound, Ted Bowsfield, who held Omaha to four hits through six innings but taking advantage of four Millers errors, Omaha scored three runs in the seventh to win 4-2.

In Minneapolis, Cardinals' lefthander Ray Sadecki struck out 12 and pitched a three-hitter in a 7-0 Omaha win to even the series at two games apiece. Another of Mauch's lefties, starter Chet Nichols took the loss.

Minneapolis beat Omaha 3-2 in ten innings in the series fifth game but Omaha protested claiming that the Millers had used an ineligible player, newcomer Carl Yastrzemski, who had scored the winning run.

Yastrzemski's eligibility date had been set for September 18, the day that outfielder Lee Howell was to report for military service. When Howell decided to leave on September 15, Gene Mauch and Millers General Manager George Brophy thought the insertion of Yastrzemski was legal.

Omaha General Manager Bill Bergesch protested and League President Ed Doherty threw the victory out and called for a last minute, makeshift doubleheader. No problem for Gene Mauch.

On a brutally cold, rainy, windy day in Minneapolis, only 455 fans saw the Millers sweep both games. Roy Smalley doubled in two runs in the sixth in a 5-3 win. In the second game, reliever Billy Muffett hammered Cards' pitcher Tom Cheney's first pitch in the twelfth inning over the fence for a 3-2 victory as the Millers took the series four games to two. Next up was a surprising Ft. Worth team that had swept regular season champ Louisville 4-0.

With empty seats outnumbering fans, in 22,000 seat Metropolitan Stadium, 615 braved the cold weather to watch the Millers open the next series against the Ft. Worth Cats, who had swept Louisville 4-0 in their first series. The Millers exploded for six runs in the third inning in an 8-6 win.

After the next day's game was postponed because of rain and freezing temperatures and preparations for a pro football exhibition game occupied the stadium for the next two days, the league decided to move the series to Ft. Worth for the next four games. If a sixth and seventh game were needed, they would be played in Minneapolis. The clubs also agreed to wait another day before resuming the series.

Gene Mauch was happy about the delay, figuring his beleaguered pitching staff could use some rest.

In Ft. Worth, rookie Carl Yastrzemski had three hits, scored three runs and drove in two in a 9-6 Minneapolis win giving the Millers a 2-0 lead in the series.

Going for three straight, Millers leadoff hitter Tom Umphlett homered to start the game and then was involved in an odd play that decided the outcome. With the score tied 3-3 in the eighth, Ft. Worth had a runner at first when the Cats' Emil Syngel hit a sinking liner to center. As Umphlett raced in to field it, the ball darted about 15 feet to the left and rolled for a triple, allowing the deciding run to score. Ft. Worth tacked on another run in the 8th and won 5-3, to cut the Millers series lead to 2-1.

Ft. Worth's Al Lary, brother of Detroit Tigers ace Frank Lary, took a no-hitter into the sixth in Game Four until the Millers Herbie Plews singled. Lary wound up with a four hit shutout to win 6-0 to even the series.

In Game Five in Minneapolis, Seth Morehead stopped the Millers on five hits and won 2-1 as Ft. Worth took a 3-2 lead in the series. Billy Muffett, the only right-handed starter Gene Mauch used in the series, pitched well but took the loss.

Lefty Ted Wills pitched six strong innings and John Goryl had two hits and two RBI as the Millers won 6-3 to force a seventh game.

On a cold, rainy night at Metropolitan Stadium, Gene Mauch sent lefty Tom Borland to the mound. He stopped the Cats on five hits 4-2 as Minneapolis won the series 4-3. Shortstop Johnny Goryl was a hitting barometer for the Millers. In the four victories, he went 8-for-16 but was hitless in ten at bats in losses.

For the second straight year, Gene Mauch had taken the Millers to the Junior World Series.

A Sporting News headline read, "Millers' Fans Cheer Star Juggler Mauch." Mauch's slight of hand produced an amazing comeback. With Pumpsie Green, Art Schult, Jim Mahoney, Earl Wilson and Chuck Tanner, the Millers were eight games ahead of the field on July 4 and shutout the league's all-star team. Then, the parent Boston Red Sox gutted Mauch's infield and outfield. When the regular season ended, Chuck Tanner, the team's leading hitter left to join the Cleveland.

In the Junior World Series, the Millers met the Havana Sugar Kings who finished third in the International League and then upset Columbus and Richmond.

Managed by Preston Gómez, the Sugar Kings were a mixture of mostly Cubans, some Puerto Ricans and Venezuelans and a handful of Americans. Several Havana players enjoyed major league careers including Leo Cardenas, Elio Chacón, Mike Cuellar; and two players who would eventually play for Gene Mauch, outfielder Tony González and infielder Cookie Rojas.

Gene Mauch's Millers were the defending Junior World Series champions, making their third appearance in the minor league classic in five years. Minnesota was bolstered by the addition of 20-year-old second baseman Carl Yastrzemski, who won a batting title, hitting .377 in Class B.

The first three games of the series were scheduled for Metropolitan Stadium in Minneapolis. Despite freezing rain and the thermometer at 37 degrees, 2,486 braved the weather to watch the opener. Even though they were 1,500 miles from Cuba, the Sugar Kings had more fans. Cuban natives living in the Twin Cities bought box seats behind the Havana dugout and cheered wildly when the Sugar Kings scored four runs in the third inning and won 5-2.

It was colder the next day and as the rain turned to snow, the crowd dwindled to 1,062. Sugar Kings' players tried to stay warm drinking massive quantities of coffee and huddling around a fire in a wastebasket in the dugout.

The Millers trailed 2-0 in the second but Gene Mauch's brother-in-law Roy Smalley tied the game with a two-run homer. Havana led 5-2 in the eighth until homers by Lou Clinton and Red Robbins retied the score at 5-5. Ed Sadowski led off the ninth with a home run as the Millers won 6-5 to even the series at a game apiece.

With the next day's forecast calling for "more rain and colder weather," the Series Commission voted unanimously to cancel the third game and move the series to Cuba. George M. Trautman, National Association President and the heads of the two leagues, Ed Doherty of the American Association, and Frank Shaughnessy of the International League agreed the good weather in Cuba would produce bigger crowds.

Despite sunshine and clear skies, Cuba, in 1959 was not a vacation spot for Americans. On January 1, Cuban President Fulgencio Batista y Zaldívar took exile in the Dominican Republic and revolutionary leader Fidel Castro took over the country.

As the Millers flew to Havana they were well aware of previous violence at Gran Stadium, home of the Havana Sugar Kings. In a July game, the Sugar Kings and Rochester Red Wings were in extra innings after midnight, when, outside the stadium, a celebration erupted with music, shouting and gunfire.

With Rochester player-coach Frank Verdi in the third base coaching box, the Red Wings' Dick Rand grounded out to shortstop Leo Cardenas. Before the next pitch, gun shots rang out and both Verdi and Cardenas dropped to the ground in pain. Verdi was hit in the head, but fortunately was wearing a plastic batting helmet liner which deflected the bullet through his ear and onto his shoulder. Cardenas was grazed by a bullet in the shoulder. Neither was seriously injured, but the umpires immediately called off the game as everyone ran for the clubhouses. The Red Wings refused to play the final game of the series and left the country.

Now, two months later, an apprehensive Millers team arrived but were immediately surprised by the warm reception of the Cuban people. Cuban fans cheered as the players rode in convertibles in a parade from the airport to the Havana Hilton.

When they arrived at the ballpark, the Millers saw a sellout crowd approaching 30,000, but also 3,000 soldiers with loaded guns, munition belts and bayonets, lining the field and flanking the dugouts.

Remembered Johnny Goryl, "Fidel Castro came through the gates in centerfield with his entourage and soldiers carrying machine guns and the fans pulled their white handkerchiefs out and started waving them. I think everybody had a hanky and sitting in the dugout, you could hear them whipping through the air. It sounded like bees."

For each game, Castro was surrounded by an estimated 35 soldiers. "Young people not more than 14 or 15-years-old were in the dugout, waving their guns around like toys," remembered Ted Bowsfield."

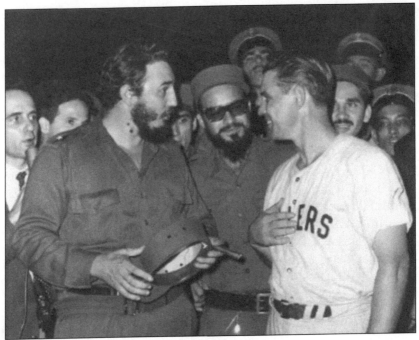

Gene Mauch with Fidel Castro.

"We had soldiers lining up outside our dugout and you know Gene, he was not the most cordial guy in the world when it came to baseball," said Johnny Goryl. "It was a problem for us to get out on the field when we were changing between innings. I think Gene actually shoved one of the soldiers so he could see the field."

As centerfielder Tom Umphlett entered the dugout at the end of an inning, a soldier made a slicing motion across his throat. "Our players were truly fearful of what might happen if we won," said Mauch.[19]

At home plate, Castro spoke to the sellout crowd, "I came here to see our team beat Minneapolis, not as a premier but as just a baseball fan. I want to see our club win the Little World Series. Castro then shook hands with players from each team and settled into his box behind home plate. He stood and cheered with fans and saw live chickens sailing out of the stands. The chickens, black in color with their legs tied together with red bands, were tossed onto the field whenever the Cubans got a rally going.

As the series resumed with Game Three, Havana came back to win 3-2 in ten innings as the Sugar Kings scored two in the eighth to tie it and added another in tenth to win it. Carl Yastrzemski hit a 400-foot home run in the game.

For Game Four, again Fidel Castro sat in his box behind the plate and watched the Minnesota bullpen blow a late innings lead. He stood and cheered as his team tied the game 3-3 on a run scoring single by Dan Morejon in the bottom of the ninth. Then More-jon drove in the winning run with a single in the 11th, giving the Sugar Kings a 4-3 win.

Gene Mauch was ejected from that game but no one knew it, not even Mauch, until later. With one out in the eighth, Umpire Bill Kinnamon ruled that Yo-Yo Davalillo had been nicked by Tom Borland's pitch. Mauch raced to the plate and heatedly argued that the hitter had swung at the pitch. Later in the inning, Mauch came out to change pitchers. However, when Mauch went to the third base coaching box to start the ninth inning, Kinnamon told him that earlier he'd been thrown out of the game. "That's the first I heard of it," said Mauch. Even the three members of the Junior World Series Commission hadn't been told of Mauch's ejection. To avoid confrontations and a possible riot, Ed Doherty, American Association President said, "We told the umpires that no one was to be thrown out except for flagrant misconduct." The Sugar Kings led the series 3-1 and were within one game of the title.

For Game Five, Fidel Castro joined the fans in the right centerfield bleachers and sat quietly as Millers lefthander Ted Wills silenced the Sugar Kings, scattering seven hits with twelve strikeouts in a 4-2 Millers win.

Hoping to change his team's luck, in Game Six, Fidel Castro took a seat in the Sugar King's dugout. It didn't matter. Minneapolis knocked lefthander Mike Cuellar out of the game with a four run uprising in the third and won again 5-3 to tie the series and set up the decisive Game Seven.

Because of heavy rain in Havana, the next game was postponed. "We were warned not to leave the hotel between games," recalled Carl Yastrzemski. "There was a revolution in the streets but with the guns and noise it was just scary."[20]

"One of the highlights of staying in the hotel was Martha Raye was also staying there," said Johnny Goryl. "She was a U.S. citizen and we were all U.S. citizens so she came and joined our beer party in one of the rooms. We wanted her to sing but by the time she drank a couple of beers, I don't think she was in any mood to sing. She was very gracious and cordial with all of us."

As the series resumed, an overflow crowd of over 30,000 crammed into Gran Stadium for Game Seven and several thousand more stood along the outfield foul lines. Fidel Castro was not about to let his team lose. Before the game he made his entrance through centerfield and surrounded by bodyguards, walked around the warning track to his box seat. According to Millers' outfielder Stu Locklin, as Castro passed the visiting bullpen, he paused, looked at the players, patted his revolver on his hip and said, "Tonight we win." Because the Cubans like most players are superstitious, Castro returned to his box seat behind home plate. That seat had brought good luck in games three and four.

The Millers took the lead as Joe Macko homered leading off the fourth and Lou Clinton did the same in the sixth as Minneapolis took a 2-0 lead.

In the eighth inning, with one out, Havana had runners at second and third and Gene Mauch brought in veteran righthander Murray Wall to replace starter Tom Borland. After Wall struck out Ray Shearer for the second out, Mauch headed to the mound to talk with Wall. Third baseman Johnny Goryl joined the meeting. "Gene came out with runners at second and third and we were up by two runs and Gene told Murray, 'Look Murray, I don't want you to throw this guy any fastballs. We've got an open base at first. All I want you to do is throw your slider and see if we can get him to chase, if we don't get him to chase and walk him, that's alright.'"

With left-handed hitting Larry Novak, a .216 hitter with nine homers, batting for Rogelio Alvarez, Wall threw sliders for two quick
strikes. "Then Murray was trying to set up his fourth pitch," said
Goryl, "He wanted to throw a slider the hitter would chase. He
threw a slider but it got too much of the plate and the guy drove
it up the middle for a base hit and I thought Gene was going to go
nuts." Novak's two-run single tied the game at 2-2.

In the bottom of the ninth, reliever Billy Muffett walked Havana's
leadoff batter, Raul Sanchez. Yoyo Davalillo sacrificed him to second and after Elio Chacon flied out, Tony González was walked
intentionally. Dan Morejon who hit .407 with 7 RBI in the series,
stepped in, the last guy the Millers wanted to see. Morejon came
through again, with a single, driving in Sanchez for a 3-2 win and
the Junior World Series title that sent the huge crowd into hysteria.

The Cubans danced and sang and celebrated their heroes, party-
ing into the morning.

The Millers returned to their hotel where Gene Mauch, hoping to
keep his players inside, threw a party in his suite on the twenty-
third floor. The team was composed of mostly veterans, much
older than rookie Carl Yastrsemski so Mauch paired Yaz with
twenty-year-old Lou Clinton, the only player near his age.

As the vets drank and partied deep into the night, Mauch sent
the two rookies out to a rib joint to buy spareribs for the whole
party. As the players continued to drink and wolfed down the
ribs, Mauch went to bed.

With the manager gone, one of Mauch's well-oiled players threw
a glass out the window. It landed in the swimming pool, twenty-
three floors below. That prompted a visit from the hotel manager
accompanied by two policemen. To keep his charges out of jail,
Mauch had to get up and make peace. Then, he headed back to
bed.

At seven in the morning, packing for their flight, somebody decided to continue the fun. "So while Clinton and I watched in
morbid fascination," said Carl Yastrzemski, "the boys began pop-

ping glasses on the pavement which scared Cubans driving in rush hour. They got out of their cars to see who was shooting at them. That brought the cops right back."[21]

When Mauch came in and saw what was happening, he said, "Don't take anybody anywhere until I call Fidel," which brought an immediate halt to the activity.

Mauch reached Castro, who was staying in the same hotel. He came right down, told the cops to let the players go, and warned them not to throw any more glasses.

Mauch thanked Castro and then said, "Pack up. We're leaving in twenty minutes."[22]

The Millers quietly boarded a plane home as pitcher Ted Bowsfield said, "Nobody minded losing the game in that country and under those conditions. We were just happy to get it over and get out of town with our hides."[23]

As a result of moving to Havana after drawing just 3,543 for the two games in Minneapolis, the teams set a Junior World Series record for gate receipts with $124,592 for the seven game series. The five games in Cuba drew 100,260.

Each member of the Havana Sugar Kings received a winner's share of $888.27 while the losing Millers got $592.18 apiece.

For the second straight year, Gene Mauch was voted American Association Manager of the Year.

Gene Mauch had studied with masters like Leo Durocher, Ray Blades, Billy Southworth and Bob Scheffing. From Durocher he'd learned how Leo could get opponents to try to beat him, distracting attention from his team. He'd also developed Leo's preference for veteran players.

Watching Ray Blades, Mauch had learned to make creative defensive shifts and for better or worse, he absorbed his manager's "win today" theory of pitching.

Billy Southworth told Mauch not to fall in love with his players, but like his mentor, he did. Southworth also taught him that every player is different and how to find the key to unlock each athlete's talent.

Bob Scheffing also saw the future manager in Mauch and allowed him to be his manager on the field.

Mauch had studied under the best and had gotten a taste of managing in Atlanta. After adding more seasoning in Los Angeles and two successful years in Minneapolis, all the pieces were in place. The mosaic that was Gene Mauch, manager, was complete. All he needed now was a museum in which to hang it.

Gene Mauch says goodbye to the Millers. Credit: Bill Swank

Chapter Thirteen

"All Things Considered, I'd Rather Be in Philadelphia"

– W.C. Fields

Gene Mauch went to spring training in 1960 looking to win a third straight American Association title. Carl Yaztremski was back but Mauch knew Yaz wouldn't be there long. He called Yaz "Irish" because he'd gone to Notre Dame, took him to breakfast a few times and told him the Red Sox were moving him to left field. Mauch hit fungoes to Yaz by the hour and explained the peculiarities of left field in Fenway Park.

"You're no Ted Williams yet," Mauch said, "but some day you can be better than he is." Carl Yastrzemski played one more year in Minneapolis, hitting .339 in 1960. Then, he began a 23-year career with the Boston Red Sox, was A.L. MVP in 1967 and was elected to the Hall of Fame in 1989.

The Minneapolis Millers trained in Deland, Florida until early April, then went to Pompano Beach for four days. "We were staying in a small motel in Pompano and things were so crowded that the people who ran the place gave up their regular quarters and were sleeping in the office," Gene Mauch recalled. "That's where the call came, but they told me there was an extension in the lavatory and that's where I talked to John."[1]

John was John Quinn, General Manager of the Philadelphia Phillies, who explained that Eddie Sawyer had resigned as Phillies' manager after just one game, a 9-4 season opening day loss in Cincinnati.

"John Quinn asked me to manage the Phillies and I said, 'Let's go. I'm ready,'" recalls Mauch.[2]

Mauch and Quinn talked several times that night, agreeing on a salary. Mauch tried to call his wife with the news but the hotel where she was staying had disconnected the switchboard so Mauch had to wait until 7 a.m. to call. "I woke her up to tell her and she was pretty excited but I didn't have too much chance to discuss it with her."[3]

Mauch spent most of the day on the phone talking to reporters and the next morning flew to Philadelphia. For several hours Mauch did radio and TV interviews, posed for photos and answered questions from the media.

Mauch admitted he'd turned down a previous offer from another team and accepted the Phillies' job because he'd seen John Quinn rebuild a team before in Milwaukee. When reminded his club had been picked for last place, Mauch said, "I won't go for that. We must have some pretty good players. You don't get to the big leagues by accident."[4]

In Philadelphia the Phillies brain trust was scrambling. The morning of the home opener, Phillies owner Bob Carpenter and G.M. John Quinn the media to come to the Phillies' office. "Gentlemen, I'm going to make an announcement which will be a shock to you and a great surprise and disappointment to me," said Carpenter. "I talked to Eddie Sawyer last night and he has resigned as manager." Carpenter said Sawyer told him, "I just don't want to manage a major league club or any club.'"[5]

Sawyer also told one reporter, "I am 49 and I want to live to be 50."

John Quinn took the podium and announced that Gene Mauch had signed a two-year contract to be the new Phils' manager. Quinn said he selected Mauch because he had admired his spirit as a player, his knowledge of the game and his managing record.

First base coach Andy Cohen held down the fort until Mauch arrived. Cohen, who'd played second base for John McGraw's New York Giants in 1926, piloted the Phillies to a 5-4 10-innning win over the Milwaukee Braves. He had waited thirty years for a chance to manage in the big leagues. "Now I'm hired and fired all in one day," Cohen said, "but my winning percentage is as good as anyone ever had."[6]

Gene Mauch and G.M. John Quinn.

"I'm going to be myself and manage my way," the 34-year-old Gene Mauch said. As Phillies players would find out, Mauch had great confidence in his baseball knowledge and ability to run a team. He was becoming "the Little General."

"If you've got pitching, you've got a chance," said Mauch, refer-ring to veterans Robin Roberts and Curt Simmons. The 33-year-old Roberts had won 221 games with Philadelphia and Simmons, a 31-year-old lefthander, had 115 victories with the Phils.

Roberts had his best spring in five years but when the season opened, he was a disaster, giving up eight runs in an opening day loss to the Reds and seven more against the Braves. Control had been Roberts' trademark and now he couldn't locate his pitches. After Roberts' third poor start, Mauch gave him a ten-day vacation, using him occasionally in mop-up relief.

Simmons was returning after elbow surgery, appeared to be recovered and also pitched well in spring training. But in the home opener he gave up back-to-back homers to the Braves' Hank Aaron and Joe Adcock in the first, and was lifted with one out in the second. In his next start against Pittsburgh, Simmons failed to get anybody out in the first inning, giving up 2 runs, 3 hits and 2 walks. Simmons had gone 17-8 for the Whiz Kids in 1950, but a stint in the Korean War, and a losing battle with a lawn mower that sliced up his toe, had derailed his career. After a couple of ineffective relief appearances, the Phillies released Curt Simmons, a move they would forever regret.

Simmons figured he might be traded but getting released was the low point of his career. He was still young and his arm felt good. Ken Silvestri, a former catcher and a Phillies' coach told Simmons he "got screwed" and suggested that he contact every team to request a tryout.

After moping for a few days, Simmons reached Cubs manager Lou Boudreau who offered a tryout. Simmons threw to former catcher, Cubs' coach Del Rice, who said, "How the hell did they ever release you?"

As the Cubs twiddled their thumbs over a few dollars, Solly Hemus and Bing Devine of the Cardinals called to invite Simmons in for a tryout. "He's down at the park, trying out for the Cubs," said his wife. Forget the tryout! The Cardinals blindly signed Simmons, one of the best moves they ever made.

The Phils lost six straight at the end of April and dropped into last place with a 5-11 record. Quinn had previously said that pitchers Robin Roberts, Gene Conley, Jim Owens and Don Cardwell, were untouchables but losing changed his mind. After conferring with Mauch, Quinn said he would trade anyone on the roster if it helped the club.

If the threat of being traded wasn't enough to get players' attention, in a clubhouse meeting in San Francisco, Mauch told his players that if they didn't observe the rules, they would be fined, "and it won't cost them any piddling $5, $10 or $25."[7]

When the Phillies swept a doubleheader from the Pirates, eight players returned to the clubhouse to find out they'd been fined $25 apiece for not being on the field when pre-game practice began.

Mauch had heard about "The Dalton Gang." *Sports Illustrated's* Walter Bingham wrote a story about them, "The Dalton Gang Rides Again."

The three were pitchers Dick "Turk" Farrell, Jim "The Bear" Owens, and Jack "The Bird" Meyer. In a nightclub in Pittsburgh, Meyer and his roommate Harry Anderson were sitting near beat writers, Ray Kelly and Allan Lewis and broadcaster Byrum Saam.

Meyer was talking loudly about horse racing and Lewis asked him to quiet down. Enraged, the inebriated Meyer tried to punch Lewis and had to be taken back to the hotel by Anderson. After Meyer had been put to bed, Farrell decided it would be fun to pour cold water on him. Meyer jumped up and began fighting and had to be restrained by Anderson and teammate John Buzhardt.

Back in bed, Meyer received a disturbing phone call, jumped out of bed and trashed the room. Again his teammates calmed him down. Meyer suffered a herniated disc in his back and the next day had to tell Gene Mauch what happened. The Phillies sent Meyer to the hospital, placed him on the disabled list, and fined him $1,000. To put the enormity of the fine in perspective, $1000 was nine per cent of Meyer's $14,000 salary.

"What do they think I am, a millionaire?" Meyer shouted "I've got four kids to support." Meyer asked for his release and threatened to sue, but later retracted his comments saying he just wanted to help the team win.

In Chicago, Mauch left the dugout for the third base coaching box. "Most people say a manager can stay more on top of things if he's in the dugout, but I feel I can do a better job from third base."[8] The

Phils won the next game and took three of the next four.

Besides dumping Curt Simmons, the Phils traded first baseman Ed Bouchee and pitcher Don Cardwell to the Chicago Cubs for infielder Tony Taylor and catcher Cal Neeman.

Two days later, pitching for the Cubs, Cardwell threw a no-hitter against the St. Louis Cardinals, the first no-no against the Cards in 41 years.

The same day Cardwell pitched his no-hitter, Gene Mauch and his Phillies were involved in a brawl in Cincinnati. The slugfest broke out in the eighth inning of the first game of a doubleheader. With the Phillies leading 13-1, Reds' reliever Raul Sanchez hit back-to-back hitters, Ted Lepcio and Cal Neeman. He tried to hit the next batter Joe Koppe but missed and walked him. Then Sanchez planted a fastball in pitcher Gene Conley's ribs.

Gene Mauch bolted out of the dugout, charged Sanchez on the mound and began throwing punches. Reds' first baseman Frank Robinson tried to collar Mauch and took a punch in the face.

Both dugouts emptied as players raced onto the field. The Reds Billy Martin, no stranger to fights, charged Gene Conley. The tale of the tape was not in Martin's favor: Martin at 5-11 and 160 pounds versus the 6'-8" 230-pound Conley. Conley threw a haymaker and caught Martin above the left eye. "I was holding back Mauch," said Martin, "when Conley belted me. But I got Conley too. I had to jump to hit him. Fighting him is like fighting a two story building."[9] Later, Martin was rushed to a hospital for X-rays.

Meanwhile, two Phillies players were sitting on Reds catcher Ed Bailey. Umpires Chris Pelekoudos and Bill Jackowski helped calm the fray, but then Robin Roberts, who had raced in from the bullpen, began sparring with Frank Robinson near first base.

When the brawl was finally stopped, plate umpire Stan Lawles, cleared both dugouts and bullpens. Roberts and Martin were escorted off the field as fans booed and threw paper cups onto the field.

After being released from the hospital where he had his jaw X-rayed, Billy Martin said, "I'll fight Conley any time. He's so big I might need a stool to belt him in the face but I'll get my opportunity."[10]

Cincinnati manager Fred Hutchinson blamed the brawl on Gene Mauch. "There wouldn't have been any trouble at all if Mauch hadn't charged the mound," said Hutch.[11] a TKO, the Phillies won 14-3.

Mauch was fined $100 and reprimanded by National League President Warren Giles. Giles told Mauch the penalty would have been more severe but Mauch was new in the league and this was his first offense.

The ultimate juggler, Mauch began to manipulate his roster, trying to win. He used Joe Koppe, Ted Lepcio, Bobby Del Greco, Tony Curry and Bob Malkmus in the leadoff spot. Pancho Herrera, a 240-pounder played first and second. Johnny Callison moved into the third spot in the batting order while playing all three outfield positions.

The Phils lost seven straight, falling into last place with a 12-27 record. By now, Mauch and Quinn realized they had squeezed every drop out of this lemon. There would be no quick fix. The team would have to be imploded and rebuilt from the ground floor.

In a game against Cincinnati, outfielder Johnny Callison collided with Reds' catcher Ed Bailey and was carried off the field on a stretcher. Callison went to Temple University Hospital where his leg was put in a cast. He had reinjured a knee he'd originally hurt in winter league play. Callison's injury was the most serious in an epidemic that included catcher Jimmie Coker breaking his thumb and shortstop Joe Koppe and outfielder Tony Curry colliding, knocking both out of the lineup.

All Mauch and Quinn could do now was evaluate players, look for possible trades and try to wring a few more wins out of a terrible team. They tried to deal infielder Joe Koppe for a shortstop but with no takers, they recalled Ruben Amaro from the Mexican League. They swapped outfielders with Cincinnati, sending Wally Post and Harry Anderson to the Reds for Lee Walls and Tony González.

As the trading deadline passed, Mauch said, "We have the arms and the legs to steal a game when we're not hitting and the arms and legs to save one on defense."[12]

Making Mauch look like a prophet, the Phils won six straight. Robin Roberts and Dick Farrell each won two games, rookie outfielders Ken Walters and Tony González and first baseman Pancho Herrera had big hits and the defense improved. But the streak ended when former Phillie Curt Simmons, now a St. Louis Cardinal, combined with Lindy McDaniel to shut out the Phils 1-0.

Second baseman Tony Taylor and shortstop Ruben Amaro gave the Phils a superb keystone combination. Taylor was a good leadoff hitter, above average fielder and their best base stealer since Richie Ashburn.

Most of the Phils anemic offense was provided by Pancho Herrera, the rookie who played both first and second base, led the team in homers and put together a 20-game hitting streak.

With his club at 29-42, Mauch tried everything, including teaching his team trick plays. He showed his players how the Phils' defense could turn a popped-up bunt into a double play but the play backfired in an 11-5 loss to San Francisco. With the Phils' Joe Morgan, the future Red Sox manager, on first base and Ken Walters batting, Walters popped up a bunt. Giants' pitcher Sam Jones faked a catch and let the ball drop. Then he picked up the ball, fired to first to get Walters and the throw to second cut down Morgan, who had held up at first, thinking Jones would catch the ball.

In July, Mauch made another move to try to help his team. He switched the bullpen locations at Connie Mack Stadium. For years, the Phillies' bullpen was in foul ground down the left field line, on the same side as the dugout. The visitor's pen was in foul ground against the right field fence with their dugout on the same side.

But Mauch moved the Phillies' bullpen to right field while keeping the dugout on the third base side of the field. And the visitors' bullpen shifted to left field while their dugout remained on the first base side. Only Mauch could explain the move. "Most of the balls hit to left field are straight away and are usually caught or are home runs," the manager explained. But right field is different.

"Say the Phillies have runners on second and third and one of our players hits a ball to right field. It's always tough to decide whether it will be caught or hit the wall. But now our bullpen coach Ken Silvestri is in position to judge the ball right away and can start whirling a towel around to tell our base coaches to get the runners moving, the ball is going to hit the wall. And on defense, they can also help direct our right fielder who is chasing the ball and tell him where to throw it and also warn him about the fence. It is common knowledge that balls hit to right field are tougher to handle than those in left."[13]

As usual, Mauch had a hidden motive for the switch. He couldn't see the left field bullpen from the third base dugout and there were rumors that Phillies' relievers went underneath the stands to get food and beverages. Now, Mauch could see what was going on in the bullpen during the game.

The Phillies were encouraged by the resurgence of Robin Roberts who'd suddenly found the plate and pitched well in seven straight games.

Roberts had never pitched a no-hitter but came close against the Giants in Candlestick Park. The only Giants hit was a fluke. Felipe Alou came up with two outs in the fifth and hit a hard shot to rookie third baseman Joe Morgan, not the Hall of Famer Joe Morgan but the other one who managed the Red Sox. Morgan backed up to field the ball on the big hop but his right leg buckled and he fell on his back, unable to get Alou.

The official scorer called it a hit which elicited howls from Mauch and his players. Mauch complained that the rule book said the first hit of the game had to be a legitimate hit but he was wrong. A hit is a hit, an error an error.

For this game, he looked like the old Robin Roberts, but for the most part, the season was a struggle as Roberts wound up 12-16.

Robin Roberts was impressed by 22-year-old righthander Art Mahaffey who was recalled from AAA Buffalo in late July. After a relief appearance, the rookie staged a spectacular run. On a disastrous 6-13 road trip, he went 5-0 including a two hit shutout in San Francisco. Then, in September Mahaffey got his first taste of Gene Mauch's temper.

Before Mahaffey's start in Chicago, Mauch had a pregame meeting and said, "Whatever you do, don't let Ernie Banks hit a home run." Easier said than done. "Mr. Cub" had already hit 38 that year en route to 512 career homers and the Hall of Fame." Mahaffey was working on a perfect game until Banks came up with two outs in the fourth inning and homered.

Mauch stormed the mound and with blood vessels popping out on his neck, he screamed obscenities at Mahaffey. "Nobody had ever said anything like that to me," said the rookie. The Cubs won 2-1 and Mahaffey finished the season 7-3 with a 2.31 ERA but he never forgot his first bad encounter with the Little General.

Art Mahaffey (L) with Gene Mauch (R).

Mahaffey had the most unique pickoff move in baseball. A right-hander, after he stretched, he kept his right foot on the rubber as he twisted his upper body to throw to first base. It appeared he was throwing home and the deception fooled the runner. Opponents yelled, "balk" but he was rarely called for it. When he was recalled by the Phils, he predicted that he would pick off the first runner to get on base against him. He did better than that, picking off the first three, the Cardinals' Curt Flood and Bill White in the same inning and in the next game, the Giants' Jim Marshall.

On a national telecast, catcher turned broadcaster Joe Garagiola said said of Mahaffey's move, "Gene Mauch said he's like a drunk falling off a bar stool. You don't know which way he's going with that motion."[14]

Mahaffey's move to second was even more unusual because no one covered the bag. While the second baseman and shortstop stayed in their usual positions, Mahaffey spun and faked a throw.

The runner, thinking that he'd be picked off at second, either froze or headed for third. Mahaffey ran toward the runner and either got him in a rundown or tagged him out. Every year, Mahaffey caught three or four base runners with the move.

6'8" 225-pound Gene Conley starred in baseball and basketball at Washington State and played both major league baseball and pro basketball. He had pitched for the 1957 World Champion Milwaukee Braves and then played on three NBA title teams with the Boston Celtics from 1959-61. After going 12-9 for the Phillies in 1959, Conley had slumped to 8-14 in 1960. After a poor relief job by Conley, an angry Gene Mauch said, "What, are you doing saving your best for Red Auerbach?"[15]

Conley handed the baseball to Mauch and answered, "I'll never pitch for you again."[16] Conley quit the team a few days before the season ended.

The Phillies offered Conley an additional $20,000 to forgo basketball for the next year. Conley made a counter-offer and when the Phils and Conley couldn't agree, G.M. John Quinn traded him to the Boston Red Sox. Gene Mauch called it "the biggest trade in baseball," since the Phillies received 6'7" pitcher Frank Sullivan in return.

The Phillies finished last in the National League with a 59-95 record, thirty-six games out of first place.

This was a bad team. Gene Mauch and John Quinn knew they had to make major changes. Unlike today, in the 1960's, there was no amateur draft and no free agency. The only way to acquire players was to sign them and hope they developed in the farm system or trade for them.

The biggest need was a power hitter to bat behind Pancho Herrera and give him some protection in the batting order. In 1960, the Phillies had been last in runs scored and home runs, hitting only 99. Herrera led the team with a meager 13.

The Phils also wanted a left-handed pitcher and knew they had to straighten out the catching situation. Jim Coker and Clay

Dalrymple shared the position but Coker couldn't hit and Dalrymple had a sore arm and couldn't throw. If Gene Mauch could have cloned them together to make a complete catcher, he would have.

But Robin Roberts told Mauch he'd been impressed by Dalrymple's pitch-calling. After working with veteran catcher Cal Neeman, Dalrymple improved defensively and also hit .272. Eventually, his arm healed, he became a strong and accurate thrower and developed into one of the best catchers in baseball.

Like his first manager Leo Durocher, Mauch preferred veteran players. He felt young players made too many mental and physical mistakes. But with the Phillies, he had no choice. He had so many young players with limited experience that he felt he had to work on fundamentals.

Gene Mauch in Spring Training.

"The most overlooked part of managing is what happens in the spring," Mauch said.[17] "The most important month is March, not September." Mauch ran spring training like a drill sergeant in 1961. Since his team had no power, they would have to manufacture runs. Mauch was a great believer in bunting. For several days, in batting practice, the team did nothing but bunt. Just bunting, over and over and over. Mauch's philosophy was that if his team scored first, then it would take two runs to beat him. So, he often employed the sacrifice bunt in the early innings.

Mauch also wanted to reduce the team's base running and defensive mistakes. Each morning, Mauch and coaches Peanuts Lowery, Al Vincent and Bob Lemon would drill the players on running the bases, executing pickoff plays, throwing to the right base and mastering rundown plays.

Lee Walls, who had played for the Pirates, Cubs and Reds, said, "It's the finest camp as far as fundamentals are concerned that I've ever been to. Fundamentals aren't generally stressed enough in spring training especially when you have younger players."[18]

Utility infielder Bobby Malkmus, said, "This is the best organized spring training I've ever been in and I trained under Charley Grimm, Fred Haney, Cookie Lavagetto and Eddie Sawyer."[19]

Gene Mauch boldly predicted that the Phillies would win more games in 1961 than they did the previous year. Upbeat and prepared by Gene Mauch's boot camp, the Phillies flew to Los Angeles to open the season. The night before the opener, 1,000 fans packed the ballroom at the Beverly Hilton Hotel. Dinah Shore and Tony Martin sang and Don Rickles and Joey Adams cracked jokes. Gene Mauch was among the featured speakers which included Dodgers' owner Walter O'Malley and manager Walter Alston.

The next night, 50,927 fans at the L.A. Coliseum saw a pitcher's duel between Robin Roberts and Don Drysdale.

Gene Mauch and Walter Alston visit with Richard Nixon.

The Dodgers took the lead in the first inning on an RBI single by Tommy Davis. Wally Moon homered leading off the second to give his team a 2-0 lead but the Phils' Johnny Callison tied it in the third with a two run blast off Drysdale.

Roberts and Drysdale battled until the eighth, Roberts struggling to locate his fading fastball and Drysdale brushing back hitters and striking out eight with his gas.

Charlie Neal singled in a run in the 8th to give the Dodgers a 3-2 lead and then Ron Fairly, pinch hitting for Drysdale, doubled to drive in two more. The Dodgers added another run and won 6-2.

Looking at the lineup card for the next game, it didn't seem fair. The Phils with Malkmus, Callison, Taylor, Walters, Herrera, Dalrymple and Amaro against Wills, Willie and Tommy Davis, Snider, Moon and Neal. Come on. As Ruben Amaro said, "We went out there and played our asses off but we were overmatched. We were so young. It was like a kindergarten team playing a fourth grade team."[20]

Mauch felt that pitching would be the team's strength and hitting the weakness. He was right. Frank Sullivan, Dallas Green and Art Mahaffey all pitched well.

Although Robin Roberts lost his first two starts, Green blanked San Francisco and Sullivan and Mahaffey pitched shutouts in a doubleheader sweep of the Chicago Cubs.

Mahaffey was overpowering, allowing just four hits and breaking the club record with seventeen strikeouts in a 6-0 win. "That was the most powerfully pitched game I ever saw," said Mauch, "and I've been in baseball for 20 years."[21]

In May, the Phillies finally acquired the power hitter they needed, getting outfielder Don Demeter and infielder Charley Smith from the Dodgers for Dick Farrell and Joe Koppe.

Mauch felt that Demeter had never had a chance to prove how good he could be. The tall Texan was one of the league's better centerfielders and if he played a full season, Mauch thought he'd hit more than 20 home runs.

Mauch needed every extra bat when his team faced former Phillie Curt Simmons in St. Louis in late April. Since being released by the Phils, the lefthander had worked with Cardinals' coach Darrell Johnson and changed his repertoire. He had developed a screwball changeup off his fastball, a slow curve, a fast curve and spotted his fastball to set up the other pitches. Simmons had beaten his old team four straight times and had a shutout for seven innings, coasting with a 6-0 lead.

But in the eighth, the Phillies erupted for seven runs and knocked Simmons and two relievers out of the game. In the rally, Mauch sent up four pinch hitters. Three of them singled as the Phils took a 7-6 lead and went on to win 11-7.

After giving up five runs and ten hits in the season opener, Robin Roberts went into a tailspin. In a 7-0 loss to the Giants, Roberts gave up home runs to Felipe Alou, Orlando Cepeda and Ed Bailey. The seven runs were more than he'd given up in any game in over a year.

Roberts challenged hitters with his fading fastball, mixing in a breaking ball and changeup. But at 34, he'd lost the velocity and location on his fastball. Gene Mauch tried to convince the one-time ace that many aging pitchers adjusted by learning to change speeds or by developing another pitch like a cut fastball or forkball. But Roberts was proud and stubborn and refused to give in. Many of his "hit me" fast balls came whizzing back by his ear.

Trying to break a 10-game losing streak in May, Gene Mauch played a hunch in a game against St. Louis. Although it was Dallas Green's turn to pitch, Mauch instead started Art Mahaffey.

Mauch knew that the left-handed batting Green hit 13 home runs in the minors and hit three in only 27 at bats at Buffalo before being recalled. Mauch reasoned that Green would have better luck against Cards' righthander Larry Jackson than southpaw Ray Sadecki.

Mahaffey ended the losing streak, winning 3-1 and then the next day, Mauch looked like a genius when Green delivered a bases loaded single, driving in two runs in a 6-4 Phils win.

On June 28 at Connie Mack Stadium the Phillies and San Francisco Giants played the longest night game in major league history to that point, a five hour, eleven minute marathon that was called after 15 innings because of curfew with the game tied 7-7. According to baseball rules, the records and stats would be recorded, but the game had to be replayed, forcing a doubleheader the next night.

Before the first game, Gene Mauch tried more chicanery. As the game was ready to start, no one had the starting lineups. Mauch, again wanted to have left-handed hitting pitcher Dallas Green bat against a righthander, Sam Jones, so he refused to name his starting pitcher. Giants' manager Alvin Dark, a Mauch disciple, did the same thing.

As the Phillies prepared to take the field, five pitchers were warming up. Green and Art Mahaffey were up in the Phils bullpen and lefty Ken Lehman threw on the sidelines. Sam Jones warmed up in the Giants pen, with lefty Billy O'Dell heating up on the sidelines.

Since Mauch was the home team manager, he had to present his lineup card first to the umpires at home plate. Giants coach Whitey Lockman, subbing for Dark, had two lineup cards. After seeing that Ken Lehman was listed as the Phils' starter, Lockman handed umpire Frank Secory, the lineup designed to face Lehman.

Secory forgot to give the public address announcer the lineups so only as hitters came to the plate and were announced, could fans determine who was playing where.

The lineup Mauch had presented before the game, listed the names of four pitchers. Three were in spots where Mauch usually platooned.

Don Ferrarese was listed as the leadoff hitter, playing centerfield. Jim Owens, the so-called right fielder, hit third. The left-handed Chris Short was listed as the catcher, batting seventh and Ken Lehman, the pitcher hit ninth. When the Phillies took the field in the first inning, Ferrarese, Owens, and Short were replaced by Bobby Del Greco, Bobby Gene Smith, and Jim Coker.

Lehman gave up a single to Chuck Hiller and walked Harvey Kuenn. Gene Mauch then pulled Lehman and brought in Dallas Green, who induced Orlando Cepeda to ground into a double play with Hiller going to third. Willie Mays then blasted a two-run homer off Green to give the Giants a 2-0 lead.

For the Giants, lefty Billy O'Dell started and faced one batter, Del Greco, before being replaced by Sam Jones.

In the top of the third, Green gave up another two-run homer to Willie Mays, which tied the score at 4-4. Mays also singled, going three-for-three off Green.

San Francisco Giants	AB	R	H	RBI	Philadelphia Phillies	AB	R	H	RBI
Hiller 2b	4	2	3	0	Ferrarese cf	0	0	0	0
Kuenn rf	3	0	0	1	Del Greco cf	5	2	3	1
Cepeda lf	5	1	2	1	Taylor 2b	4	1	2	1
Mays cf	5	3	4	5	Owens rf	0	0	0	0
McCovey 1b	5	1	1	0	Smith B. rf	0	0	0	0
Haller c	2	0	0	0	Gonzalez ph,rf	5	1	1	1
Bailey ph-c	1	0	1	0	Herrera 1b	4	0	1	1
Davenport 3b	5	0	2	1	Demeter lf	4	1	2	1
Pagan ss	2	0	0	0	Smith C. 3b	4	0	0	0
Alou M. ph	1	0	0	0	Short cf	0	0	0	0
Bressoud ss	1	0	0	0	Coker c	0	0	0	0
O'Dell p	0	0	0	0	Dalrymple ph, c	5	0	0	1
Jones p	2	0	0	0	Amaro ss	3	1	0	0
Marshall ph	1	1	0	0	Lehman p	0	0	0	0
Loes p	0	0	0	0	Green p	1	1	0	0
Miller p	0	0	0	0	Sullivan p	2	0	0	0
Alou F. ph	1	0	1	0					
Marichal p	0	0	0	0					
Totals	38	8	14	8	Totals	37	7	9	6

San Francisco	2	0	2	0	0	1	2	0	0	1	8	14	0
Philadelphia	4	0	0	2	0	0	1	0	0	0	7	9	1

June 29, 1961 at Connie Mack Stadium in Philadelphia

San Francisco Giants	IP	H	R	ER	BB	SO
O'Dell	0.0	1	1		0	0
Jones	6.0	6	5	5	2	5
Loes	0.2	2	1	1	0	0
Miller	1.1	0	0	0	0	1
Marichal W (6-4)	2.0	0	0	0	0	1
Totals	10.0	9	7	7	2	7
Philadelphia Phillies	IP	H	R	ER	BB	SO
Lehman	0.0	1	1	1	1	0
Green	5.2	8	4	4	0	3
Sullivan L (3-8)	4.1	5	3	2	2	2
Totals	10.0	14	8	7	3	5

E-Taylor (8) **DP**-San Francisco 1, Philadelphia 2 **2B**-Hiller (10), Cepeda (13) **HR**-San Francisco, Mays 3 (20, 1st inning off Green, 3rd inning off Green, 10th inning off Sullivan **SH**-Hiller (4), Taylor (4) **SF**-Kuenn (6), **Team LOB**-5 **HBP** Green (Jones), Herrera (Loes), Demeter (Marichal) **IBB**-C. Smith (Jones) **Team**-6 **CS**-Mays (7), Bailey (4), Demeter (1) **HBP**-Jones (Green), Loes (Herrera), Marichal (Demeter), **IBB**-Jones (Smith) **Umpires**-Frank Secory, Tony Venzon, Ed Sudol, Al Forman, Frank Dascoli **Time**: 3:20

Mauch did get the Green vs Jones matchup he wanted. Green was called out on strikes his first time up and then was hit by a pitch in his second plate appearance.

In this crazy game, the Giants used 18 players and the Phillies 16, including the phantom starters. With the score tied 7-7 in the tenth, Willie Mays struck again, with a leadoff homer off Frank Sullivan as the Giants won 8-7.

The Phillies continued to lose, dropping six in a row and 13 out of 14. The Phillies were making losing an art form, but the pièce de résistance was just around the corner.

On July 28, John Buzhardt got some rare run support and beat San Francisco 4-3 in the second game of a doubleheader. He was wearing uniform number 23. An omen?

The next day, Phillies lefthander Don Ferrarese walked Giants' leadoff hitter Joe Amalfitano to start the game. Then Harvey Kuenn singled. Matty Alou's groundout advanced the runners to second and third with Willie Mays coming up and the dangerous Orlando Cepeda on deck.

Mauch considered the alternatives. The percentage move was to walk Mays to load the bases, setting up a force at any base and a possible double play. But how could you overlook the names? Willie Mays was an established star and "The Baby Bull," Orlando Cepeda, at 22, an emerging star. A firing squad or the gas chamber? Take your pick. In two previous games, Mauch had elected to walk Mays intentionally. The first time, Cepeda doubled in two runs and the second time, he'd hit a three-run homer.

Again, Mauch had to decide what to do. Mauch was stubborn and stuck to his strategy come hell or high water. Would he walk Mays again? It was just the first inning in a scoreless game. Unbelievably, Mauch ordered Ferrarese to walk Mays intentionally, loading the bases and Cepeda belted a fastball into the left field stands for his first career grand slam home run as the Giants won 4-3. Cepeda went on to lead the National League with 46 homers and 142 RBI and was second in MVP voting to Cincinnati's

Frank Robinson.

After losing the last two games to the Giants, the Phils dropped three straight in Cincinnati and all four in St. Louis, including a 7-0 shutout by old friend Curt Simmons. In the final game at Busch Stadium, the Phils had the tying run at second base in the ninth, then made three straight outs without advancing the runner. The Cardinals won 3-2 and after the game, Gene Mauch threw batting helmets all over the field.

Having lost nine straight, the Phils returned home, lost all three to Pittsburgh and then were shutout by Cincinnati's Joey Jay. As the tension built, Gene Mauch put his fist through his office door and broke all the dugout light bulbs at Connie Mack Stadium. When the lights were replaced, a protective device was placed over the bulbs so Mauch took a bat and broke them all again.

Back on the road, Pirates' ace Bob Friend shut them out in the opener in Pittsburgh. Fourteen straight losses. As they continued to lose, records fell like dominoes.

The Phillies were shut out for a third straight game when the Pirates' Wilmer "Vinegar Bend" Mizell, blanked them 4-0. It was the Phils' fifteenth straight loss, a new club record. Phils' owner Bob Carpenter didn't blame Mauch, saying, "Middleweights can't fight heavyweights."[22]

With another loss in Pittsburgh and a three-game sweep in Chicago, the Phillies losing streak had stretched to nineteen in a row.

Gene Mauch tried everything to break the streak: different line-ups, five different leadoff hitters, a rabbit's foot, even mind games. On one road trip, Mauch told his players there would be a 2 a.m. bed check. Any player found in bed would be fined. For a game in Chicago, he told the players to arrive at Wrigley Field at game time and not a minute earlier. Nothing worked.

With nineteen straight losses, the hapless Phillies were one loss away from setting a new National League record when they began a four game series in Milwaukee. Robin Roberts started, but gave up three straight hits and two runs in the first inning. After he walked the leadoff batter in the second, Mauch waved to the bullpen for Art Mahaffey. Mahaffey pitched brilliantly into the eighth with the Phils leading 6-4 and with a chance to end the losing streak.

Then Mahaffey walked Hank Aaron, bringing the tying run to the plate in massive Joe Adcock, who'd hit twenty-four home runs. When Mahaffey got two quick strikes on Adcock, Mauch went to the mound. "If you're gonna waste a pitch," Mauch told his pitcher, "don't throw it high."

Just as Mauch returned to the dugout, Mahaffey delivered and so did Adcock, belting the next pitch into the centerfield bleachers to tie the game at 6-6. Mauch was furious. The Braves won the game 7-6 on Al Spangler's eleventh inning single as the losing streak stretched to 20, breaking the National League record of nineteen straight, set in 1906 by Boston, and tied in 1914 by Cincinnati.

The next day, the Braves Lew Burdette showed off a new knuckleball, handing the Phils a 4-1 loss. Twenty-one straight losses. A new major league record. When Burdette struck out Lee Walls to end the game, Mauch yelled, "Keep throwing that knuckleball and you'll wind up with us"[23]

The Braves scored four runs off Frank Sullivan in the third inning and won 4-3. Twenty-two straight losses.

In the first game of a doubleheader, Warren Spahn beat the Phils 5-2 as they broke the National League record for consecutive losses on the road with 17. Overall, 23 straight losses.

"It's tough to go to the park each day when all you're doing is losing, losing, losing," said second baseman Tony Taylor. "Gene Mauch was outstanding," Taylor said. "He never got down on us or made drastic changes. He was mad at losing but not mad at any individual. He knew we were trying."[24]

Wearing number 23 and trying to snap his team's twenty three game losing streak, John Buzhardt scattered nine hits and pitched a complete game as the Phils beat the Braves 7-4. Finally, the streak was over. Fifty-three years later, the Phils' 23 game losing streak is still the longest in modern major league history.

"I'm glad to get that monkey off my back," said Gene Mauch.[25]

Second baseman Bobby Malkmus who drove in two runs said, "Believe me, we really wanted to break out for Mauch. He took all the blame himself-never took it out on us. He knew we were in there trying all the time."[26]

Mauch said he'd never seen a club try harder, winning or losing than this club did. "It's a good that something like this happens when you're young," said the 34-year-old Mauch. "When you're older, it could kill you."[27]

When the Phillies charter arrived in Philadelphia at 1 a.m., they were surprised by roughly 2,000 fans who had waited two hours in a torrential downpour to help their team celebrate. As he waited to deplane, team comedian Frank Sullivan looked out at the crowd and said, "They're selling rocks at $1.50 a pail. Leave the plane at one-minute intervals. That way they can't get us all with one burst."[28]

Instead of rocks, the fans threw confetti as the players came up the escalator to the terminal. Some held up handmade signs. One read, "Who said it couldn't be done? Phillies 7 Braves 4." Another, "Just relax fellas. You are home now."

When Gene Mauch arrived, met by his wife Nina Lee and daughter Lee Anne, fans lifted him to their shoulders and carried him through the terminal.

"I thank you all for your wonderful enthusiasm," Mauch told the crowd. "All the Phillies thank you," he said, his voice choked with emotion.[29]

That team compiled the worst record in the majors-47 wins and 107 losses. "From the end of one game to the beginning of the next," said Mauch, "I experienced every conceivable emotion known to mankind. The only thing I didn't think about at least twice was suicide, because I was afraid it would work if I tried it."[30]

Chapter Fourteen

If It's Broke, Fix It

Assessing the wreckage of 1961, John Quinn and Gene Mauch agreed that pitching was the biggest problem. The Phillies didn't have a stopper, someone to win consistently

Mauch hoped Art Mahaffey would fill that role. Through May, the 23-year-old pitched well and had some brilliant efforts including his 17-strikeout performance in a shutout against the Cubs. Mahaffey began the season winning six of his first nine and led the league in complete games with eight. Then he lost ten of his next 11 decisions with no complete games.

Besides hoping that Mahaffey could become their ace, Quinn and Mauch felt the team needed a power hitter, another starting pitcher and a backup catcher.

First, they had to deal with the expansion draft with the Houston Colt 45's and New York Mets coming into the league in 1962. Robin Roberts had no future with Philadelphia and Quinn hoped one of the expansion teams would take his $40,000 a year contract. They didn't, passing on Roberts and former Phillie favorite Richie Ashburn of the Cubs.

The Mets selected veteran utility man Lee Walls and outfielder Bobby Gene Smith, who'd been with the Phillies all season. They also took catcher Clarence "Choo Choo" Coleman, infielder George Williams and minor league pitcher Jess Hickman. Lee Walls, who'd been a great pinch hitter and utility man for the Phils, was the only player who'd be missed.

Then, the Phillies ended an era when they sold Robin Roberts to the New York Yankees. The 35-year-old righthander was the last remaining player from the 1950 pennant winning Whiz Kids.

Roberts's departure freed up money so the Phils could sign a power hitter. They landed Roy Sievers, the slugging first baseman who hit .295 with 27 home runs and 92 RBI for the Chicago White Sox. Sievers would be the Phillies top-salaried player making a reported $40,000. To get Sievers, the Phils sent pitcher John Bu-zhardt and infielder Charlie Smith to Chicago.

Gene Mauch wanted a big stick. "When I was with the Red Sox," remembered Mauch, "I saw pitchers begin worrying about Ted Williams while they were pitching to our leadoff man and their knees were still shaking two or three batters after Ted came up."[1] Mauch was hoping Roy Sievers might provide such a threat.

Figuring Sievers would need some days off, Quinn also signed former Brave Frank Torre, at one time, the top fielding first baseman in the league.

The Phillies made a couple of minor deals, getting Gene Mauch's former teammate, infielder Billy Consolo from the Red Sox in the draft and swapping catcher Cal Neeman to Pittsburgh for good field-no-hit receiver Bob Oldis. They added a third catcher, signing former Red Sox receiver Sammy White. The two vets would backup Clay Dalrymple.

The Phillies also acquired third baseman Andy Carey from the White Sox in a deal involving cash and three minor leaguers but Carey announced his retirement.

Unlike the previous year's boot camp, Mauch took a different attitude into spring training in 1962. "We're going to stop hammering or nagging-them this season," said Mauch. "I feel the players know what to do. Now it's up to them. The ones who want to play will do it that way."[2] Mauch also predicted his team wouldn't finish last again.

"Let's work on flyballs today."

Al Widmar replaced Bob Lemon as the Phillies pitching coach. Widmar had pitched for the Red Sox, Browns and White Sox and had been a pitching instructor in the Quakers system since 1959. He was considered a great tutor.

Widmar's major task was to help Mauch mold Art Mahaffey into a consistent winner. In 1961, Mahaffey had been brilliant at times with three shutouts, a 17 strikeout game, and a one-hitter. But for long portions of June, July and August, he was a loser, winding up at 11-19.

First, though, Mahaffey, Widmar, Mauch and other Phillies had to compete in the first annual Major League Baseball Bowling Championship at Tampa's East Gate Lanes. Gene Mauch predicted that Mahaffey, a serious bowler with a 200 average, would win the tournament. Chris Short, Bob Oldis, Bobby Malkmus, Dallas Green, John Callison, Don Demeter, Clay Dalrymple, and Jackie Davis represented the Phillies along with Mauch and his coaches Peanuts Lowery and Al Widmar.

Don Landrum, St. Louis Cardinals outfielder, rolled a 422 for the two game series to win the $500 first prize and a trophy from *The Sporting News*. Mahaffey's total was 400 and he picked up $350.

Despite the Phillies abysmal 1961 season, Gene Mauch thought Ruben Amaro had become the best shortstop in the league. Amaro had served in the six-month Army reserve program and although he reported for spring training, the team knew he'd soon be called to active duty.

The Phillies opened the 1962 season in Cincinnati, winning 12-4 behind Art Mahaffey's complete game. After taking three of their first four, the Phils went into a tail spin, losing six of their next eight. They finished April with an 8-9 record and in early May lost Ruben Amaro to the Army.

Roy Sievers was supposed to supply badly needed power, but adjusting to a new league and pitchers he'd never faced, he had just 5 hits in his first 45 at bats. As fans booed and the media circled like vultures, Gene Mauch remained steadfast. "I'm willing to bet that Roy will hit over .280 the rest of the season and will wind up with at least 20 home runs."[3]

In May, the Phillies suffered through their worst month, going 9-19. With Ruben Amaro in the Army, Mauch used former Bosox teammate Billy Klaus and utility man Bobby Malkmus at shortstop. Billy Consolo had been sold to the Angels and Bobby Wine was recalled from AAA Buffalo.

Bobby Wine recalled his first impressions of his new manager, Gene Mauch, "Back in our day, the manager was like God and the King. There wasn't a lot of fun and games with Gene. He was all baseball, from sunup to sundown and he had a lousy team, so there wasn't a lot of laughs."

Although Don Demeter, Johnny Callison and Tony González carried the offense, the pitching was erratic. Mauch's preference was for veteran pitchers who'd been through the wars. He shared that view as noted before with his mentor and old manager Leo Durocher. But after trying everything to get his pitching straightened, he finally decided to go young with pitchers who might improve with experience. Southpaw Dennis Bennett and righthander Paul Brown were recalled from AAA Buffalo, joining another rookie, Jack Hamilton, Art Mahaffey and spot starter Cal McLish in the rotation.

As the Phillies began a series in Los Angeles, Mauch spent several days in the hospital with a bronchial condition but returned to see 22-year-old lefty Dennis Bennett shutout the Dodgers 7-0, with a four hit, eleven strikeout performance for his first major league victory.

20-year-old Paul Brown had made a miraculous recovery from mononucleosis which caused him to miss most of spring training. But Brown didn't fare as well as Bennett. He was knocked out early in several starts, lacked stamina, and was eventually placed on the disabled list.

Cal McLish threw a shutout and Art Mahaffey pitched a four-hitter as the Phillies swept a doubleheader from the New York Mets.

Wes Covington hit two homers and drove in four runs in a 7-5 win over Cincinnati. Then the Phils beat the St. Louis Cardinals and their old nemesis Curt Simmons 8-5 ending the lefthander's eight game winning streak against his old club.

In the third inning of a 13-8 battering of Cincinnati, the Phils exploded for ten runs in the third inning. Roy Sievers hit a grand slam homer and added an RBI single in the inning. His five RBI fell one short of the major league record of six RBI in one inning.

Gene Mauch called the 4-3 win the next day, "The most satisfying game we played since I came here. Everything came out right, we came from behind and we got the pitching we had to have to win it."[4] Reds lefthander Ted Wills blanked the Phils for the first six innings and the Reds led 3-0. Then Roy Sievers led off the seventh with a home run, one of his three hits. The Phils scored three to tie it and one in the eighth to win.

In that game, after Cincinnati's Leo Cardenas was ejected by plate umpire Jocko Conlan for arguing a called third strike, Reds third base coach Reggie Otero shouted at Conlan, "You're too old and you're just like Fidel Castro, Nobody can talk to you."[5] The 59-year-old ump dropped his mask and chest protector and started after Otero but Gene Mauch bolted out of the dugout and led Conlan away while the other umps restrained Otero.

Suddenly on fire, Roy Sievers doubled, tripled, and drove in two runs as the Phils completed a three-game sweep of the Reds winning 7-2. "Now you see what I mean," said Mauch, "when I said Roy Sievers was the kind of hitter we needed to lead us."

Mauch felt that Sievers had been pressing but was becoming more familiar with pitchers. After Mauch made his April prediction, for the next two months, Sievers hit .313 with 15 doubles, four triples, 11 home runs and 43 RBI.

In that victory against the Reds, Jack Baldschun pitched five and two thirds innings of shutout relief to get the win. Twice within eight days, Baldschun pitched more than five innings and won both games. The rubber armed 25-year-old righthander was a godsend for Gene Mauch.

Unlike today's closers who usually pitch no more than an inning, Baldschun could pitch one inning or five and could pitch almost every day. In 1961, he'd been the only pitcher on the staff with a winning record at 5-3 and he'd led the league with 65 appearances. In 1962 he topped that with 67 outings, a 12-7 record a 2.96 ERA and just six home runs allowed.

After relying on his screwball, in 1962 Baldschun had gained confidence in his fastball, curve and slider and made a believer out of Gene Mauch. "There used to be some clubs I was hesitant to use him against," said Mauch, "but no longer. He went out there believing he could get anybody out and he usually did."[6]

In an 11-3 win over St. Louis, Roy Sievers and Don Demeter drove in a total of nine runs. Sievers had two hits including a homer and four RBI while Demeter was four-for-four with five RBI.

The Phils swept a doubleheader from Houston as Jack Hamilton pitched the best game of his career, throwing a two-hit shutout at 2-0 and then Art Mahaffey added a complete game victory, 6-4 in the nightcap.

The Phillies won more games in June than in any month in almost five years going 17-13.

In a game in San Francisco, rookie umpire Doug Harvey ejected Phils' catcher Sammy White for arguing about a call. Mauch rushed to the plate, spewing obscenities and bumped Harvey, who referred to himself as "God." Mauch was fined $100 and suspended for four days.

While managing in Minneapolis in 1958, Gene Mauch had seen Johnny Callison hit 29 home runs for Indianapolis and compared his swing to Mel Ott's. Callison, who'd been traded by the White Sox in 1959, had shown promise in his first two years in Philadelphia.

Gene Mauch saw greatness in Johnny Callison and made him his personal project. Mauch worked on smoothing out Callison's left-handed swing and encouraged him to stop trying to pull the ball and use the whole field. Callison had above average speed and Mauch urged him to bunt for base hits occasionally. Mauch also moved Callison from left field to right, allowing him to cover more ground and use his strong, accurate arm. Johnny Callison was the only Philly player selected for the All-Star Game July 10 in Washington D.C., one of two that were played that year. Callison singled in his only at bat in the National League's 3-1 victory.

The American League took the second game 9-4 at Wrigley Field in Chicago. Johnny Callison walked in his only plate appearance and Art Mahaffey pitched two innings, giving up home runs to Leon Wagner of the Angels and Pete Runnells of the Senators.

In late July, reality said hello. Nearly 200 fans boarded the Pennsylvania Railroad train from Harrisburg, PA. Headed to Philadelphia for a game between the Phillies and Pittsburgh Pirates. Nineteen people were killed and 116 were injured when three cars left the tracks and plunged down a 40-foot embankment into the Susquehanna River.

The following day at Connie Mack Stadium, fans rose in a moment of silence for those who lost their lives.

The Phils took time out to play an exhibition game against their Class A farm team, the Williamsport Grays, before an overflow crowd of 6,796 at Bowman Field. The Grays were running away in the Eastern League with a 68-32 record. A pair of 20-year-olds, pitcher Ray Culp and outfielder Richie Allen showed why they were top prospects. Allen hit a three-run homer in the first and Culp pitched a five-hitter as the farmhands won 5-1.

Don Demeter had done everything Gene Mauch had asked. He had moved from the outfield to first base, then to third base and now with Gonzalez out, his manger asked him to move back to center field. Despite the position changes and a bad knee, Demeter kept hitting and was a major reason why the team had their second winning month, going 17-15 in August.

Going 24-13 in the final five weeks of the season, the Phillies were playing as well as any team in the league. They went 15-7 in September and finished seventh with an 81-80 record, the first time they'd been over .500 since 1953.

Gene Mauch had done one of his best managing jobs. His gamble with young pitchers was successful; his belief in Roy Sievers had been rewarded. Despite the howl of critics, his shuttling of Don Demeter had been a big key. "The main thing is," said Mauch, "they found out they can win. You have to let young players find out how good they are."[7]

Mauch was named National League Manager of the Year for 1962 by both the Associated Press and United Press International.

The Phillies appeared to have found their stopper in Art Mahaffey, who snapped two eight-game losing streaks and one seven-gamer and just missed winning twenty games, finishing 19-14 with 20 complete games.

Lefties Dennis Bennett and Chris Short pitched impressively down the stretch.

Don Demeter led the club in hitting, home runs and RBI. Playing three different positions the big Texan's .307 batting average, 29 homers and 107 RBI were all career highs.

Gene Mauch handled Johnny Callison perfectly. The 23-year-old hit .300 with 23 homers and 83 RBI and had become a complete player.

Before he was injured, Tony González hit .312 with 20 homers and sixty-three RBI and catcher Clay Dalrymple hit a surprising .276 with 11 homers and had greatly improved behind the plate.

Even the veterans, Roy Sievers and Cal McLish contributed. Despite his early struggles, Roy Sievers hit twenty homers, many of them clutch and drove in eighty runs. Used as a spot starter, the 36-year-old McLish was 11-5.

As Gene Mauch and John Quinn looked forward to 1963, the team suffered a crushing blow. While playing winter ball in Puerto Rico, in January, promising pitcher Dennis Bennett, pitching coach Al Widmar, rookie hurler Joel Gibson, and his wife Gail were returning from a picnic, when their car crashed into a stone culvert. Bennett was thrown through the windshield, suffering a shattered ankle, broken pelvis and facial lacerations. He also suffered a cracked left shoulder blade which doctors didn't detect until three years later. Gibson suffered a fractured bone near the shoulder in his left arm and Al Widmar and Gail Gibson suffered minor injuries. The driver, a director of the Arecibo club for which Bennett and Gibson had played, was killed. A Puerto Rican doctor said, "Gibson will be able to play baseball again soon but I cannot say anything about Bennett."

The two pitchers, Widmar and Mrs. Gibson were flown home.

Phils' General Manager John Quinn arranged for Bennett to be flown on a stretcher to Philadelphia and Temple University Hospital, where he was placed under the care of an orthopedic surgeon. The Phillies figured Bennett would miss most if not all of the season.

Bennett had been the Phils most effective starter in the final two months of 1962 and without him, Mauch knew he'd have to rely on unproven youngsters like Ray Culp, Chris Short, Marcelino Lopez and Paul Brown.

Midway through spring training, they suffered another major injury. Cincinnati's hard throwing Jim Maloney drilled Roy Sievers and fractured his rib.

Mauch, the mad scientist, was always tinkering. In spring training he suggested that pinch hitters bat for pitchers, although the hurlers would remain in the game. He said he had pretty much of a set eight man lineup, which means that other players may not see as much action in exhibition games as in the past and he'd like to get permission to hit for his pitchers every time they come up, except in bunt situations. Mauch and Quinn knew they'd have to get permission from National League President Warren Giles to implement the idea.

Mauch said his pitchers hit .125 the previous year and if they hit .080 this year, what difference does it make? And meantime he can find out what other players can do at the plate. National League President Warren Giles vetoed the idea although it was instituted several years later.

Mauch had been right the previous year when he predicted his team would win half their games. In 1963, Mauch said only that his team would win more games than they did the previous year.

With Dennis Bennett out, pitching was Mauch's main concern. He envisioned Art Mahaffey as a twenty-game winner but after that he was worried. In March, the Los Angeles Angels put 34-year-old fireballer Ryne Duren on waivers. When none of the other American League clubs claimed him, the Angels sold Duren to the Phillies for $20,000.

The Phillies needed an everyday third baseman and when Pittsburgh's Don Hoak became available, John Quinn went after him. Hoak had been part of the 1961 World Championship Pirates and had name value, enhanced by being married to popular singer Jill Corey.

Hoak was also Mauch's kind of guy; nicknamed "Tiger," a tough ex-Marine, a battler who would do anything to win. Hoak would even berate teammates if they weren't hustling. Although Hoak was 34 and coming off a poor year, Mauch felt he had plenty of baseball left. In November, the Phils traded 26-year-old outfielder Ted Savage to Pittsburgh for Hoak.

Art Mahaffey applauded the acquisition of Don Hoak. Again setting a goal of twenty wins, Mahaffey said, "Just having Hoak at third should mean two or three more runs for every starter. I'm sure there's not a pitcher on our staff who doesn't love that trade."

Having filled one need, Quinn was still on the lookout for a relief pitcher to take some of the pressure off Jack Baldschun and a right-handed hitter who could play several positions.

The Phils filled the second need when they sent disgruntled pitcher Jim Owens to Cincinnati for utility man Cookie Rojas. Owens was the last remaining member of the infamous Dalton

Gang. The Phillies also sent outfielder Jackie Davis to the Los Angeles Angels for Earl Averill, who, like Rojas, could play several positions.

With Dennis Bennett sidelined and Billy Smith sent to AAA, Mauch had one left-handed pitcher, Chris Short. Mauch needed a southpaw who could pitch at least 200 innings. Lefthanders Johnny Podres of the Dodgers, Denny Lemaster of the Braves, Dick Ellsworth of the Cubs, Al Jackson of the Mets and righthander Roger Craig of the Mets were mentioned in trade talks. But the price to acquire any of these pitchers was too steep and the Phils stood pat.

Gene Mauch rewarded 19-game winner Art Mahaffey by making him the opening day starter in 1963, on a cold, windy day, before 28,291 bundled up fans at Connie Mack Stadium. Portable heaters were stationed around the clubhouse with one aimed squarely at Mahaffey's locker. Mahaffey was brilliant, pitching a four-hitter with ten strike outs in a 2-1 Phillies win.

It was even colder the next day as the crowd dwindled to 6,000. Trailing Cincinnati 6-2, the Phils exploded for eight runs in the seventh to win 10-7. Wes Covington had three hits; Don Hoak and Johnny Callison two apiece and all three of them drove in two runs.

After winning their first three games, the Phils began their first road trip in St. Louis, opening day for the Cardinals. Nearly twenty beautiful girls, candidates for Miss Red Bird, were driven around the stadium in convertibles. Former Phillie Curt Simmons had won nine of his first ten decisions against his old team and shut them out 7-0 on five hits to improve his record to 10-1 against the Phillies.

In the first inning, Simmons came high and inside with a pitch and sent Don Hoak sprawling in the dirt. "He's been doing that to me for years," said an angry Hoak, "and I've taken all I'm going to. The next time, I'm going after him."[8]

Simmons denied throwing at Hoak and added, "He's not a good

enough hitter to bother throwing at."

In a doubleheader, Don Demeter, went six-for-ten with a homer and three RBI, the Phils won 4-3 and 5-4 as reliever Jack Baldschun got wins in both games.

On to Milwaukee and a matchup of Cal McLish and Warren Spahn. Spahn changed speeds, mixing fastballs, curveballs and changeups and shutout the Phils 8-0.

Playing first base, Don Demeter went seven-for-thirteen with two homers against the Braves but Milwaukee swept the three game series.

Back home, the Phils again faced Curt Simmons and the St. Louis Cardinals. Simmons went the distance, winning 5-1 and improving his record to 11-1 against the Phillies.

Watching Don Hoak struggle, Mauch knew he had misjudged the veteran third baseman. Hoak was aging fast, his talents eroding. In the second spot in the batting order Mauch needed someone who could bunt, play hit-and-run and advance runners. When Hoak's average dropped to .167, Mauch benched him. Hoak loved playing for Gene Mauch and was frustrated. "I'm struggling just to get a loud foul," said Hoak.

Again, Mauch called on jack-of-all-trades, Don Demeter. Mauch wanted Demeter in the outfield, but when Roy Sievers got hurt, he moved Demeter to first and now asked him to move to third.

Although struggling in his previous three starts, Art Mahaffey was overpowering at Wrigley Field, beating the Chicago Cubs 5-2 with a three hit, eleven strikeout performance. The Phillies finished April with an 8-10 record.

The Phillies had won five-out-of-six when they met Houston at Colts Stadium on May 17, 1963. Righthander Don Nottebart mixed sinkers and sliders and pitched the first no-hitter in Houston's history as the Colts won 4-1. The only Phillies run came on an error, a sacrifice bunt and a sacrifice fly. Nottebart first realized he hadn't allowed a hit when he took the mound for the fourth inning. "I looked up at the scoreboard and saw the zeroes and said to my-self, 'This is no joke.'" As Nottebart reached the late innings, he could hear Gene Mauch yelling from the Phillies dugout: "You'll never make it, Notty, you'll never make it."[9]

As the team searched for its identity, Cal McLish was a beacon in the darkness. With a win over Los Angeles, a shutout in San Francisco and victories against Cincinnati, Pittsburgh and Chicago, McLish had five straight complete game wins, the longest streak by a Phils' pitcher since 1956.

Rookie Ray Culp had developed into a reliable starter. He started against Curt Simmons and the St. Louis Cardinals and pitched a three hit shutout as the Phils won 6-0. He also had a five hit, eleven strikeout shutout in beating the Mets in New York 2-0.

The biggest disappointment was Art Mahaffey. After winning nineteen games, he was an enigma, a shutout in one start and a butt-kicking in the next outing. Mahaffey had a sore shoulder in spring training but had pitched well in his opening day start against the Reds.

But in a loss to St. Louis, Gene Mauch took him out in the fourth inning after Mahaffey gave up six runs and five hits. He bounced back with a three hit, 11 strikeout game against the Cubs, and then lost six straight. After getting pummeled in back-to-back starts, Mahaffey was sent to the bullpen.

In San Francisco, in relief, just as Mahaffey threw his last warmup pitch, he fell to the ground, grabbing his right ankle. At a hospital, the injury was diagnosed as a dislocated tendon in his ankle and his leg was placed in a cast.

Mahaffey returned in late September at Candlestick Park and in relief, pitched seven and one-third innings, allowing one run and picked up a 6-4 victory. But four days later, a Don Drysdale fast-ball clipped him on the elbow and he had to leave the game. He finished the season 7-10.

Dennis Bennett returned in late June. After several relief appear-ances, he started against the Mets. The 23-year-old lefthander went five and one third innings allowing just one run in a 7-2 win. "Gene Mauch was the best manager I played for," Bennett said. "He was great with young pitchers. He would take us aside and talk to us. We'd go over how we'd pitch different guys. He was a great manager."[10]

Dennis Bennett must have been the good luck charm because from the day after his first appearance until the end of August, the Phillies won 40 of their next 60 games to move into pennant contention.

Growing stronger with each start, Bennett went 6-2 in his nine starts and his comeback came at just the right time. Art Mahaffey's ankle injury finished his season and Ray Culp and Cal McLish bit the dust with injuries, leaving only Bennett and Chris Short as regular starters.

Gene Mauch had acquired Ryne Duren for situations like this. Although he'd been a reliever most of his career, Mauch figured he could be a spot starter, hopefully pitching six or seven innings before turning it over to the bullpen.

Duren threw as hard as any pitcher in baseball, was often wild and wore coke-bottle thick glasses. If that wasn't enough to intimidate hitters, he always fired his first warmup pitch over the catcher's head and squinted when he looked in for a sign. In July, Duren started at home against the San Francisco Giants.

The Giants Willie McCovey had gone five for thirteen with four homers in the first three games of the series. Duren asked catcher Clay Dalrymple how to get the big left-handed hitter out.

"I have no fucking idea," said the catcher, "he's red hot, he whips our ass."

"If he's that hot," said Duren, "I'm going to hit him in the right knee."

Dalrymple figured Duren was kidding because he didn't have enough control to hit a particular spot. "So, I called for a fastball," Dalrymple said, "and he hit that fucking guy on the right knee so solid that it stuck there for a second and then fell to the ground."

"McCovey went down and had to be helped off the field," said the catcher. "Willie Mays was the next hitter and Duren was out there trying to take the sign from me. Mays was in the back of the box and when Duren shook me off several times, Mays stepped out, looked down at me and I said, "Well, I guess he can't see my signs."

Willie said, "I don't care if he can see your signs. I just hope the hell he sees me." Duren's next pitch sent Mays sprawling in the dirt. After Mays waved at a pitch, Giants' manager Alvin Dark shot out of the dugout and demanded that plate umpire Shag Crawford at least warn Duren. Crawford refused and told Dark, "If your pitcher hits Duren, you're out of the game."

"Then you might as well throw me out now because Duren is going to go down," Dark yelled.

In the bottom of the inning, Giants lefthander Billy Pierce hit Duren in the back and Crawford immediately ejected Dark.

In the fourth inning, after the umpires had warned Duren about bringing his fingers to his mouth, a further warning from ump Augie Donatelli brought Gene Mauch out of the dugout to argue and he got thrown out.

After the game, an angry Alvin Dark said, "Even if I draw a life suspension, I am going to stop this continual throwing at my players the only way I know how-by ordering retaliation against the pitchers who throw at us."[11] Duren and the Phillies won the game 4-3.

Then, Tony González, hitting .317, injured his left leg on the damp outfield grass at Wrigley Field. On the day of the injury, the Phillies were only seven games behind the first place Dodgers and a game and one-half out of second place. With their most consistent hitter sidelined and John Callison, Roy Sievers and Don Demeter, all slumping, the Phillies lost nine of their next 13 games.

As August ended, Gene Mauch held a clubhouse meeting. "We'll snap out of it," he told his team, "we've just run into one of those down periods. We have a month to go and we'll bounce back." And, they did.

In September, Cal McLish pitched a complete game in a 9-4 win over Milwaukee, Ray Culp two-hit the Braves, winning 2-0 and Dennis Bennett went the distance in a 3-2 win over the Reds.

On September 22, the Phillies were leading Houston 1-0 in the ninth inning. The Colt 45's scored a run to tie the game and then 5' 7" rookie Joe Morgan, in his second major league game, got a game winning single to beat Philadelphia 2-1.

As the Phillies entered their clubhouse, they saw three tables, piled high with food, put out by the visiting clubhouse attendant.

"Johnny Callison was the first one in the clubhouse," said Bobby Wine, "and he picked up a piece of chicken. As he started to eat it, we heard a 'click, click, click,' sound, which we all new was Gene Mauch's spikes hitting the floor. As Mauch entered, Callison threw the chicken down."

Mauch exploded. "You guys are more worried about the food than losing the game. You just got beat by a guy who looks like a little leaguer." Wine said Mauch continued yelling, even inventing words and then he took his arm and swept all the food off the tables as chicken, ribs and watermelon flew through the air. Tony González and Wes Covington were to the left of the table and they had chicken grease all over their clothes."

As Mauch entered his office, there was dead silence, nobody moved and food was scattered everywhere. Then Mauch came back out and said to González and Covington, "Go buy yourselves a suit and give me the bill."

González looked at Covington and said, "Hey roomie," and they looked down and saw a chicken leg in a shoe. "Do you think that chicken is good?"

The chicken may been fine but the defense was awful and combined with weak hitting, dropped the Phillies out of contention.

The Phillies won their final three games and five of their last six, to finish the season at 87-75.

Chapter Fifteen

1964... The Phillie Phold

Although only ten of the 232 members of the Baseball Writers Association picked Philadelphia to win the pennant in 1964, Gene Mauch liked his club, an improving team, solid at almost every position with some promising pitchers.

The Phillies had young arms with Art Mahaffey, Dennis Bennett, and Chris Short but Gene Mauch needed a true number one pitcher, who could stop losing streaks, pitch complete games and set a good example for the youngsters. Mauch got his man when John Quinn traded Don Demeter to the Detroit Tigers for pitcher Jim Bunning and catcher Gus Triandos.

In nine years in Detroit, Bunning had won 118 games including a 20-8 season in 1957 but Bunning was unhappy after disagreements with manager Charlie Dressen. "He wouldn't give me the ball," said Bunning. "He didn't think I could pitch and win anymore. I was 31 years old." When Dressen bypassed Bunning and gave his five remaining starts to lefty Mickey Lolich, Bunning went to Tigers' G.J. Jim Cambell and said, "Trade me.' Bunning loved to pitch in Fenway Park so he told Cambell, "If you can make a deal with Boston, I'd appreciate it."

No deal with Boston but Gene Mauch had played against Bunning in the minor leagues and when Mauch was with the Red Sox. Mauch knew Bunning was exactly what the Phillies needed.

"You're my number one starting pitcher," Mauch told Bunning, "so just get in shape and get ready to pitch."

"He let me get in shape the way I wanted to," said Bunning. Mauch let his ace go to the Phillies' spring training complex and pitch in minor league games as much as he wanted to. "I got almost 50 innings in spring training, so when the bell rang I was ready."

Mauch tried to keep Bunning away from National League teams who'd never faced him but his final spring appearance was against Pittsburgh in Asheville, North Carolina. "He wouldn't let me throw breaking balls," said Bunning, "so they're hitting the ball all over the place."

When the Pirates' pitcher plunked Bunning's second baseman Tony Taylor, he retaliated. "We had a big brawl," said Bunning, "it was fun."

Bunning was a leader by example. He showed up every day. In four years with the Phils, he averaged 40 starts per season. He showed the young guys how to train, prepare for starts and win.

Mauch also felt that Bunning would take some of the pressure off his young lefthander Chris Short, who hadn't seemed comfortable with being the ace of the staff.

Without Don Demeter, the Phils needed a right-handed power hitter. Orlando Cepeda of San Francisco and Dick Stuart of Boston were mentioned. The Phils didn't make a deal but Mauch thought powerful rookie Richie Allen could pick up the slack. Allen had led the International League with 33 homers and 97 RBI in 1963. Although Allen had been the league's All-Star left-fielder, Mauch thought he could be the Phillies' opening day third baseman.

Except for an inning at third base late in a game, Allen had never played the hot corner. Allen was signed as a shortstop, played both short and second base and then moved to the outfield. But Mauch felt Allen was such a great athlete that he could adjust. He also asked the rookie to come to spring training early to work on his new position.

Gene with Richie Allen.

At Wampum (PA) High School, Allen and his three brothers led the basketball team to two State Championships and an 82-game winning streak. Although just 5'11", from a standstill, Allen could leap and dunk a basketball. Just before the Phillies broke camp, Mauch timed his players running from first to third. Allen was the fastest with Alex Johnson second and Johnny Briggs third.

For Gene Mauch, watching Don Hoak was like watching himself. As players, both were marginally talented but combative and driven. Mauch knew the fading veteran couldn't play with Allen, but when asked who his third baseman was, out of respect he said, "Don't count out Don Hoak."[1]

"There's nothing Hoak can do that I can't do," responded Richie Allen.[2] Allen blasted nine home runs in spring training, to lead all major leaguers.

"He has the short stroke that's indicative of most good hitters and he has tremendous hand action," said Mauch. "There's no telling how good this kid can be. I wouldn't be surprised if he singled to both right and left field on the same pitch someday. He'll split the ball right in half."[3]

Gene Mauch predicted the Phillies were capable of winning 95 games. A major reason for Mauch's optimism was his pitching staff: Jim Bunning, Art Mahaffey, Chris Short, Dennis Culp, and Dennis Bennett, as well as a bullpen that included Johnny Klippstein and Jack Baldschun. Mauch admitted that the Phils didn't have a Sandy Koufax or Don Drysdale, but felt that Bunning might be "the man."

The Phillies opened the 1964 season against the New York Mets at Connie Mack Stadium. It rained most of the day and the field was muddy. 21,016 showed up anyway. Mayor James H. Tate threw out the first ball. Batting third, Richie Allen had two hits and an RBI and cleanup hitter Roy Sievers belted a three-run homer in the first inning. Opening day starter Dennis Bennett lasted just four and two thirds innings but Johnny Klippstein pitched four and one third innings of shutout relief and got the win as the Phillies prevailed 5-3.

The next day, Jim Bunning made his first Phillies start against the Mets. He pitched a complete game and Tony González's three-run homer in the eighth inning gave the Phils a 4-1 victory.

Two days later at Chicago's Wrigley Field, the Phils and Cubs slugged it out, hitting a total of eight home runs, including five in one inning in a 10-8 Phillies win. In the fifth, Richie Allen, Roy Sievers and Art Mahaffey connected for the Phils and Lou Brock and Billy Williams homered for the Cubs. It marked the eighth time in major league history that two teams had hit five home runs in one inning.

The next day, Richie Allen hit two home runs and Dennis Bennett pitched a complete game as the Phils beat the Cubs 2-1. After the Phils took two out of three at Wrigley Field, Gene Mauch said, "Allen hit three home runs in Chicago and under normal conditions, he would have hit five. He tore up two balls in the Saturday game when the wind was blowing in a gale."[4]

The Phils went 10-2 to start the season as Allen hit safely in eleven of twelve games, batting .431 with twenty two hits in fifty one at bats with five homers and thirteen runs batted it.

In a mid-May, Phillies' pitchers piled up shutouts like a South Philly pizza cook stacking pies. Dennis Bennett pitched a five-hit 4-0 shutout in Houston. Chris Short blanked the Colts 2-0 on five hits and then on May 18, the Phillies moved into first place as Jim Bunning fired a one-hitter, beating the Colts 4-0. The only hit off Bunning was a leadoff single by Jimmy Wynn in the fifth.

The Phillies five game win streak was stopped cold by Sandy Koufax. On June 4, the Dodgers' lefthander threw a no-hitter. His third no-hitter in three years, Koufax called it his "best of all" with only one walk preventing a perfect game. The Phillies hit only four balls out of the infield and Koufax struck out twelve.

"If you're going to have a no-hitter pitched against you," said Gene Mauch, "you might as well have it done by the greatest pitcher in the world."[5] Koufax's no-hitter sent the Phils into a tail-spin as they dropped six of their next eight games.

In a 13-4 loss in Pittsburgh, in the third inning, Mauch sent little used backup infielder Cookie Rojas up to pinch hit. He grounded out but stayed in to play second base and Ruben Amaro took over at short. In the fifth, Rojas broke up Vernon Law's shutout with an inside-the-park homer and then singled in a run in his final at bat.

One of a few players who wore glasses, Rojas started the next game at second base, led off and went two for four. Mauch moved Rojas to center field and he went three for four. Then, back to second and a four for five game in a 7-6 win over Houston. At the end of the three game sweep of Houston, Rojas was hitting .536 and had reached base 26 straight times with an on-base percentage of .692. With Rojas leading off, the Phillies won seven out of eight to improve to 36-22.

June 20 1964. Father's Day.

With the Phillies in New York, Mary Bunning didn't want her husband Jim to be alone on Father's Day. Mary and Jim had seven children and their oldest, 12-year-old daughter Barbara joined her mom on the 100-mile drive to New York, while the other six kids stayed home with a baby sitter. Mary figured it would be fun to see Jim pitch and they could also visit the World's Fair, across the street from Shea Stadium.

32,026 fans had settled into their seats as Jim Bunning took the mound in the first game of a doubleheader, on a 92 degree day in New York. Just the way Bunning liked it. "I sweated a lot and I'd go through three jerseys in every game," Bunning said, "but I welcomed it because I knew I was in better shape than the hitters."

Richie Allen singled in a run in the first inning to give Bunning the lead. As Bunning finished his warmup tosses, he told catcher Gus Triandos he had good stuff and felt great. Facing leadoff hitter Jim Hickman, Bunning hung two sliders that Hickman fouled off before taking a called third strike. Ron Hunt grounded out and Ed Kranepool popped to short. Bunning was off and running.

By the fourth inning, Gene Mauch knew Bunning might be unhittable. To provide the best possible defense, he switched Cookie Rojas from shortstop to left field, replacing Wes Covington and put Bobby Wine at short.

Bunning was in complete command when left-handed hitting

Mets' catcher Jesse Gonder came up with one out in the fifth. He swung and missed at Bunning's first pitch and then Bunning threw a straight change, right down the middle. Gonder jumped on it, hitting a low liner, headed for right field. Both Gonder and Bunning thought it would be a hit but Phils' second baseman Tony Taylor took a couple of steps toward first base, dove and knocked the ball down. While on his knees, he grabbed the ball and threw Gonder out.

"It was a great play," said Bunning. "When he did that, I knew I had something special going." That was as close as the Mets would come to a hit. From that point on, Bunning was untouchable.

Bunning's battery mate Gus Triandos doubled in a run in the second to put the Phils ahead 2-0. Then in the sixth, Johnny Callison led off with a home run, Triandos singled in a run and Bunning helped himself with a two run double to give the Phils a 6-0 lead.

Three weeks earlier, Bunning had a perfect game for six and two thirds innings against Houston. "There was total silence on the bench," said Bunning. After Mike White broke up his perfecto with a double, Bunning swore, "If I ever get into this situation again, I'm going to talk about it the whole time."

So, in New York, knowing he was working on a perfect game, when he got to the sixth inning, he yelled, "Hey guys, this is a perfect game....start diving." His teammates remained silent. Gene Mauch left the bench. "He thought I was out of my cotton-picking mind," said Bunning.

As Bunning took the mound in the bottom of the ninth, the Mets crowd cheered. Leadoff hitter Charlie Smith hit a foul popup caught by Phils' shortstop Bobby Wine. The cheering got louder as dangerous left-handed hitter, George Altman pinch hit for Amado Samuel and struck out on a curveball.

With two outs, Bunning called his catcher Gus Triandos to the mound. "Hey, it's a little tense out here," Bunning said. "Do you have any good jokes?" Triandos just laughed at Bunning and went back behind the plate.

The fans were on their feet, cheering, as left-handed hitter John Stephenson pinch hit for pitcher Tom Sturdivant. Stephenson was hitting .074. "When I faced him earlier in the season," Bunning said, "Gene Mauch told me, 'this guy can't spell curveball.'"

Bunning struck him out on three curveballs and pounded his fist into his glove as his teammates rushed onto the field. With only 90 pitches, he had just thrown the ninth perfect game in major league history and the first by a Phillies pitcher in 58 years.

"It meant so much to me because my wife and daughter came up for the game and they never would have if it wasn't Father's Day," said Bunning.

Bunning wanted to go to Toots Shor's restaurant to celebrate but it was closed for Father's Day. Then, Bunning was asked to appear on "The Ed Sullivan Show." When he arrived at the CBS Theater, Bunning met golfer Ken Venturi, who had just won the U.S. Open in a dramatic finish. Venturi had played 36 holes in grueling heat and needed intravenous fluids to finish.

"You S.O.B, you knocked me off the front page," said Venturi.

"I'm sorry but it just happened I pitched a perfect game," responded Bunning. Bunning told Venturi that the New York writers would think a perfect game in New York was more important than winning the U.S. Open. Bunning and Venturi became good friends.

The two athletes were supposed to be introduced by Sullivan, take a bow and pocket $1500 for the appearance.

"Ed Sullivan was such a baseball nut, that when he introduced me, he called me to the microphone and asked some questions about the perfect game. Then, he introduced Venturi but didn't speak to him.

Still having not eaten, the Bunnings stopped at a Howard Johnson's on the New Jersey Turnpike and then headed for Philadelphia.

Overshadowed by Bunning's performance, 18-year-old Rick Wise won his first major league start beating the Mets 8-2 in the second game of the twin bill. Clay Dalrymple was behind the plate when Wise walked the second batter of the game and "everybody in the grandstand stood up and cheered because it was the first runner the Mets had all day."

The great pitching continued two days later at Connie Mack Stadium. After another bout with "lefthanderitis," a five-hit 2-0 shutout by the Cubs' Dick Ellsworth, 21-year-old Ray Culp fired a one-hitter in a 9-0 Phillies win, allowing just a sixth inning single to Len Gabrielson.

Just before the All-Star break, the Phils won the final game of a series in L.A. and then swept the Giants three straight in San Francisco. They were 47-28, with a game and a half lead on the second place Giants.

The 1964 Major League Baseball All-Star Game was played at Shea Stadium in New York. Jim Bunning, Johnny Callison and Chris Short represented Philadelphia. Richie Allen was left off. "Richie should have made the team," said Callison. "He should have started at third base instead of Kenny Boyer."[6]

Allen was being mentioned as a leading candidate for Rookie of the Year honors. "So what," Allen said, "No money goes along with that award, does it? If they put ten or eleven thousand dollars in a pot and gave it to the Rookie of the Year, I might be interested."[7]

Jim Bunning pitched two scoreless innings and Chris Short gave up two runs in one inning of work.

In the fifth inning, Callison pinch hit for Bunning and popped out. The Braves' Hank Aaron would have gone in to play right field but the Hammer wasn't feeling well so Callison stayed in the game in right field. After the American League took a 4-3 lead in the seventh, A.L. skipper Ralph Houk brought in the "Monster," 6-foot-6, 250-pound Dick Radatz of the Red Sox. Callison hit the ball hard of Radatz but Mickey Mantle ran down the drive in deep right-center.

In the ninth, with the American League leading 4-3, Willie Mays walked and stole second. Orlando Cepeda's bloop single to right and a throwing error by the first baseman Joe Pepitone allowed Mays to score the tying run with Cepeda going to second. After Ken Boyer popped out to third and Doc Edwards was walked intentionally, Dick Radatz struck out the ailing pinch hitter Hank Aaron on three blazing fastballs. With two outs, Johnny Callison stepped in to face Radatz.

Callison rememberd how Radatz had pumped fastballs by Aaron and decided he needed a lighter bat. So, Callison borrowed a bat from the Cubs' Billy Williams. On Radatz' first pitch, Callison swung and hit a drive to deep right field. "Stayed fair by ten feet," recalled Callison. "I floated around the bases." Callison's grand slam home run gave the National League a 7-4 win and he was named the game's MVP. "That homer was the greatest thrill of my life," Callison said, "but I remember thinking it was only the beginning. It was going to be the Phillies' year. We had everything going our way. Everything."[8]

Callison was the only left-handed hitter who was not platooned. Opponents knew the Phillies couldn't hit lefthanders. Teams started altering their rotations to make sure southpaws faced the Phils. They would pull a lefty out of the bullpen or bring one up from the minors or as Mauch said, "They bring them in from Nome and points north."

After the All-Star break, the Phillies lost six out of seven, with five left-handed pitchers beating them including Jim O'Toole and Joe Nuxhall of the Reds. Nobody enjoyed beating Gene Mauch more than Nuxhall. After a four-hit shutout against the Phils, Nuxhall said, "I like to win anytime but I especially like to beat that little so-and-so Mauch. Did you see him showboating out there? He wasn't even saying anything to the umpires, but he still stood there. And I don't like the things he does. He'll yell at a pitcher. Who does he think he is?"[9]

On August 3, the Phillies and Dodgers were set to play the fourth game of a series in Philadelphia. Sandy Koufax, who had no-hit the Phils in June, was scheduled to pitch for the Dodgers. Gene Mauch's team was playing well and he knew Koufax, who'd beaten the Phils eight straight times, could stop his team's momentum. So Mauch, who's memorized the rule book, consulted rule 3:10 (a): "The manager of the home team shall be the sole judge as to whether a game shall be started because of unsuitable weather conditions."

It had rained in nearby South Jersey that afternoon so Mauch met with G.M. John Quinn and they decided to postpone the game because of "threatening weather." By the usual gametime, the skies were clear but Mauch had avoided Sandy Koufax. The game was rescheduled for September 8, which happened to be a Jewish holiday so they would miss Koufax again. Later this move would come back to haunt Mauch.

For more than a year, G.M. John Quinn had dickered with George Weiss of the Mets trying to acquire veteran slugger Frank Thomas. Finally, on August 7, the Phils sent three young prospects to New York for Thomas, who didn't have to go far to join his new team. With the Phils beginning a three-game series with the Mets, Thomas just walked from the Mets' clubhouse to the Phillies, where he saw the lineup card taped the wall. He was batting fourth and playing first base.

In his first game in Philadelphia flannels, Thomas doubled and singled and drove in two runs in a 9-4 victory over the Mets. The Phils swept the three-game series as Thomas had three singles, a double and three run homer in thirteen at bats.

With the addition of Thomas, the return of Gus Triandos from the injury list and the recall of rookie Alex Johnson from Little Rock, the Phillies won six of their next eight against lefthanders.

After Thomas joined the team, the Phillies went 20-12 as he hit .302 with seven homers and 26 RBI in the 33 games he played. Then on September 8th, the Phils and Dodgers met in a game that made up for the postponement in August, the game Gene Mauch had cancelled because of "threatening weather" and Sandy Koufax. In that game, Thomas fractured his thumb sliding back to second on a pickoff. Thomas tried to play with the injury, but was ineffective and spent most of his time on the bench.

After Chris Short notched a complete game victory and Dennis Bennett and Jack Baldschun combined to shutout Houston, improving the Phillies record to 88-57, Gene Mauch figured he'd go for a sweep. Unlike most managers who stayed with a set pitching rotation, Mauch would often have a starter pitch out of turn to face an opponent he owned. Jim Bunning had already beaten the Colts four times. Mauch thought that even with just two days rest, Bunning would have no problem. It turned out to be one of the biggest mistakes Gene Mauch made.

Rusty Staub hit a two-run homer off Bunning in the first and then it got worse. Bunning lasted just four-and-one-third innings, allowing six earned runs and eight hits as the Colts won 6-5.

Three days later in Los Angeles, the Phillies and Dodgers were tied 3-3 in the sixteenth inning. With two outs, the Dodgers' Willie Davis singled off Jack Baldschun and stole second. After Tommy Davis was walked intentionally, with Ron Fairly up, Baldschun threw a wild pitch advancing Willie to third and Tommy to second. Mauch came out and waved to the bullpen for rookie lefthander Morrie Steevens, just recalled from Little Rock. Facing the left-handed hitting Fairly, Steevens was using a full windup. Dodgers' third base coach Leo Durocher, Gene Mauch's first big league manager, whispered to Davis, "You can steal home on this kid." With two strikes on Fairly, Stevens wound up and Davis took off. He slid across home plate giving the Dodgers a 4-3 win. "There's a kid out there," Davis said, "You always try to do something to shake up a kid."

Phillies' catcher Clay Dalrymple was furious and called for a post-game meeting with the pitchers. "If this happens again, if a guy is trying to steal home," he told them, "don't throw the ball outside, just throw the ball to the catcher. It doesn't even have to be a strike and the catcher can tag him out."

After splitting the four-game series in L.A., the Phillies flew home and were greeted by the mayor and two thousand fans who hoped to see their team clinch the pennant on the upcoming home stand.

On September 21, the Phillies had a six-and-a-half game lead with 12 games to play when they met the Cincinnati Reds at Connie Mack Stadium. With skipper Fred Hutchinson battling cancer, Coach Dick Sisler was the Reds' interim manager. Sisler had played for the 1950 Phillies, the "Whiz Kids," who blew a seven-and-a-half game lead and had to beat the Dodgers in the final game of the season to win the pennant. Sisler's three-run homer at Ebbets Field had won the game.

Although the Reds were six-and-a-half games back of the Phillies, Sisler thought his club still had a chance, "If we can get within two, two-and-a-half or three games of them. The closer we get, the more pressure will be on them. If it gets that close, they might get a little tight. That's what I noticed on the 1950 Phillies. When you see 'em right behind you, it begins to tell."[10]

Art Mahaffey and the Reds John Tsitouris hooked up in a scoreless duel until the top of the sixth. After Pete Rose grounded out, Chico Ruiz singled to right. Vada Pinson followed with a single sending Ruiz to third, but Pinson was thrown out trying to go to second. So, Ruiz was at third with two outs and the Reds cleanup hitter Frank Robinson at the plate.

As Ruiz led off from third, he studied Mahaffey's slow deliberate windup. A light bulb flashed on. "It just came to my mind," Ruiz said, "you either do it or you don't." With two strikes on Robinson, as Mahaffey wound up again, Ruiz bolted for home plate.[11]

"Just as I'm ready to throw, Ruiz ran at the fraction of a second that my head is turning and my arm is coming down," remembered Mahaffey. "My brain panicked and I held my arm up and threw a pitch two feet wide of the plate." Catcher Clay Dalrymple had no chance to catch the ball as it went all the way back to the screen. Ruiz stole home and gave the Reds a 1-0 win.

"If you steal home and Frank Robinson is the fucking hitter," said an incredulous Dalrymple, "and the game is on the line, you gotta have some big balls."

Just four days after Willie Davis stole home to beat the Phillies, it had happened again. Dalrymple was especially angry that Mahaffey hadn't heeded his advice in the L.A. clubhouse meeting. "All he had to do was throw the ball to me and I could have tagged Ruiz, but he threw the sumbitch so far outside I couldn't reach it."'

Mahaffey said, "If I throw a strike, Frank Robinson swings the bat and knocks Ruiz's head off.

"He surprised everyone in the ballpark, including me, "said Sisler. "I saw him and I said 'Holy Smokes' what's he doing? I would never call for a steal with the big man up there. But it worked. We got by with it. If the pitch is over though, even at the batter, he's out. He goes crazy on the bases sometimes."[12]

Gene Mauch went nuts after the game, "Chico Fucking Ruiz beats us on the bonehead play of the year! Chico Fucking Ruiz steals home with Frank Robinson up! Can you believe it?"

The next night, Mauch screamed insults from the dugout and told his pitcher Chris Short to hit Ruiz. Short tried and missed twice but reliever Ed Roebuck finally drilled Ruiz in the ribs.

With one out in the third, Short walked pitcher Jim O'Toole. Pete Rose singled, Chico Ruiz walked, loading the bases and Vada Pinson grounded into a force play with O'Toole scoring to give the Reds a 1-0 lead. With runners at first and third, the Reds tried a double steal. Pete Rose stole home and Pinson stole second as catcher Gus Triandos' throw went into centerfield for an error, sending Pinson to third. With the Reds now leading 2-0, Frank Robinson stepped in. Mauch feared Robinson more than any hitter in the league.

Earlier, in a slump and grumbling about his salary, Robinson had threatened to retire. Nobody believed him and Mauch said, "I know 91 pitchers in the league and nine managers who will chip in $500 apiece if Robinson will retire. That's $50,000." Robinson didn't retire and belted a two run homer make it 4-0.

Another lefthander, Jim O'Toole went the distance in the 9-2 Reds win, reducing the Phils lead to 4 ½ games.

Sore-armed Dennis Bennett started the next game, tried to pitch but gave up six earned runs in four and two-thirds innings. Two home runs by Vada Pinson carried the Cincinnati to a 6-4 win, the Phillies third straight loss, reducing their lead to 3 ½ games.

Ironically, the same day the Phillies were accepting orders for World Series tickets. The postman delivered 18 sacks of mail with an estimated 63,000 ticket requests.

Vada Pinson said, "We're smelling that Series money now and we don't intend to let it go."

"Baloney," said Mauch, "We're on top and that's where we're going to stay."

Jim Bunning started the next game. He walked leadoff batter Eddie Mathews in the second and then Joe Torre tripled in a run to give the Braves a 1-0 lead. The Braves scored two more off Bunning in the fourth and won 5-3. The Phils lead was down to three games.

In the Reds' clubhouse Dick Sisler said, "I don't think I'd change places with the Phillies. My team is loose and relaxed. They are tight. They're under terrific pressure. Less than a week ago they had the flag all wrapped up. Now they can feel us breathing down their neck. They're uncomfortable."[13]

Of all the losses during their collapse, the game on September 25 stands out. "It was like a World Series game," said Braves manager Bobby Bragan. After two bad outings and then Chico Ruiz's steal of home against him, Art Mahaffey had fallen out of favor with Gene Mauch. Instead of starting Art Mahaffey, Mauch used Chris Short with only two days' rest.

The Phillies led 1-0 going to the top of the seventh, when catcher Clay Dalrymple tipped Dennis Menke's bat and was called for interference. The Braves took advantage to score two runs and led 3-1 in the top of the eighth. Johnny Callison's two-run homer in the bottom of the eighth, tied the score 3-3.

With the score tied 3-3 in the 10th, the Braves Ty Cline led off with a single off Phillies reliever Bobby Locke. After Gary Kolb's sacrifice moved Cline to second, Joe Torre was up. Torre had two triples the night before and already had two hits and an RBI in this game.

Mauch had to decide what to do:—walk Torre intentionally and pitch to Gene Oliver or have Locke pitch to Torre. Mauch decided to let the righthander try to get Torre out. But Locke hung a curveball and Torre blasted a two-run homer to give Milwaukee a 5-3 lead.

Richie Allen's two-run inside-the-park home runs tied the game at 5-5 in the bottom of the tenth but in the twelfth, Eddie Mathews drove in the go-ahead run with a single off pitcher John Boozer that deflected off the glove of first baseman Frank Thomas. The Braves added another run to win 7-5. The Phillies had lost five in a row and eight of their last ten. Their lead was down to one and a half games over the Reds and the Cardinals were just two-and-a-half back.

Mauch then started Art Mahaffey on four days of rest. The Phillies led 4-2 in the sixth when Milwaukee loaded the bases with one out. Jack Baldschun was warming up in the bullpen but Mauch stayed with Mahaffey and he got out of the jam.

When Joe Torre and Rico Carty singled in the eighth, Mauch called for Jack Baldschun. Dennis Menke bunted and Baldschun threw to third for the force out. Mike de la Hoz's grounder skidded off Richie Allen's glove for a single. With the bases loaded and left-handed hitting Ed Bailey set to pinch hit for pitcher Chi Olivo, Mauch brought in lefty Bobby Shantz. Coach Peanuts Lowery asked Mauch if he wanted to take out Gus Triandos and bring in a better defensive catcher, Clay Dalrymple. "No," said Mauch, "my daughter could catch Shantz."

Shantz threw Bailey a high changeup that glanced off Triandos' glove for a passed ball allowing Carty to score and cutting the

Phillies lead to 4-3.

In the ninth, Hank Aaron and Eddie Mathews singled and after fouling off two bunts, pinch hitter Frank Bolling grounded to Ruben Amaro, who flipped to Tony Taylor for a force at second. But Taylor dropped the throw, an error, loading the bases. Rico Carty then hit Shantz's first pitch off the centerfield wall for a three run triple. Braves' ace Warren Spahn came in and retired the Phils in order in the ninth as they lost again 6-4.

With their sixth straight loss, the Phils were clinging to a half game lead over Cincinnati, who beat the Mets 6-1. St Louis also won, beating Pittsburgh 6-3, to move to within a game-and-a-half of Philadelphia.

For 150 games the Phillies had played winning baseball and now it was all coming apart. The defense, which had been air tight, sprung leaks. When they hit, they got no pitching. When they pitched well, they got no hitting. The ship was sinking fast.

With one game left on the final home stand, Gene Mauch called Bunning into his office. "I kind of hinted that I would like another shot at Milwaukee," Bunning said. "I told Gene that if we were short of pitchers, then I would take the ball but he made the final decision."

The Phillies were short of pitchers. Dennis Bennett's arm was so bad that, according to Bunning, "He couldn't throw the ball sixty feet-six inches. His arm was just hanging."

Ray Culp had a bad elbow and Mauch had no confidence in Art Mahaffey. "Art could have started and should have," said Bunning, "but Gene lost faith in him."

That left Mauch with two pitchers, Jim Bunning and lefthander Chris Short.

In the 1960's teams used four man rotations, not the five of today. Pitchers got three days rest. So asking Bunning and Short to pitch on two days rest was just a slight variation from their normal schedule.

"We were dead willing," said Bunning. "We thought somebody had to take the ball and some of the people didn't want it and since Shorty and I had gotten them that far, they thought we could get them the rest of the way."

So, Bunning took the ball against Milwaukee. Bunning's sacrifice fly in the second gave the Phillies a 3-2 lead but on the mound, Bunning had nothing. The Braves battered Bunning, knocking him out of the game. In three innings, Bunning allowed seven earned runs, ten hits and was tagged with the 14-8 loss. Milwaukee pounded out 22 hits with Joe Torre going three-for-five with a home run. In the Braves four-game sweep, Torre had eleven hits, including two homers, two triples, and seven runs batted in. The Phils lost, despite Johnny Callison having the first three-home run game of his career.

When Cincinnati swept a doubleheader from the Mets, the Phillies tumbled into second place. Gene Mauch had done what he thought was best for his team to win. But in the final two weeks of the season, in six games, Mauch had started Bunning and Short on two days rest. The Phillies lost all six games.

Gene makes a pitching change.

Catcher Clay Dalrymple respected Mauch, but 50 years later, in 2014, he said, "Gene Mauch's biggest fault was that he didn't know when to take pitchers out. I didn't know this at the time, but later when I played for Earl Weaver in Baltimore, he had a knack for knowing when to make a pitching change. One of the biggest reasons we lost our pennant chances in 1964, was because Mauch used Bunning and Short every other day for the last two weeks of the season."

Mauch was blamed for the team's collapse but Jim Bunning said it wasn't just his manager's fault. "In hindsight, maybe he could have brought somebody up from Little Rock or could have started a relief pitcher. But we had to look at the entire 25-man roster and say *we* didn't play well for ten days."

Bobby Wine agreed with Bunning. "I don't think a lot of people realized it," said Wine, "but we played 'stinko' that last couple of weeks. We'd played so great all summer with the pitching and defense, getting a guy over and getting him in, squeeze bunts, – everything. But in the last two weeks, a ground ball would come to somebody, take a bad bounce and go over his head. A double play ball? We couldn't turn it and the next guy gets a hit. It threw everything out of whack."

Allen Lewis, the beat writer for the *Philadelphia Inquirer* called the Phillies seven-game losing streak, "the blackest seven days in Philadelphia baseball history."

Cincinnati and St. Louis headed home. The Reds had three games with Pittsburgh and two with the Phillies. The Cardinals had four with the Phillies and three with the Mets.

Hoping that another day's rest would help Dennis Bennett's ailing shoulder, Mauch again started Chris Short on two days' rest. In five-and-a-third innings, Short allowed three runs, but was no match for Cardinals' ace Bob Gibson, who pitched eight innings of one run ball in St. Louis' 5-1 victory and the Phillies eighth straight loss.

Despite a black-and-blue area on his shoulder, caused by internal bleeding, Bennett told Mauch he didn't know how long he'd last but he'd try to pitch five or six innings.

He lasted just an inning-and-a-third, giving up five hits and three runs. With the 4-2 win, their seventh straight, the Cardinals were tied for first place with the Reds, who lost to Pittsburgh 2-0, ending their nine-game win streak.

The Phillies were now in third place. If there was anyone the Phillies didn't want to see on the mound it was Curt Simmons, who had already rubbed salt in their wounds with a 15-2 career record against the Phils. Simmons had a no-hitter until Richie Allen singled with two outs in the seventh. Pitching on two days' rest, in just three-and-one-third innings, Bunning was battered for six hits and six runs as the Cardinals won 8-5.

When Simmons was asked if he enjoyed sticking it to the Phils, he said, "No, no, no. That story's four years old. They just wanted to get rid of old guys."[14] Simmons wound up with a lifetime 19-6 record against the team that released him.

With two games left in the season, St Louis was in first, with Cincinnati a game back and the Phils, who'd lost ten straight, in third, now two-and-a-half games out.

Although on life support, the Phillies were still breathing. If they won twice in Cincinnati and the Mets swept two from the Cardinals, a three-team playoff would be necessary.

As Gene Mauch stood near the batting cage at Crosley Field, Fred Hutchinson walked up and said, "I wish there was something I could say to help." Mauch was overwhelmed by Hutch's comments, a man dying of cancer thinking about him.

In the bottom of the seventh, with the Reds leading 3-0, Deron Johnson singled and went to second on Tommy Harper's bunt. With Leo Cardenas up, Mauch went to the mound and told Chris Short, "Don't give him a good pitch."

Short's curveball hit Cardenas in the left shoulder. Cardenas glared at Short. Waving his bat, the Reds shortstop took a step toward the mound and yelled, "You sonuvabitch, I'm going to hit you with a bat."[15]

Phillies catcher Clay Dalrymple grabbed Cardenas and said, "You're not going to hit anybody." Then, the Reds' Jim Coker, a former Phillie and Frank Robinson took Cardenas bat.

With one out in the top of the eighth and trailing 3-0, the Phils rallied. Pinch hitter Frank Thomas popped up a ball that landed on the infield dirt behind second base. Cardenas, the shortstop and second baseman Pete Rose, both froze as Thomas reached on a hit.

Dick Sisler and several of his players felt Cardenas' head wasn't in the game and that he was still thinking about his shouting match with Short. Unnerved by Cardenas' mistake, pitcher Jim O'Toole walked Cookie Rojas, then Tony Taylor singled him home. Sisler brought in lefthander Billy McCool who struck out Johnny Callison. Although righthander Sammy Ellis was ready in the bullpen, Sisler let McCool face the Phillies right-handed hitters, Richie Allen and Alex Johnson. Allen tripled in two runs to tie the score and then Johnson's single brought in the go-ahead run as the Phillies won 4-3.

When the game ended, Jim O'Toole was still furious at Cardenas, waited for him to arrive, grabbed him and threw him across the clubhouse. "Leo grabbed an ice pick," Frank Robinson said later.[16]

Robinson and some other players pulled Cardenas away and in Sisler's office, the manager ripped Cardenas for perhaps having awakened the Phillies.

After a day off, the Phils played their final game of the season with Jim Bunning pitching. Bunning pitched a six-hit shutout and finished the year 19-8 with a 2.63 ERA. Richie Allen had a double and two home runs with the Phillies winning 10-0 to finish tied for second with Cincinnati with a 92-70 record.

Richie Allen hit .318 with 29 homers and 91 RBI and led the league with 125 runs scored. On the other side of the ledger he committed 41 errors and set a National League record with 138 strikeouts. He was the only Philly to start every game and was named

National League Rookie of the Year.

When the Phillies returned home, about 10,000 fans greeted them as their charter landed at the Philadelphia International Airport. Gene Mauch stood and faced his players. "I want to be the first one off," Mauch told them. "You guys didn't lose it. I did."

As the players looked out the windows of the plane, they saw homemade banners that read, "We still love you Phillies." "Thanks for a great year" and "Wait until next year."

A downcast Gene Mauch walked along the fence shaking hands with fans. G.M. John Quinn said, "What a tribute to the Phillies. I am inspired and thrilled."

Mauch and his team wouldn't be going to the World Series along with thousands of fans who had bought tickets. The Phillies began returning checks and money orders for World Series tickets. The number of ticket applications exceeded 250,000.

The Phillies collapse also cost the city of Philadelphia an estimated $3.5 million. When the Phillies had a 6½ game lead with 12 games left, the front office ordered for extra box seats to be built, the press box was enlarged, programs were printed and hotels were sold out. Restaurants, bars and souvenir shops were expecting booming business.

Despite the collapse, Gene Mauch was named Associated Press Manager of the Year for 1964.

Larry Shenk, the Phillies longtime public relations director felt that if it wasn't for Mauch's managing, the Phils never would have been in position to win a pennant. "Listening to Gene talk baseball was like listening to the Philadelphia Orchestra. Pure entertainment."

On the Phillies gave Gene Mauch a new two-year contract with a substantial raise over the $40,000 per year he had been making. "I think he's done a fine job," said club President Robert R.M. Carpenter, who tore up the old contract with one year remaining.

General Manager John Quinn said the contract would assure

Mauch of the longest tenure by a Phillies' skipper since Burt Shotton, from 1928 to 1933.

Although to this day, Mauch is blamed for the incredible collapse of the 1964 Phillies, many felt that the Phils never should have been in contention to begin with. This was not a great club. The only Hall of Famer was Jim Bunning, who was elected by the veterans' committee.

Mauch had just three names he would pencil in the lineup every day: Johnny Callison, Richie Allen, and Tony Taylor. He platooned at every other position. John Herrnstein, Roy Sievers and Frank Thomas all played first base. Bobby Wine and Ruben Amaro shared the shortstop position. Tony González and Adolfo Phillips both played centerfield and Alex Johnson and Wes Covington each patrolled right field. Clay Dalrymple was usually the catcher but at times Gus Triandos was there. Cookie Rojas was the jack-of-all-trades who played everywhere, including catcher.

Mauch hoped Art Mahaffey would become a 20-game winner; instead he was up and down, a shutout one day and a two-inning bombing the next start. Dennis Bennett tried to pitch but had a bad shoulder, Ray Culp had a sore elbow and bad back. Rick Wise was only 18-years-old. So what was a manager to do? Mauch probably out maneuvered himself when he decided to start Jim Bunning and Chris Short with only the limited amount of two days of rest. Pitchers are creatures of habit, they rely on a structured approach to their next start and any disruption is liable to cause problems.

To Mauch's credit, he took all the blame. The collapse hurt him deeply. Although he didn't always show it, Mauch loved these players and the potential of this team. He was crushed when they crumbled and heaped the blame on himself. He struggled with this guilt for years, thinking about it every day. One of his biggest disappointments was Johnny Callison not winning MVP honors. Mauch felt, that if the Phillies won the pennant, Callison would have won the award. Instead it went to St. Louis third baseman Kenny Boyer.

The city of Philadelphia spent the winter in mourning. Mauch returned to California and took out his anger on golf balls.

Mauch family off to Hawaii-Nina Lee (L), Lee Anne (C) Gene (R).

Chapter Sixteen

Let's Make a Deal

Gene Mauch and John Quinn attended baseball's winter meetings in Houston, looking to make trades. They made three of them.

They acquired pitcher Bo Belinsky from the Los Angeles Angels for first baseman Costen Shockley and pitcher Rudy May. In 1962, the 28-year-old Belinsky became the first Angels pitcher to win his first four starts. The fourth was a no-hitter against the Baltimore Orioles, the team that had originally signed him

Bo played as hard off the field as he did on it. He loved to party and hang with the beautiful people in Hollywood including starlets Ann Margaret, Tina Louise, Connie Stevens, and Mamie Van Doren, his eventual fiancée.

Bo's lifestyle and major league hitters caught up with him in 1963, when he slumped to 1-7 and was sent to the Angels AAA team in Hawaii. After going 4-1 with a 2.50 ERA there, he was brought back up and finished the year 2-9 with the Angels.

Bo was enjoying his best year, with a 9-8 record and 2.86 ERA Then he was involved in a hotel room fight with drunken, elderly sportswriter Braven Dyer, of the *Los Angeles Times*. He was suspended by the Angels and then traded to the Phillies after the 1964 season ended.

Gene Mauch, (L to R) Bo Belinsky, Jim Bunning, Ray Herbert, 1965.

Besides Belinsky, the Phils added another controversial player, 32-year-old Dick Stuart who was acquired from the Boston Red Sox for pitcher Dennis Bennett. "Dr. Strangeglove" and "Stonefingers," were two of Stuart's nicknames because he was such a butcher at first base. But Stuart had the power the Phillies needed and pounded left-handed pitchers.

Stuart became a legend in 1956 when he hit 66 home runs for Lincoln in the Class A Western League. He spent five years with the Pittsburgh Pirates, playing on their 1960 World Championship

Team and had his two best years with the Boston Red Sox from 1963-64. In his first year with Boston he hit 42 home runs and led the American League with 118 RBI. The next year, he had 33 homers and 114 RBI.

The Phillies could certainly use Stuart's bat but how would the outspoken slugger get along with the no-nonsense Mauch?

"Mauch will get no trouble from me," Stuart said. "As long as I start, I'm happy."[1]

The Phillies made a third deal, acquiring righthander Ray Herbert from the Chicago White Sox for utility man Danny Cater. Herbert was a solid veteran who could be a spot starter much the way Cal McLish had been for the Phils.

"This is the strongest team I've had in my six years in Philadelphia," said Mauch. We kept the good things we had last year and added Stuart, Herbert and Belinsky. Mauch also predicted that Stuart would hit 40 home runs and Belinsky would win at least 12 games.

Richie Allen and G.M. John Quinn couldn't agree on a salary so the Phils star held out until after the first Grapefruit League game. Although not happy with the terms of the contract, Allen finally signed because his mother asked him to.

Bo Belinsky picked up the Phillies first spring training win, with three scoreless innings, allowing just one hit in a 1-0 win over the New York Mets in Clearwater, Florida.

An eager Dick Stuart said, "I hope Gene will let me play in as many exhibition games as possible. I'm a slow starter and I need the work in spring training." As expected, Stuart had a weak spring, hitting only .250 with two home runs as the team readied to head north.

"Dick has never been a good spring hitter," explained Mauch. "Hitters like Stuart, who are established, usually find their level. He'll hit. I know he will."

The Phillies opened the 1965 season in Houston and Mauch handed the baseball to Chris Short, a 17-game winner in 1964. It was the first time in Short's pro career that he'd been the opening day starter.

Richie Allen christened the Astrodome, with a two-run blast, the first homer in Houston's new home. That was all Short needed in the Phils 2-0 win. The 25-year-old lefthander had all four of his pitches working: fastball, curve, slider, and changeup. In complete control, he struck out eleven and said, "I hope this is an omen. I feel like I can win 20 games this year."[2]

Back home at Connie Mack Stadium, 31,923 Phillies fanatics turned out to watch Jim Bunning's first start against San Francisco. Bunning had gone 4-0 against the Giants in 1964. Bunning lasted just three-and-two-thirds innings, allowing three runs and eight hits as the Giants won 5-2.

Aside from a home run off Sandy Koufax in a loss to the Dodgers, Dick Stuart was hitting just .222 and his five errors outnumbered his two home runs. After a 0-13 stretch in which the Phillies lost all four games, Mauch benched Stuart for three days. "I'm not worried about Stuart," Mauch told the media. "He'll hit a couple on that roof and everybody will come down from the stands and start hugging him."

In Philadelphia, Jim Bunning pitched a five-hit shutout, beating Houston 8-0. In the third inning, with 6'7" 230 pound Walt Bond at the plate, Bunning sent Bond sprawling in the dirt with a fastball. Then, Bunning drilled him in the arm. Bond got up, yelled at Bunning, "If you hit me again. I'm gonna fight," and started toward the mound until teammates and umpires broke it up.[3]

"I have to pitch him inside," Bunning said, "And as long as I'm in this league, I'll do it."[4]

In Los Angeles, the Phillies lost to the Dodgers 9-3 and Mauch got into two arguments with Umpire Al Barlick. Barlick called a balk on Bo Belinsky in the second inning, which led to a Dodgers' run. Mauch tried to convince Barlick that Belinsky had pitched the same way in the American League, in spring training and in his first National League start.

Then the Dodgers scored six runs in the sixth, Barlick ruled that first baseman Dick Stuart didn't hold a throw which would have been the third out. Four unearned runs scored after the play. Mauch lost that argument too.

After the game, Mauch locked the clubhouse doors and told his team, "I've seen more mistakes in our first nine games than we made in our first 130 last year."[5]

During the Dodgers big inning, Mauch went out to make a pitching change and out of frustration, he fired a ball against the screen. Before the next day's game, Dodger manager Walter Alston sent Mauch a message: "When you threw the ball against the screen, you definitely balked."[6]

The Phillies finished April at 6-8. "We don't have the feeling of superiority we had last year," Mauch said. He was especially concerned with a defense that committed 14 errors on a 12 game road trip, including four in one game.

Dick Stuart was incensed over a newspaper story saying he'd ripped Gene Mauch, "I play 15 games. All of a sudden he finds out I can't hit and I can't field. The team's going bad so he's looking for a guy to blame."[7]

Stuart denied making the comments and he and Mauch had a 20-minute meeting in the manager's office. Stuart was in the line-up that night.

Stuart went one-for-four, but hit the ball hard every time up. Jim Bunning pitched a four-hit shutout and the Phils beat the New York Mets 1-0.

After a frustrating 4-3 loss to Cincinnati, Mauch locked out the media and in a post-game rant, broke a window and punched a clubhouse locker. "That's just me," he said. "Some people can keep things inside of them; some people can't.....and I'm not going to talk about it anymore."

The Phillies won the next game 7-6 in ten innings as two sluggers played Gene Mauch's "small ball." With two outs in the 10th, Frank Thomas bunted home Dick Stuart.

Despite a sore shoulder, Art Mahaffey pitched well in two starts including a 5-2 win over Milwaukee in which Mahaffey struck out ten.

Dick Stuart wasn't hitting and with the team struggling to get to

.500 mark, Mauch benched him, putting Frank Thomas at first base. Thomas had 3 of the Phillies 18 hits as they battered New York 10-3.

When the writers asked about Stuart, Mauch said, "I told Stuart to sit here and help me manage."[8]

"I have no comment at all," said Stuart. "I don't want to start any more trouble, period."[9]

And Bo Belinsky? A disaster. He lost his first two starts to the Dodgers, failing to go more than five-and-one-third innings. Finally in his sixth start, he beat the Cardinals 2-1, besting Curt Simmons in a pitcher's duel for his first National League victory.

His next win didn't come until a month later, a 7-1 victory over Houston, a six-hit, ten strikeout performance.

Then, Bo announced that he had pitched for eight weeks with a cracked rib. The Phillies trainer said the injury occurred ten to twelve weeks earlier, but was fine now. Belinsky also complained about his back stiffening up. Mauch finally took Bo out of the rotation and stuck him in the bullpen.

Although Dick Stuart and Bo Belinsky were busts, Richie Allen was having another outstanding season. After committing 41 errors as a rookie, his improvement defensively was astounding. "Allen will eventually become as good a fielding third baseman as there is in baseball," Gene Mauch said. "He has quick reactions that come from playing basketball and his arm is four times as strong as it was when I saw him work out before we signed him."[10]

"I've never known an athlete with a better mental attitude," continued Mauch. "He never gets too high when things are going good and he never gets downhearted when they are going bad. He can become just as great as he wants to be."

Although just 5'11" and 185 pounds, the broad-shouldered, slim waisted 24-year-old was hitting monstrous home runs that would become the stuff of legends. Allen had exceptionally long arms, forearms like steel cables, and huge hands. "His muscles rippled like those of a racehorse," said Gene Mauch.

In a win over the Chicago Cubs, Allen hit one of the longest home runs in the history of Connie Mack Stadium. He hammered a Larry Jackson pitch high and far over the 80 foot high billboard atop the left field stands. The ball traveled more than 500 feet and hit a tree on Woodstock Street.

"The funny part is that he didn't look good hitting it," said Gene Mauch. "He actually sort of fell into the ball, which shows what a hitter like Rich can do."[11]

Johnny Callison also flexed his muscles, hitting three homers in the second game of a doubleheader at Wrigley Field, a 10-9 win. In the first inning, Callison hit a Larry Jackson changeup into the first row of right field seats. "I never hit a ball harder in my life," Callison said.[12]

Then, in the third, Jackson challenged him with a fast ball. As he connected, his bat split in half and he headed toward first base, holding the handle of his bat. "Halfway to second base, they signaled home run," Callison said, "I couldn't believe it." Neither could Gene Mauch, "I've seen Steve Bilko hit the left field fence on the fly when that happened," said Mauch, "but I've never seen anyone hit one out of the park." Just for good measure, Callison also homered off Ernie Broglio in the ninth.

Callison's explosion overshadowed Cookie Rojas, who had four hits, including a three-run homer. Rojas may have been the team's first half MVP. In April and May, he'd been the centerfielder against left-handed pitching, hitting over .300, and he also played every position except first base and pitcher.

With great pitching, the Phillies won five in a row to reach the .500 mark at 28-28. During the streak, Chris Short scattered ten hits in a 7-3 win over the Dodgers then Ray Herbert shut out the Bums 4-0 as Richie Allen and Dick Stuart hit back-to-back homers in the eighth. Allen's blast was one of the highest and longest home runs ever hit at Connie Mack Stadium. The ball soared over the left field roof and landed in a parking lot across the street." Stuart's homer cleared the left field stands but he said, "Mine looked like a drag bunt in comparison to Richie's."

In the next month, Gene Mauch put on a juggling act that rivaled any in his career. Only Johnny Callison and Richie Allen played every day. Depending on the situation, Mauch mixed and matched. He used five different left fielders; three first basemen; three centerfielders; and two different players at shortstop, catcher and second base; as well as three different leadoff hitters. He platooned, he juggled the lineup, and he used the squeeze play. He used starters as relievers and several different closers as the Phils just kept winning.

In a 4-2 win over San Francisco, in the sixth inning, when Willie McCovey came up with Matty Alou on third with one out, Mauch moved first baseman Dick Stuart to third, third baseman Richie Allen to shortstop and rifle-armed Bobby Wine from short to first. Mauch hoped that if McCovey grounded to Wine, Alou could be thrown out at the plate. But, McCovey hit a sac fly to center.

Although his team was winning, Gene Mauch snapped when he saw Tony González loafing in centerfield. He pulled González out in the middle of a 5-4 win over Houston and the next morning, met with him to discuss the outfielder's lack of effort.

After lecturing him, Mauch put him González back in the lineup and he responded with a home run, double, and single supporting Chris Short's five-hitter in the 5-0 win over the Colts and lifting them to the .500 mark for the first time in almost a month.

During this month long surge, the Phillies went 17-6. Chris Short won five times with two shutouts, Jim Bunning had four wins, Ray Culp three. Even Bo Belinsky pitched two gems, including a 10 strikeout, one walk effort in a 7-1 win over Houston. Ray Herbert had a shutout and save and besides Jack Baldschun and Ed Roebuck, Gene Mauch found another reliever in 24-year-old Gary Wagner who had two wins and two saves.

Richie Allen was leading the league in hitting and Dick Stuart finally got hot, with five home runs during the streak.

Every move Gene Mauch made seemed to work. Then, one swing of Frank Thomas' bat broke the piñata and ruined the party.

On July 3, two hours before game time, the Phillies were taking batting practice before playing Cincinnati.

Frank Thomas was in the batting cage, when Richie Allen, Johnny Callison and others began needling him. It was normal pregame banter that quickly took a serious turn. Allen shouted, "Do what you did last night," referring to Thomas striking out as a pinch-hitter in the seventh inning with the Phils leading 3-2 with runners at first and third[13].

When Thomas dropped a bunt toward third base, Allen yelled, "That's 21 hours too late."

Thomas answered, "You are running off at the mouth like Muhammad Cassius Clay."

Allen threatened to come after Thomas, who said, "I'll be right here." As Allen approached, Thomas said, "I'm sorry I hurt your feelings."

"That don't go with me," answered Allen, who then punched Thomas in the jaw[14]. Thomas was holding his bat and retaliated by swinging and hitting Allen on his shoulder. Teammates separated the two.

"The incident was really nothing," said Bobby Wine. "It was blown up like it was a massive fight. I was standing ten feet from them. It was really nothing, just a minor skirmish."

Pat Corrales was standing down the third base line talking with Gene Mauch when he saw the commotion around the batting cage. "It really started earlier on a road trip. Thomas had been picking on Johnny Briggs, saying, 'boy this' and 'boy that,' and Dick told him to stop it.

Both Thomas and Allen played that night in a loss to Cincinnati. Thomas had a pinch-hit home run and Allen went three-for-four with two triples and four RBI.

After the game, the Phillies released Thomas, who claimed he was the victim of circumstances. He said Mauch told him, "That's what happens when you're 36 and the other fellow is 23 and leading the league in hitting."

Gene Mauch ordered his players not to talk about the incident and threatened them with a $1,000 fine if they did. When reporters asked Richie Allen about what happened, he said, "What fight?"

Publicly, the team seemed to move past the incident but what would the long-term effects be?

"Most of us," said one player, "felt it was the only thing to do, letting Thomas go after he hit Allen with the bat. Now we're beginning to have second thoughts. We're after a pennant and it was good to have Thomas' bat around."

After dropping the final two games to Cincinnati, the Phillies swept a doubleheader from Pittsburgh that left the team alone in fourth place.

But nearly 30,000 fans in Connie Mack Stadium didn't let Allen off the hook, booing him every time he came up.

After Thomas had been sold to Houston, some fans blamed Allen and some Thomas. When Allen picked up a bat, boos and cheers were mixed.

Two games before the All-Star break, Jim Bunning flirted with another no-hitter against San Francisco. With one out in the seventh, the Giants' Tom Haller homered, the first hit off Bunning. Bunning wound up with a five-hitter and a 10-2 win as the Phils moved into third place.

Since Johnny Keane, who led St. Louis to the pennant in 1964, was now piloting the New York Yankees, Gene Mauch replaced him as manager of the N.L. team for the All-Star Game in Minneapolis. Dick Allen was the starting third baseman and Mauch selected Johnny Callison and Cookie Rojas as reserves. Mauch thought Jim Bunning and Chris Short deserved to be on the team but every team had to be represented and the other managers left the two off the roster. The National League beat the American League 6-5.

After the All-Star break, the Phillies lost eight of eleven including losses at the hands of Mauch-hater Joe Nuxhall of the Reds and ex-Phillie Curt Simmons, who improved his record to 17-3 against his old club since they released him in 1960. When Simmons ended his career in 1967, he wound up with a 19-6 record against the Phillies.

In August, the Phillies began a ten game road trip to Houston, San Francisco and Los Angeles. In the opener in Houston, they ran into old friend, Robin Roberts. Since being let go by the Phillies after going 1-10 in 1961, the 39-year-old revived his career with three winning seasons in Baltimore. When the Orioles released him, Roberts signed with Houston and would make his first start against his old team.

Roberts pitched a four-hit shutout, winning 8-0. In the second game, Jim Bunning returned the favor, blanking Houston 2-0 and the Phils went 7-3 on the trip, then returned home and sunk like the Titanic. Below average defensively all year, the Phillies hit a new low when the once strong bullpen fell apart. The Phillies lost 13 of 17 games and ten of the losses were charged to relievers.

The Phillies finished the season in sixth place with a disappointing 85-76 record, eleven-and-a-half games out of first place. Jim Bunning had the best year of his career, going 19-9, Chris Short was 18-11, Johnny Callison's average dropped to .262 but he had a career high of 32 home runs and 101 RBI.

When John Quinn and Gene Mauch began to rebuild the Phillies in the early 1960's, they swapped age for youth. In the last couple of years, needing veteran players, they dealt youth for experience. Gene Mauch's biggest disappointment in 1965 had been the defense. In an effort to shore up the D, John Quinn traded young players Alex Johnson, Art Mahaffey, and Pat Corrales to the St. Louis Cardinals for veterans, first baseman Bill White, shortstop Dick Groat, and catcher Bob Uecker. White, Groat, and Uecker were all in their 30's. Johnson, Mahaffey, and Corrales were in their 20's.

Pat Corrales was a 24-year-old catcher who'd played just two games for the Phillies in 1964 and 63 in 1965. But playing time didn't measure Corrales' value to the team. Corrales was Dick Allen's alarm clock. He made sure Allen got in before curfew and was always on time for meetings, workouts, and games. "I wouldn't let him be late," Corrales said, "We'd ride together to the park."

The two formed a friendship in the minor leagues when Corrales pulled Allen out of a near fight with another player who'd called him the "N" word. "I went up to Dick," remembered Corrales, "and said, 'that idiot is not worth getting into trouble over.'" They became friends and Corrales pointed out that most of Allen's problems occurred after Pat was traded.

The Phillies had once hoped Art Mahaffey would become a 20-game winner but the Phillies felt they had given him plenty of chances. G.M. John Quinn didn't think Mahaffey fit into the team's future plans."

Mahaffey didn't like Gene Mauch. "One day," he said, "Mauch had a meeting and said, 'I hate every pitcher who ever lived.'" Mahaffey felt Mauch was too negative and he was tired of his manager's constant criticism. After being traded to the Cardinals, Mahaffey pitched in only five more games before retiring at 28.

White was the best defensive first baseman in the league and replaced the worst, Dick Stuart, who was traded to the Mets. Groat could play short, second or third and Uecker was a good backup catcher and budding comic.

The Phillies went into spring training in 1966 knowing they needed more pitching. Righthanders Jim Bunning and Ray Culp were set. The team had traded Jack Baldschun because 24-year-old Gary Wagner who had been so good as a rookie, had a sore arm which plagued him during spring training.

Gene hitting fungoes in spring training.

Lefthanders Grant Jackson and Darrold Knowles pitched well in camp. Just before the Phils left spring training, they acquired two veteran righthanders, 35-year-old Roger Craig, who'd been released by Cincinnati and former Phillie Steve Ridzik, purchased from Washington. Ed Roebuck, who'd shared bullpen duties with Jack Baldschun, was released.

April 21, 1966 was a day that would live in infamy. The Phillies traded three young players, outfielders John Herrnstein, Adolfo

Phillips and pitcher Ferguson Jenkins to the Cubs for two pitchers in their mid-thirties, Larry Jackson and Bob Buhl.

The Phils obviously had no idea how good Fergie Jenkins would become. The 23-year-old Canadian was with the team in spring training, but threw only 20 innings.

Jenkins was shagging fly balls in the outfield when a bat boy told him to go to the manager's office. When he walked in, Mauch told him to sit down. They were soon joined by Phils' G.M. John Quinn and players John Herrnstein and Adolfo Phillips. Gene Mauch told them they had been swapped to the Cubs for veterans Larry Jackson and Bob Buhl. Phillips started to cry. Jenkins and Herrnstein were newly married and Herrnstein had two kids. Quinn told them they had 24 hours to report to Chicago. "It was like a kick in the stomach," said Jenkins. "I kind of had a bad taste in my mouth because I expected to be a Phillie."[15]

In his first year with the Cubs, Jenkins was 6-8, pitching mostly in relief. In 1967, his first full year as a starter, he was 20-13, the first of seven, twenty-win seasons. He pitched for 19 years, ten of them in Chicago, won the Cy Young Award and was elected to the Baseball Hall of Fame. His lifetime record against the Phillies was 26-8.

Larry Jackson threw five shutouts and went 15-15 for the Phillies in 1966 but Bob Buhl was a disappointing 6-8.

Unlike the previous spring when he was embroiled in a contract dispute, Richie Allen and John Quinn agreed on a salary of a reported $80,000. "I'm a changed man," said Allen, "I'm feeling pretty good about everything and I'm anxious to get going."[16]

Allen got off to a typical fast start with three singles in six at bats in the opener in St. Louis, a 3-2 Phillies' win in 12 innings. The next night he belted a three-run homer in a 5-4 victory.

Back at Connie Mack Stadium for the home opener, 29,007 saw the Phillies beat Cincinnati 4-3, handing the loss to former teammate Jack Baldschun.

After the Reds' Jim Maloney shutout the Phillies 4-0, Joe Nuxhall, who took great pleasure in beating Gene Mauch, took the mound for the Reds. Nuxhall hadn't lost to the Phillies in nearly two years and hadn't lost a game in Philly since 1958.

In the first inning, Allen smashed a home run that hit off the sign board atop the left field stands to give Chris Short all the support he needed in a 3-1 win. "I just look for something I can hit," Allen said, "and when I get that 40 ounces on it, it's got to go."[17]

Allen had also improved defensively at third base. One of the reasons was six-time Gold Glove first baseman Bill White. "All I do when I get the ball," said Allen, "is let it go in the general direction of first base. I know White's going to get it."[18] Richie Allen was doing it all; hitting for average and power, playing defense and stealing bases, when it all came crashing down.

At Wrigley Field in Chicago, in the fourth inning of a 3-1 win over the Cubs, Allen tried to steal second base. As he beat the throw but slid past the base, he tried to grab the bag but wrenched his right arm and shoulder. He stayed in the game but when he went out in the field, he couldn't throw. Allen was taken to the hospital for x-rays and then flown to Philadelphia to be examined further. The injury was diagnosed as a dislocated shoulder and severe bruise and would sideline Allen for a month.

With Allen out, the Phillies got good pitching but couldn't score and Mauch tired of seeing the pitching go to waste. Although he still couldn't throw, Allen was "going nuts on the bench" and pestered Gene Mauch to somehow get him back in the lineup. He did make four pinch-hitting appearances and then Mauch put him in left field. Mauch told the shortstop that on a ball hit to Allen, he should run into the outfield and relay the ball back into the infield.

Realizing that Allen was playing hurt, rather than booing, fans cheered in appreciation. During a June homestand, he thanked them with a power display for the ages. In an 18-day stretch, Allen belted nine tape measure home runs.

He hit one in New York believed to be the longest home run in

Shea Stadium history. It sailed over the centerfield wall and hit about one-third of the way up on the batting screen, nearly 500 feet away.

Then, in the first game of a doubleheader at Connie Mack Stadium, against the Cubs, he hammered a drive into the enclosure that houses the batting cage in deep center field, a 460-foot blast.

The next night, he hit a 430-foot bomb off the top of the centerfield wall.

One night later against San Francisco, Allen jacked one into the upper stands in centerfield, 450 feet.

In the final game against the Giants, he put one on the left field roof.

Against the Cardinals, Allen lined a shot off the roof façade for another homer.

Five days later, at Crosley Field in Cincinnati, he cleared the center field side of the huge scoreboard in left center. Reds' centerfielder Vada Pinson watched it go out and said it was the hardest hit homer he'd ever seen at Crosley Field. Asked where he thought the ball landed, Pinson said, "Dayton."

The next night, Allen hit one completely over the high left field screen and the ball carried into the parking lot.

Besides the monstrous homers, Allen hit .333 and drove in 26 runs in 23 games. With Allen carrying the club on his broad shoulders, the Phillies were 14-8, in fourth place, four and a half games out of first.

"He's the best young ballplayer to come into the league in all the time I've been up (1956)," Bill White said. "Frank Robinson and Vada Pinson and a lot of good players have come up in that time, but he's the best. He hits a baseball like a golf ball. He can be as good as he wants to be."[19]

No manager had a better knowledge of the rule book than Gene Mauch. On July 4, Mauch was involved in a play for which he became famous. At Connie Mack Stadium, the Phillies and New York Mets were in the fifth inning of the first game of a double-header. Bill White lifted a high foul ball to the third base side of the field. The ball drifted toward the Phillies' dugout as Mets' catcher Jerry Grote gave chase. As Grote reached into the dugout to make the catch, Gene Mauch whacked him across the arms and the catcher dropped the ball.

Grote and Met manager Wes Westrum argued with plate umpire Bill Jackowski, claiming that White should be out because of Mauch's interference.

"A player goes into the dugout at his own risk," Jackowski explained. "It's like a player reaching into the stands for a ball-it's the position of the ball that counts."

The rule was explained in the booklet, "Instructions for Umpires" and the Official Playing Rules, which Gene Mauch had memorized.

"In one way," Mauch explained, "it's the same as going into the stands for a ball. If a fan reaches out onto the field and prevents a player from catching a ball, the umpire can call the batter out, but if the player reaches into the stands and is interfered with, it's just a foul ball. There's one difference between the stands and the dugout. A player can catch a ball as he's falling into the stands, but he can't jump into the stands and then make a catch. He can, however, walk or jump into a dugout and then catch a ball."

Mauch also liked to have fun with umpires. He went up to one ump and asked, "If I call you a horse's ass, are you throwing me out of the game?"

"You bet I'm throwing you out of the game," answered the ump.

"Well, what if I'm just thinking you're a horse's ass?" Mauch asked.

The umpire said, "Well, I can't throw you out for what you're thinking."

So, Mauch said, "Well, I think you're a horse's ass."

Richie Allen couldn't carry the club by himself. A notorious slow-starter, Bill White wasn't hitting and Johnny Callison was suffering through a 0 for 20 slump and power outage.

Gene in clubhouse with Richie Allen and Johnny Callison.

In late July, the Phillies began a road trip to Texas and the West Coast unlike any in club history. Because of an airlines strike, the travel was tortuous. On a turbulent flight from Philly to Houston, players got no sleep. Then, on their flights from Los Angeles to Pittsburgh by way of Dallas, Memphis, Nashville and New York, they had to wait four hours for a charter to arrive from Canada to finish the trip.

In Houston, the Phillies lost two out of three; in San Francisco, the same and in Los Angeles, they were swept three straight, with the Dodgers winning every game in their final at bat.

Gene Mauch fined Richie Allen for missing the curfew in San Francisco and Johnny Callison for not hustling. This came after a game against the Giants when Willie Mays' pop fly dropped in front of Callison in the first inning. Mauch benched both players for the final game of the series with the Phillies beating the Giants

8-0. Then, Callison told reporters he could no longer play for a manager who accused him of loafing and said the Phillies should trade him.

Mauch knew something was wrong with Callison. Thinking his star might have vision problems, Mauch had him take an eye exam in Los Angeles. Johnny Callison needed glasses.

Callison and Mauch apologized to each other. Wearing his new glasses, in the next eight games, Callison went 17 for 34, hit two home runs in one game and raised his average to .295. "I'm seeing the ball so well it scares me." Callison said.

But soon, Callison's numbers began to sink and so did the Phillies. After an eight-game hitting streak, Callison had just three singles in 24 at bats. His average dropped to .276 with just eleven homers and 55 RBI.

Bill White finally started to hit near the end of the season but it was too late. He wound up hitting.276 with 22 homers and 103 RBI

Despite missing a month of the season with injuries Richie Allen hit .317 with 40 homers and 110 RBI.

Chris Short went 20-10 and Jim Bunning 19-14 but the bullpen collapsed late in the season and the Phillies wound up a disappointing 87-75 in fourth place, a distant nineteen-and-a-half games out of first place.

Chapter Seventeen

The End is Near

Gene Mauch had been around long enough to notice the cracks in the foundation. A front office's vote of confidence was usually the kiss of death. Conflicts with star players like Johnny Callison, Richie Allen and Ray Culp spelled trouble. A disappointing fourth place finish didn't sit well with management. The hard to please Philly fans and ownership had seen improvement but demanded more. Gene Mauch had one year left on his contract. Phillies owner Bob Carpenter gave Mauch an ultimatum to win or lose the job he'd held longer than any Phillies manager in modern times. Was Mauch worried?

"Seven years ago, the Phillies were in last place and I was in the minor leagues," Mauch recalled. "Now the Phillies are fighting for first place and I'm here. Why should I worry?"[1]

Mauch's coaching staff was wiped out. Longtime friend and ally Cal McLish was reassigned from pitching coach to minor league pitching instructor. Peanuts Lowery, Mauch's longtime golfing buddy, had supposedly retired. Third base coach George Myatt was the only survivor.

Veteran minor league manager Larry Shepard replaced McLish, Don Hoak left a broadcasting job with the Pirates to coach first base and former Phils' catcher Andy Seminick became the bullpen coach. With a straight face, Gene Mauch said this was the best coaching staff he'd ever had.

With coaching changes and his contract set to expire at the end of 1967, it appeared Gene Mauch's job might be in jeopardy. But team owner Bob Carpenter ended the speculation, giving Mauch an extension through 1968.

Mauch had been the Phillies manager since 1960. Asked if he knew he was going to grow old in the job, Mauch said, "I grew old in one year," referring to 1961.[2]

Surprising to many, Gene Mauch said his 1967 club was the best he'd ever had. Mauch based his optimism on an outstanding pitching rotation, an improved bullpen and what he felt was the best defensive team he'd had in Philly.

With the Dodgers' Sandy Koufax having retired because of arm problems, Mauch felt he had the best starting pitching in baseball with Jim Bunning, Chris Short, Larry Jackson and Dick Ellsworth, acquired from the Cubs.

Despite Mauch's optimism, this club had major concerns. Bill White tore his Achilles tendon playing paddleball in the off season and had suffered a setback in spring training. Who would play first base? Former Oriole slugger Jim Gentile was brought in for a look-see but wasn't signed. Finally, Mauch handed the first baseman's glove to versatile Tony Taylor, a second baseman most of his career.

The bullpen, which had failed down the stretch the previous year, had been dismantled. Lefty Darold Knowles was traded to Washington for outfielder Don Lock. Veterans Dick Hall, Pedro Ramos and Ruben Gomez were in camp, trying to win jobs.

And Richie Allen held out again. As the Phillies went to spring training in Clearwater, Allen arm-wrestled with Phillies owner Bob Carpenter, reportedly seeking $100,000. Carpenter said, "I hope Allen will change his mind. We think his asking price is unreasonable and almost impossible."

In February, when Jim Bunning signed a contract for $80,000, becoming the highest-paid player in Phillies history, Richie Allen was soon to follow, signing a $75,000 contract in March.

In the season's opener at Chicago's Wrigley Field, former Phillie Ferguson Jenkins pitched a complete game and beat Jim Bunning and the Phillies 4-2.

In New York, with shortstop Dick Groat sidelined with a sore ankle, and Bill White unable to run, Mauch made out his lineup with White at first base and leading off, Tony Taylor at second base and Cookie Rojas at shortstop.

White came up against the Mets' Jack Fisher and hit a ground ball to second baseman Chuck Hiller. White started to run but slowed to a jog as Hiller easily threw him out. The Phillies went on to score two runs in the inning.

Why was the injured Bill White even in the lineup? Gene Mauch thought that White might be done, that this could be his last game. Out of respect for White, Mauch started him so he could at least make an appearance.

When the Phillies took the field, Taylor moved to first base, Rojas to second and Bobby Wine went in to play shortstop.

Later, with the Phillies trailing 6-3 in the seventh, pinch hitter Tito Francona, batting for the pitcher, walked and Wine, who was, in effect hitting tenth, was removed for pinch hitter Doug Clemens. So, Wine, who had grounded out and flied out in two previous at bats, twice was pinch hit for in the same game. "I made history," Wine said, "I'm the only regular to start a game on the bench."

With Dick Groat out for at least another week, Mauch probably would have used the maneuver again but concerned with White's condition, he didn't.

Although he occasionally pinch hit, White didn't start a game until May 29. Tony Taylor and the newly acquired Tito Francona filled in but the Phillies missed White's leadership, glove and clutch hitting.

With both Dick Groat and Bill White sidelined, the porous defense committed 17 errors in the first 13 games. The faulty fielding affected pitchers like Jim Bunning, who won only one of his first four decisions and reliever Dick Hall, a sinkerballer who induced ground balls.

A 9-8 loss in Atlanta infuriated Gene Mauch. The Phillies led 8-0, but the Braves began their comeback with five runs in the fifth. They tied the score in the eighth and then took advantage of poor defensive play by the Phils, to win it. The Phillies had blown the biggest lead they've lost since Gene Mauch took over the club and the skipper was furious.

Then, oddly, in May, they played eleven consecutive errorless games to tie a national league record. Still, the Phillies were just 5-6 during the streak.

As Dick Groat and Bill White returned, the Phillies suffered another crushing injury when pitcher Chris Short tore a ligament in his left knee in a pregame running drill. Short, a 20-game winner the year before, would be out six weeks.

In June, the Phillies traded catcher Bob Uecker to Atlanta for catcher-first baseman Gene Oliver. The Braves needed Uecker to catch their knuckleball pitcher Phil Niekro and the Phils needed a catcher who could hit since both Clay Dalrymple and Uecker were below .200. In addition to his teammates, the media would miss Uecker, one of the funniest and most popular players in baseball. "Gene Mauch was my favorite manager," said Uecker. "He said to me, 'Grab a bat and stop this rally'."

With a 29-32 record in late June, it became apparent the Phillies weren't contenders, so they sold shortstop Dick Groat to the Giants. With Groat out, rookie Gary Sutherland filled in impressively, and was given the fulltime job.

Gene Mauch loved Cookie Rojas' versatility. Rojas had played eight different positions for the Phillies. He had never pitched in a regular season game but had worked one scoreless inning in a spring training game.

Then, in a June home game against San Francisco, Mauch's pitching staff was shorthanded so he brought Rojas in to face the Giants in the 9th with the Phillies leading 12-3. Tom Haller singled and then Hal Lanier hit a routine groundball to third baseman Richie Allen, who made a bad throw for an error. Then Rojas got a grounder out of Tito Fuentes resulting in a force play at third. After Juan Marichal flied out, Rojas faced Willie Mays, who flied out to shallow right.

Bill White returned, but was never at full strength and hit just .250 with 8 homers and 33 RBI. Since White had a radio-TV job waiting for him, there were rumors that he might retire after the season.

Another disappointment was Richie Allen. Making a reported $75,000, the most ever by a fourth year player, Allen wasn't producing, was often late to the ballpark and sometimes missed pre-game practice altogether. After one incident, Mauch benched Allen for a game.

Allen returned to the lineup the next day and hit another tape-measure home run over the 32-foot high center field fence off the Cardinals' Nelson Briles in a 4-3 Phillies win.

As the team continued to play poorly, Mauch occasionally snapped. Houston lefthander Mike Cuellar was working on a one-hit shutout against the Phillies, leading 1-0 in the ninth inning.

From the dugout, Mauch had been riding Cuellar the whole game, trying to shake his concentration. In the ninth, the Astros pitcher decided he'd had enough of Mauch's lip and started toward the Phillies dugout, which is exactly what Mauch wanted. He figured a fight would get both of them thrown out of the game. At the very least, he would break the lefthander's concentration.

"He was calling me a very bad name," said Cuellar. "I no take that from anyone."[3] As Mauch charged out of the dugout, Houston third baseman Eddie Mathews bear-hugged him, preventing a fight. Both teams ran onto the field and order was restored quickly. The event seemed to rattle Cuellar who gave up a run, but he pitched all eleven innings, winning 2-1. After the game, he said he'd wanted "to punch Mauch in the nose."

Mauch replied, "All I was trying to do is win the game."[4]

An eight-game winning streak sparked Mauch's optimism. "Sure, we're 11 games out and the record says we can't do it," he said, "but you don't play baseball with a pencil. I know its August 8, but in the National League they don't settle things until the first week of October."

With injuries to key players, discipline problems, and erratic play, 1967 had already been a difficult year. Then, Richie Allen was seriously injured in a freak accident. Allen said that he had been pushing an old car up a hill, when his right hand broke through a headlight. Two tendons were cut below his last two fingers and the ulna nerve was severed. Doctors operated on him and would have to wait until the fingertip-to-shoulder cast was removed to find out if there was career-ending damage. Allen's shortened season produced a .306 batting average, 23 homers and 77 RBI.

In August at Crosley Field in Cincinnati, the Reds were playing their annual father-son game before they played the Phillies. Gene Mauch was watching from the dugout, when someone asked, "Do you have one of these games in Philadelphia?"

"No," answered Mauch. "They're afraid the fans will boo."[5]

The Phillies finished 1967 in fifth place with an 82-80 record, a major disappointment.

Finishing his eighth year as Philadelphia's manager, Gene Mauch tied a National League managerial record. Only one other manager in the modern history of the league had been with a club as long as Mauch and never won a pennant. That was Bill McKechnie of the Boston Braves who went 0-8 from 1930-37.

Phillies owner Bob Carpenter, G.M. John Quinn and Mauch attended baseball's winter meetings in Mexico City. A catcher and right handed hitting outfielder topped their shopping list. Uncertain about Richie Allen's return, they also looked for a third baseman and shortstop.

It appeared that 31-year-old Clay Dalrymple, the longtime catcher, was nearing the end of his career and Gene Oliver, acquired from the Braves, had been a disappointment.

While G.M. John Quinn scoured opposing rosters for available catchers, the Phillies sent utility man Gary Sutherland to the Instructional League to learn to catch. The 23-year-old former All-American at USC had filled in at both shortstop and left field in 1967. Gene Mauch reasoned that if nothing else, the versatile Sutherland could be used as an emergency catcher, who might even develop into a regular at the position.

The Phils brain trust came away from Mexico empty-handed. Nobody wanted to give up a catcher. Although the team made no trades, they laid the groundwork for future deals.

The Phillies lost two farm hands in the AAA draft when the Pirates took infielder Chuck Hiller and the Padres drafted catcher Jim Schaeffer from their San Diego farm club. To replace Schaeffer, the Phils drafted catcher Doc Edwards from the Astros' Oklahoma City team and also took pitcher Jerry Johnson from the Mets.

In mid-December, the team announced two trades in two days. They traded pitcher Dick Ellsworth and catcher Gene Oliver to the Red Sox for 26-year-old catcher Mike Ryan. Then, in a blockbuster, they sent their ace pitcher Jim Bunning, 36, to the Pirates for 24-year-old southpaw Woody Fryman and three minor leaguers–shortstop Don Money and pitchers Bill Laxton and Harold Clem. "That was a John Quinn special," said Bunning, "four players for one."

Jim Bunning had won 19 games three straight years in Philadelphia. He'd dropped to 17 wins in 1967, but lost five 1-0 games and another 2-0. But Bunning was 36 and reportedly seeking a contract approaching $100,000. He didn't fit into the Phillies future or budget.

In 2015, when I talked to Jim Bunning, he revealed something that nobody but he and Gene Mauch had known. "Twice, Gene came to me and personally asked me if it would be alright if he didn't select me for the All-Star Game when my record indicated I should be chosen. I'm not complaining," said Bunning, "because I was in nine All-Star games, started three of them and that would have made eleven but I knew what Gene wanted."

As always, Gene Mauch was looking for an edge, putting winning above individual honors. He told Bunning that he wanted him to start the Thursday after the All-Star Game but if he pitched for the National League, he wouldn't be able to pitch again until Saturday.

Bunning's new manager was his former Phils' pitching coach Larry Shepherd who had taken over as the Pirates' skipper. "He's one of the top five pitchers in the game," said an elated Shepherd. "I could not ask for a better Christmas present."[6]

In an unusual move, the Phillies replaced Shepherd with Al Widmar, who had been their pitching coach from 1962-64. The Phillies had removed Widmar following the Phillies' flop in 1964 but he had stayed with the organization as minor league pitching instructor.

Bunning returned to Philadelphia for the final two years of his career in 1970 and 1971. He was selected for the Baseball Hall of Fame by the Veterans Committee in 1996.

After retiring, Bunning got into politics in Kentucky. He was elected to the U.S. House of Representatives and served from 1987-99, then was elected to the U.S. Senate and served two terms.

With the trades, the Phillies' were returning to the philosophy they'd employed upon Gene Mauch's arrival, trading veterans for young players and trying to rebuild the team into a contender.

Mauch could now platoon catchers, the left-handed hitting Clay Dalrymple with the right-handed Ryan, and in the 20-year-old Money, the Phillies felt they had found their future shortstop. Although he'd never played above A ball, Money had hit .316 with 16 homers and 86 RBI at Raleigh and was named the Carolina League's MVP.

Gene Mauch admitted that the 1968 Phillies would be the "iffiest" team he'd managed. The "ifs" were Richie Allen, Bill White and Chris Short, all coming back from injuries.

The Phillies were optimistic about Allen playing again but didn't know if he'd fully regain strength in his right hand. If Allen couldn't play third base, Mauch thought about moving him to left-field or first base. If Allen played first, Bill White would be expendable.

At 34, Bill White was also making a comeback. Doctors told him the circulation in his ankle was almost back to normal and White planned to play at least one more year.

Richie Allen went to Florida early, thinking warm weather, exercise and therapy would get the numbness out of his injured hand. Driving to Clearwater, he spotted a batting cage and felt an urge to swing the bat. Allen had a leaded bat in the trunk of his Cadillac. He took off his jacket, put a quarter into the pitching machine and jumped into the cage to get his ten swings. At first, Allen swung and missed, then fouled off a few pitches but then as he loosened up, began to connect. "For me, it was a great moment," Allen said, "my hand was still numb but every time I hit the ball for distance, it was a thrill."[7] Allen stopped by the batting cages often and soon developed a fan club.

When Allen missed a workout, saying he had a touch of the flu, he disappeared for two days. Allen's wife called the club to say that Richie had flown back to Philadelphia to see his doctor. When Allen returned to Clearwater, he was reportedly fined and had a long talk with Gene Mauch.

The annual *Sporting News* poll of major league baseball writers picked Philadelphia to finish eighth in the National League.

Mauch felt his team would contend but didn't pick them to win the pennant. "If you put a gun to my head and tell me I have to pick somebody," Mauch said, "I'd say Cincinnati."

Although Mauch had shied away from predictions about his own team but at the end of spring training he said, "I know we can win 90 games. It's just a case of how many more. That's assuming of course that everybody stays healthy."

Twenty-year-old rookies, shortstop Don Money and outfielder Larry Hisle, surprised Mauch in spring training. Both played in

Class A ball in 1967 and figured they'd soon be sent to the minors. But with Bobby Wine and Tony González out with back problems, when the Phillies broke camp, Gene Mauch wanted to take a longer look at the kids.

Both rookies were in the starting lineup when the Phillies opened the 1968 season in Los Angeles. Larry Hisle and Don Money both got their first major league hits off Dodger lefty Claude Osteen. Hisle was two for three and Money one for three and drove in both Phillies runs. Lefty Chris Short was brilliant, pitching a two-hit shutout and striking out ten Dodgers in the 2-0 win. Richie Allen played left field and Bill White was at first base. Both went one-for-four.

Veteran Tony González wasn't happy about being benched for rookie Larry Hisle. "We must have a pretty good team," said González, "if we can afford to bench a .339 hitter (his 1967 average) just because a lefthander was pitching."[8]

Gene Mauch answered, "Larry Hisle is the best centerfielder I've ever had."

Hisle hit .364 in the three games he played and Money .231 in his six games. When the Phils recalled pitcher Larry Colton and infielder Roberto Pena, the rookies were sent to San Diego to play every day.

Cold weather made Richie Allen's hand ache and he had his poorest spring but during the team's first home stand, he finally started to hit. In a three game sweep of Houston he had two home runs, a double, triple, two singles and five RBI and raised his average over the .300 mark.

But Allen's discipline problems were getting worse. Driving to New York in his own car for game against the Mets, Allen showed up 20 minutes before game time. Allen had not asked for permission to drive from home and claimed he got stuck in a traffic jam. Gene Mauch benched him but used him as a pinch hitter in the eighth inning and he flied out. Allen was reportedly fined and before the game the next night, Mauch spent thirty minutes talking to Allen in the manager's office.

During a trip to Cincinnati, Mauch twice held afternoon work-outs before night games. Speaking at a luncheon, Bill White got a lot of laughs when he said, "I finally figured out why Gene is having these workouts. It's the only way he can be sure of getting Richie Allen to the ballpark in time for our games."

In May, Gene Mauch reached into his bag of tricks using a pinch hitter for a pinch hitter in a win over the Mets in New York. The first pinch hitter, John Briggs, had two strikes on him when Mauch sent right-handed hitting Ricardo Joseph up to hit for him. Joseph worked the pitcher for a walk, which figured in a five-run, elev-enth inning rally to give the Phils a 7-2 victory. Mauch said it was the first time he'd tried the move in the big leagues but had used it successfully when he managed the Minneapolis Millers.

Gene Mauch knew baseball's rules better than most umpires. In a game at Shea Stadium, Mauch made a pitching change in the sev-enth inning with the Mets leading 3-0. When reliever John Boozer was about to take his first warm-up pitch, plate umpire Ed Vargo shouted, "Ball one."

Mauch raced to home plate, yelling, "How could it be a ball? Booz-er is only warming up?"

An incredulous Mauch listened as Vargo explained a new rule. "Boozer went to his mouth and the rule says anytime a pitcher goes to his mouth when he's in the 18-foot circle, it's a ball."

So, Mauch told Boozer to go to his mouth again. "Ball two," shout-ed Vargo. Again, Mauch repeated his order and again Vargo said, "Ball three" and then threw Mauch and Boozer out of the game.

Mauch said he would protest, but National League President War-ren Giles called and told him not to, since the game's outcome wasn't affected. Giles told Mauch he was sending instructions to all the umpires that the rule did not apply when the ball is "dead," and that warm-up pitches occurred in a dead ball situation. So, Mauch was right.

In the mid-60's major league baseball was getting balls made in Haiti. "Some of them were soft, some had rips on the side," recalled Bobby Wine.

Gene Mauch suspected the ball were made by "some Haitian seamstress."

"One time, Jim Bunning was pitching and didn't like the ball, so he threw it in," said Bobby Wine. "Umpire Eddie Vargo threw the ball back to Bunning and said, 'We're not allowed to change balls. You've got to play with the ball you get."

But Bunning threw the ball in again and Vargo told the catcher to throw it back. This went on several times until Gene Mauch came to the mound. Mauch dropped the ball on the ground, stepped on it with his spikes, gave the ball back to Bunning and walked back to the dugout.

"The umpire said 'time. Let me see that ball,'" said Wine. He looked at it and it had a spike mark, so Bunning got a new baseball."

Gene Mauch would try anything including five man infields and was a pioneer in the use of the "double switch." A double switch is a substitution in which two or more players are substituted simultaneously and take places in the batting order different from those of whom they replaced.

"I was playing shortstop," recalled Wine, "and Gene came out to take out the pitcher. He told me I was out of the game, too.

"Why me?" Wine asked, "I didn't give up the home run. It was the first time I was involved in a double switch."

A back injury to Cookie Rojas forced Mauch to move Tony Taylor from third to second and bring Richie Allen in from left to third. In his first three games at third, Allen made three throwing errors but made up for them with his bat. In six games, Allen had ten hits in twenty at bats and hit four home runs.

His three-run homer was one of the longest hit in St. Louis' new Busch Stadium. The ball landed at the base of the batting cage beyond the center field fence, 450 feet away.

In Chicago, Allen left the second game of a doubleheader with a groin pull. Although Allen claimed he'd originally suffered the injury in spring training, Mauch and several players knew that Allen had suffered the injury riding horseback before the double-header.

The next night's game was rained out, but when Allen showed up late for the next game, Mauch sent him home. Allen was fined and didn't play again for a week except for pinch hitting once.

During this time, Allen didn't take part in pre-game practice for the first four days, but ran onto the field after the first half of the opening inning, spent part of the game in the bullpen, and was in street clothes before the game ended.

On June 10, Phillies owner Bob Carpenter had Richie Allen in his office for a one-hour conference. "We've gone over Allen's problems and resolved them," said Carpenter. "He said his groin injury had healed and he is now ready to play. I have talked to Gene Mauch, who is still in Los Angeles and informed him of the result of our meeting."[9]

Phillies' beat writer Alan Lewis wrote, "Allen has been repeatedly fined and disciplined for his violations of club rules over the past four years and has made it plain he wanted to get away from the Phillies, from Mauch, from Philadelphia and the segment of fans which has booed him unmercifully, mostly unfairly in the past."

Five days after Carpenter's meeting with Richie Allen, Gene Mauch was fired. With Mauch in Los Angeles with his wife who'd been hospitalized, the timing of the Phillies' decision seemed cruel.

The Phillies claimed that Mauch's differences with Allen weren't the only reason he was fired. Mauch was in the last year of his contract and a source said he'd demanded the Phillies make a decision on his status for 1969. If they didn't want him, he wanted to be free to negotiate with the expansion teams in Seattle or San Diego or with other clubs who might be interested.

Mauch was replaced as manager by Bob Skinner, manager of the Phillies Triple A team in San Diego. Asked about Richie Allen, Skinner said, "Richie Allen is a tremendous player. There are many managers in the National League who would like to have him and Bob Skinner is one of them."[10]

Chapter Eighteen

Les Expos de'Montreal

Gene Mauch wasn't unemployed for long. With the birth of expansion teams in Montreal and San Diego, Mauch was in demand. Jim Fanning, his former teammate with the Los Angeles Angels, was General Manager of the Montreal Expos. "Gene Mauch is the perfect guy for us," Fanning told Expos President John McHale. "He's rigid and tough and knows how to handle young players. I don't know of anyone else who could be our manager."

So, Mauch signed a two-year contract to become the Expos' first manager. When the media asked about Richie Allen, Mauch said little but when a reporter wondered if he'd like to have Allen playing for him in bilingual Montreal, Mauch couldn't resist. "Sure, we'll give him a chance to get booed in English and French."

Montreal fans were familiar with Gene Mauch. In 1958 he had piloted his Minneapolis Millers to a four-game sweep of the Montreal Royals in the Junior World Series. Mauch had also played for the Royals in 1943 and 1944.

Fanning and McHale hired Mauch quickly because they wanted him involved in the player draft in October. As they discussed players, Fanning was amazed by Mauch's photographic mind, "He had an absolute retentive memory. He brought up players from the PCL we knew. He had a mental scouting report on every one. I couldn't even remember who they were."

With little time before the October player draft, Fanning hired experienced scouts to watch the minor leagues, what remained of the major league season and the playoffs and World Series. He and Mauch agreed that "speed, hustle and relief pitching" topped their shopping list.

On October 14, 1968, the Montreal Expos and San Diego Padres made their draft picks. The Padres selected San Francisco Giants' outfielder Ollie Brown as the first pick in the draft. The Expos top picks were:

Manny Mota	outfielder	Pittsburgh Pirates
Mack Jones	outfielder	Cincinnati Reds
John Bateman	catcher	Houston Astros
Gary Sutherland	infielder	Philadelphia Phillies
Jack Billingham	pitcher	Los Angeles Dodgers
Donn Clendenon	outfielder	Pittsburgh Pirates
Jesús Alou	outfielder	San Francisco Giants
Mike Wegener	pitcher	Philadelphia Phillies
Skip Gunn	outfielder	Atlanta Braves
Bill Stoneman	pitcher	Chicago Cubs
Maury Wills	infielder	Pittsburgh Pirates
Larry Jackson	pitcher	Philadelphia Phillies
Bob Reynolds	pitcher	San Francisco Giants
Dan McGinn	pitcher	Cincinnati Reds

Others selected include: Mudcat Grant, Carl Morton, Larry Jaster, Ernie McAnally, Coco LaBoy, Jim Fairey, John Bocabella, and Jimmy Williams

The Expos paid $333,333 each for thirty players in the expansion draft. With emphasis on pitching, the Expos grabbed a number of prospects who became quality big league hurlers.

Gene with Ted Williams.

Gene Mauch liked to arrive at the park early, throw on his base-ball underwear and shower shoes and sit down the right field line, seemingly working on his tan. His eyes scoured the field, study-ing his opponent, searching for any weakness he could take ad-vantage of. Before a game in Houston, Mauch watched the Colt 45's young slugger Rusty Staub in the batting cage. When Staub finished, he and Mauch said hello and then the Phillies' manager started talking about Houston's hard-throwing young right-hander Don Wilson, who'd just shutout the Dodgers. "Wilson will never enter the ninth inning against me," boasted Mauch. "If he ever completes a game against my club, I'll buy you a $400 suit."

"Son of a bitch," Staub thought to himself. *"He's got Wilson's pitches. He knows what he's going to throw and that's why he's making such a bold statement."*

Staub watched Wilson throw and saw he was tipping off his pitches. Before Wilson's next start against Mauch's team, Staub counseled him. "The first inning," said Staub, "is for setting hitters up. Show them a slow curve and a fastball. Let them think they know what's coming. Then, the next time, undress the first motherfucker, then undress another motherfucker. When they come up late in the game, hold your curveball like you hold your fastball and they'll fall right on their asses." Wilson pitched a shutout against Mauch's Phillies.

"I bought a black mohair suit," said Staub, as he approached Mauch around the batting cage. "You don't have to pay for this suit if you don't want to," said Staub.

Mauch said nothing and later a $400 check arrived in Staub's locker. It was the start of a great relationship.

After a game, Gene Mauch and several Houston execs were standing outside the ballpark waiting for taxis. Mauch knew the Colt 45's wanted outfielder Jesús Alou, whom the Expos had drafted from the Giants. After throwing a few names back and forth, Mauch said, "I'll give you Donn Clendenon and Alou if you give me that Staub guy."

Shortly after the conversation, the Expos traded Clendenon and Alou for Rusty Staub. "Beautiful, beautiful, beautiful," said Gene Mauch when he heard the deal had been completed. Mauch predicted Staub would lead the league in batting twice in the next five years.

G.M. Jim Fanning welcomes Rusty Staub to Montreal. Credit: Rusty Staub

But the deal hit a snag when Clendenon announced his retirement which could have sent Staub back to Houston. But when Staub made it known that he would retire if he wasn't allowed to join Montreal, Commissioner Bowie Kuhn ruled that Staub would remain the property of the Expos.

Mauch had acquired the nickname "The Little General," but no one said it to his face. "I think the players had a fear of Gene Mauch," said Jim Fanning. "He had some rules and they walked quietly around him."

Mauch's rules included no alcohol allowed on planes or team buses. That was a problem for Rusty Staub. Staub was terrified of flying and before flights would hit the airport bar and self-medicate with shots of vodka. Staub needed to talk with his manager.

"General," Staub began. Before he could say another word, Mauch stopped him with an icy stare and slowly enunciating each word, he said, "Rusty, there is no r-a-l on my name. My name is Gene."

"Well then skipper, how much is the fine?" Staub asked.

"$100," answered Mauch.

So Staub went home that night, calculated that there were 32 road trips and the next day approached Mauch. "Skipper, here's a check for $3,200," said Staub. "I bust my ass, you've got a great player in me and I'm going to prove it. But there's no way I'm going to get on planes without drinking."

Mauch looked at Staub and said, "Take this check and get out of my office. Don't ever embarrass me."

So, on every trip, Staub filled two empty diet coke cans with crushed ice and vodka. He had one in the clubhouse and another on the bus and had a smooth flight.

Rusty Staub, Maury Wills, and Bob Bailey, purchased from the Dodgers, were the team's foundation.

Gene Mauch knew that Rusty Staub had his best years while playing the outfield so Mauch moved him from first base to right field.

Wills, the longtime Dodger shortstop, had played third base for two years with Pittsburgh. Mauch doubted the 36-year-old could play regularly at shortstop but Wills convinced him he could and he said he wanted to earn his $80,000 salary.

Mauch had seen former Pirates bonus baby Bob Bailey have some good years with the Dodgers and felt he had plenty left in the tank.

15,000 fans gathered in downtown Montreal to give the Expos a sendoff to New York for the franchise's first game. "You're all beautiful," Gene Mauch told the crowd. "We're playing pretty well now, but for you people, we'll play better." As the players were introduced, Maury Wills, Rusty Staub, and opening day starter Mudcat Grant got the biggest ovations.

On April 8, 1969, the Montreal Expos began their inaugural season at Shea Stadium against the Mets. Montreal Mayor Jean Drapeau threw out the first ball and a Canadian color guard took part in the flag raising ceremonies. Canadian opera star Maureen Forrester sang the Canadian national anthem, half in French and half in English. "It's the damndest opening day I've ever seen," said Gene Mauch.

G.M. Jim Fanning remembered the first game, "Gene and the players wore those beautiful new uniforms and tri-colored caps, Gene walked past the Mets dugout. There were probably fifteen guys in there and they're kidding Mauch about the cap. Somebody yelled, 'Put a propeller on that thing.' Mauch stopped, looked into the dugout and told the Mets, 'I saw this club when you were a lot funnier than this cap will ever be. And not only that, I've got some pitchers who don't know where the ball is going today.' Now, that's a threat."

Mauch's opening day lineup included Bob Bailey at first base, Gary Sutherland at second, Maury Wills at shortstop, and Coco Laboy at third with Mack Jones, Don Hahn and Rusty Staub in the outfield. John Bateman was the catcher and Jim "Mudcat" Grant was the pitcher.

Pitcher Dan McGinn hit the first home run in Expos' history in the fourth inning but also threw the first wild pitch and committed the first balk. First baseman Bob Bailey drove in the team's first runs with a first inning double and Coco Laboy had a game-winning three-run homer off Toronto native Ron Taylor as the Expos won 11-10.

While the Expos opened the season on the road, construction crews worked feverishly, preparing Jarry Park Stadium for the home opener. Four days before the game, the Expos feared the park wouldn't be ready but nearly 400 workers toiled around the clock.

On opening day, the gates opened late because workers, including G.M. Jim Fanning, had to put 6,000 temporary folding chairs in place. The weather was also a concern but the baseball gods cooperated with a clear, 64 degree day in Montreal.

April 14, 1969 was another historic day as the Expos won their home opener, 8-7 over the St. Louis Cardinals before 29,184 fans.

Mack Jones hit a three-run homer in the first inning and added a two-run triple in the second. Fans cheered him every time he went out to play left field and on every fly ball he caught. He became an instant hero and left field became known as "Jonesville."

The field was a quagmire and the Cardinals complained. "I pray I don't get killed out there," said Curt Flood. "It's unbelievable. The infield was soft and it was tough to go from first to third. I've played on some bad diamonds but this was the worst."[1]

Gene Mauch needled Flood, "The commissioner should turn Flood upside down and shake a little money out of his pocket. It's not in the best interest of baseball to say what he did, write it or print it in a newspaper."[2]

The problems developed because frost arose making the field soft and lumpy. When the frost began to thaw underground, the mound and the area behind home plate sank a few inches but were rebuilt quickly.

On April 17, Gene Mauch returned to Philadelphia for the first time since being fired as Phillies manager. Mauch received a warm greeting from the crowd and no one booed when he had an argument with home plate umpire Tom Gorman.

Expos' pitcher Bill Stoneman made sure the Little General's return was triumphant. In only the ninth game in franchise history, Stoneman pitched a no-hitter. It was also the first complete game of "Stoney's" career. Throwing mostly fastballs, curves and a few changeups, he struck out eight and walked five.

"I'm happy for Gene," the pitcher said. "It was great to give Mauch a home-coming like this."[3] Rusty Staub provided most of the offense with a homer, three doubles and three RBI.

Staub quickly became the most popular player in Expos' history. The handsome redhead ingratiated himself with the fans, 85% of whom spoke French, by learning to speak the language and

Montreal Gazette writer Teddy Blackman dubbed him "Le Grand Orange", which meant "The Big Orange."

Staub was besieged by autograph seekers, made public appearances and spoke to luncheons. His French became good enough that he often appeared on French-language television and did pregame shows with the team's French-network broadcasters. He was a spokesman for Orange Crush and there were even Rusty Staub watches with his face on the front.

"You want to know the best part?" Staub said. "The best part was knowing how much Gene Mauch wanted me. He's the best."

With Mauch's guidance, Staub changed from a line-drive hitter to a slugger, hitting .302 with 29 home runs and 79 RBI.

It was great to be young and a Montreal Expo until May 13 at Jarry Park when starter Mike Wegener couldn't get anybody out, walking the first three Houston batters in a 10-3 loss. The next day, Houston won 3-1 despite a complete game by Mudcat Grant, the only complete game the Expos had for a month.

Hitters pounded Expos' starters, forcing Gene Mauch to go to his bullpen early and often. The Expos lost, lost again, lost one more time and continued to lose, not tasting victory for a month.

Their 5-3 loss to the Dodgers was their eleventh straight, the longest losing streak in the majors that year. "They don't want a lot," Gene Mauch said of the Expos' fans. "They just want a little. That's about what we're giving them, too."[4]

While losses piled up, G.M. Jim Fanning scoured the major leagues for an available pitcher or two or three. Nothing. There were even rumors that the team would trade Maury Wills back to the Dodgers for pitching.

The Expos loss to the other expansion team, San Diego, was their sixteenth straight, one short of the major league record for expansion teams.

Then, Maury Wills called G.M. Jim Fanning and asked to be placed on the voluntarily retired list.

With two more losses to San Francisco, the Expos had dropped eighteen straight, a new record for major league expansion teams.

With the Expos in Vancouver for an exhibition game against their Triple A team, Maury Wills again called Fanning and said he'd changed his mind and was unretiring. "I don't know why he quit," said Gene Mauch, "and I don't know why he's coming back. But I know this-we're better off with him than without him."[5]

The Expos even lost the exhibition to the Vancouver Mounties 5-3 before 5,906 at Vancouver's Capilano Stadium. The next day, Maury Wills flew to Los Angeles to rejoin the team as they began a long road trip.

With eighteen straight losses, the Expos were within five losses of Gene Mauch's 1961 Phillies team, which lost a record twenty-three straight.

In Los Angeles, the Dodgers beat them twice. Twenty straight.

Desperate, Gene Mauch, decided to leave the dugout and coach third base. "I was the best third base coach I ever saw when I was in the minors," reasoned Mauch. "If I thought it would help, I'd coach both first and third at the same time."

The real reason he went to the third base coaching box was to distract Dodger starter Bill Singer, whom Mauch suspected threw spitters. Mauch told the umpires his plan and made Singer aware of his presence. Singer looked at Mauch every time he went into his windup. Singer gave up a two-run homer to Rusty Staub and a solo shot by Mack Jones as the Expos ended the 20-game losing streak with a 4-3 win over the Dodgers.

"I feel like I've shaken a bad habit," Mauch said. "I don't know how much more I could have stood. I'm getting older you know."

A week after Maury Wills un-retired, the Expos traded him to his former club, Los Angeles Dodgers as part of a three team deal. The Dodgers sent outfielder Ron Fairly and infielder Paul Popovich to Montreal for Wills and Manny Mota. The Expos then sent Popovich to the Chicago Cubs for outfielder Adolfo Phillips and pitcher Jack Lamabe.

With Maury Wills gone, Bobby Wine took over at shortstop. Mauch and Wine had been together in Philadelphia. He was a gifted fielder who knew how to play Mauch's "Little Ball." He could bunt, hit behind the runner, work the count, whatever it took to win. At 31, Wine was still playing despite two serious injuries, one that required spinal surgery.

Wine was one of Mauch's favorites and the player worshipped his manager. "You've got to give yourself completely to Gene," Wine said. "Trust in him, have complete faith that what he wants will be good for the team and good for you. He'll never let you down."[6] Amen.

In late June, after the Philadelphia Phillies swept a four game series in Montreal, Gene Mauch was in a dark mood as the Chicago Cubs came to town. Mauch vented, needling Cubs third baseman Ron Santo.

The Cubs accused Mauch of using foul language and when Santo had enough, he charged the Montreal dugout trying to get to Mauch. Both benches emptied near the third baseline and Mauch and Santo had to be restrained.

"I didn't say a word to Santo," Mauch said, with a straight face. "I was just talking to my catcher, saying 'Hey" and atta boy.'"[7]

But Mauch got the Cubs thinking about him, rather than the game, a tactic he'd learned from his first big league manager, Leo Durocher, now the Cubs' manager.

"As long as that little genius manages your team," said an angry Durocher "it'll finish last."[8]

The 1969 Montreal Expos did finish last with a 52-110 record, 48 games behind the eventual World Series Champions, the New York Mets.

After lots of therapeutic golf in the desert, Mauch returned to Montreal in the winter, tanned and rested, to meet with the media and predicted, "We should win at least 70 games this season." "70 in 70" became the team's mantra.

Mauch's coaching staff underwent major changes. Hours after deciding to accept Mauch's offer to become the Expos' first base coach, Don Hoak died of a heart attack. Deeply saddened by the loss of his friend, Mauch then chose Jimmy Bragan, Bobby Bragan's younger brother. Mauch's friend and golfing buddy Peanuts Lowery was homesick for California and resigned. He was replaced by another of Mauch's cronies, former Cincinnati manager Dave Bristol. Pitching coach Cal McLish and bullpen coach Jerry Zimmerman returned.

The Expos also hired former Dodger star Don Drysdale as a TV analyst and spring training pitching instructor to help Cal McLish. Once friendly adversaries, Drysdale and Mauch eventually became best friends.

Gene Mauch (4) and his coaches.

Like his second year in Philadelphia, the Expos 1970 spring training was boot camp. Disappointed with his players' lack of fundamentals, Mauch went back to basics. "We may not even take batting practice in the morning," said Mauch. "So much time was wasted in the regular season on things that should have been done in Florida. We'll get it all straightened out in spring training."

Mauch wanted his team in better shape and set maximum weights for each man. If a player came to spring training overweight, he was fined $100 for each pound over the designated weight. When 6'5" Steve Renko reported at a svelte 226, Mauch said, "He looks like a Greek God."[9]

Despite hard work in spring training, the Expos got off to a horrible start, losing their first four games and ten of their first eleven. An 11-game losing streak put the Expos at 16-33. At this rate, Gene Mauch's team would be hard-pressed to reach their manager's goal of 70 wins.

Suddenly, the Expos found a winning formula. Strong pitching, solid defense and timely hitting propelled the Expos to a 16-11 record over the next month. Bad weather and the team's poor play had kept the attendance low, but now with their Expos winning, fans flooded Jarry Park. More than 4,000 fans were turned away for one game and 2,000 for another.

On August 1 at Jarry Park, Rusty Staub had his greatest day as an Expo. Le Grand Orange hit four home runs, two in each game, in a doubleheader sweep of the Dodgers. If the Dodgers' Willie Davis hadn't made a leaping catch in centerfield, Staub would have had five home runs. The lefty-swinging Staub hit three off left-handed pitchers, made three spectacular catches, threw out a runner and triggered a double steal. "It was Rusty's Day," said Staub, "but I'm happy too for the General because he's from that neck of the woods and loves to beat the Dodgers."

A big reason for the team's improvement was rookie righthander Carl Morton, a converted outfielder, drafted from the Braves. For some reason, Morton and Gene Mauch butted heads. Morton wasn't shy about telling people that the reason for his success was renewed self-confidence, resulting from his reading a best-selling book, *"Psycho Cybernetics,"* by Maxwell Maltz. Morton felt the book helped him eradicate negative thoughts. He carried it with him constantly, reading and rereading passages and often studied 100 pages the day before each start.

Mauch wasn't into new age thinking and when writers asked about Morton's pitching, any questions about *Psycho Cybernetics*, elicited a comment of "horseshit."

Mauch also didn't permit facial hair and when Morton began growing a beard before the pitcher's last start in Philadelphia, Mauch said, "Carl, you have one more start left this season. Would you like to have it?"

"Well, yeah, of course I want it," answered Morton.

"You shave those whiskers off and you can have it," said Mauch.

Morton shaved and wound up the season with an 18-11 record, a 3.60, four shutouts, and was named National League Rookie of the Year.

The Expos finished the season 73-89. Despite their terrible start, with a strong second half, they met Gene Mauch's "70 in '70" goal.

In January, Mauch returned to Montreal for his annual visit with the media and said, "We'll make a run at 81 in '71."

The Expos got off to a strong start, winning seven of eight in a 12-day stretch in April. "Just superb baseball," said Gene Mauch. "They're doing what they're supposed to do. When that happens, the breaks fall your way, too."

Spectacular defense, timely hitting and consistent pitching had the Expos in first place. Bill Stoneman, Carl Morton and Steve Renko were either completing games or working into the late innings where they could hand the ball to relievers Claude Raymond and Mike Marshall.

Marshall had come to the Expos in a June, 1970 trade. G.M. Jim Fanning said, "John Mullen, who I used to work with, was assistant G.M. with Houston. He called me one day and said Mike Marshall was available. I said, 'I don't know Mike Marshall from a load of hay.'"

"All you gotta do is give me a live body and you've got him," answered Mullen.

So, the Expos sent outfielder Don Bosch to Houston, acquiring Marshall, whom they sent to their AAA team in Winnipeg. Clyde McCullough was the Winnipeg manager and told Fanning, "I don't know where you got this guy, but he's got the best screwball I've ever seen. Jim, you will be amazed when you see it. You can't hit it."

Because of scheduling conflicts, Winnipeg played some games in Montreal and Fanning saw Marshall pitch. Blown away by Marshall's talent, the G.M. told Gene Mauch that he'd just seen the best pitcher he'd looked at in years. "Gene, the guys got a screwball that's unbelievable. Hitters absolutely cannot hit it."

"I don't want this S.O.B.," said Mauch, "I don't want him on this club."

"Mauch must have got some bad information about Marshall," said Fanning, "and it took a long time for him to warm up to Mike but once we got him on the big league club he and Gene became very close. Many times, I saw Gene and Mike playing catch in the outfield. It became almost like a father-son relationship."

Unlike previous managers, Gene Mauch understood Marshall. "I don't argue with Mike Marshall," Mauch said. "He is extremely intelligent and he's thinking all the time. He knows what he's doing better than anyone else."

After a fast start, the Expos hit a stretch of bad road, going 9-18 in May and 11-21 in June. Morton, Renko and Stoneman pitched well but the other starters were 1-8.

After piling up nine early saves, Mike Marshall suddenly was hit hard and was booed by the Expos suddenly-not-so-faithful. Even Rusty Staub got booed after committing six errors in a three day period. A 1-10 home stand in late June, made the booing even louder.

In late August, the Expos finally caught fire, winning eight in a row as Ron Hunt, the team's second baseman and leadoff hitter, sparked the club. Hunt wasn't afraid to "take one for the team." In his three previous years with San Francisco, Hunt was hit by pitches 25, 25 and 26 times. In 1971, he was plunked a record 50 times and had an on base percentage over .400 "My ability isn't that great," explained Hunt. "When you lack something, you make up for it in other ways. I won't give that ground and if it helps get me on base more often, that's great. But I don't like it."[10]

Hunt put on an amazing show one day in spring training. Hunt was hit three times by the pitching machine and then by Steve Renko and Gene Mauch in batting practice. "I'm just getting ready for the regular season," joked Hunt.

"Ron Hunt is my kind of player," Mauch said often. "I don't think I've enjoyed watching any player in my 30 years' association with the game as much as I do watching Hunt."[11]

"Gene is my kind of manager," Hunt said. "He is tough. He won't give you a phony pat on the behind if you goof and tell you things will work out. He'll acknowledge when you're doing something well and you appreciate it because you know he only says it when he means it."[12]

Montreal went 14-11 in August as the big three pitched well and rookie Ernie McAnally solidified the fourth spot in the rotation. Mike Marshall survived a six-week funk and regained his effectiveness. Mauch's emphasis on fundamentals paid off with superb defense and Rusty Staub overcame a wrist injury and was punishing the baseball.

In a month, Staub hit safely in 27 of 31 games, hitting .405 with nine home runs and 35 runs batted in. The Expos won 20 of 31 games during Staub's hot streak.

The Expos finished the 1970 season against the Phillies in the final game in Philadelphia's Connie Mack Stadium. The old park was going to be torn down so many of the 31,822 fans showed up wearing tool belts to help them remove souvenirs from the last game. Bobby Wine had spent his entire big league career playing for Gene Mauch in Philadelphia and Montreal. The Expos' shortstop came up with the Phils leading 1-0 with one out in the ninth and a runner at first base. "Like a dope, I hit a double to tie the score," said Wine. Like everyone else, he just wanted the game to be over.

"People were going nuts," remembered Wine. "They brought tools in and they ripped seats out of the concrete, they were fighting and knocking people over, all kinds of crazy things. During the game, people were jumping out of the stands and getting hunks of grass. After the game, they even tried to steal home plate."

In the tenth, Oscar Gamble singled in the winning run as the Phillies won 2-1, and "Everyone just ran to the clubhouse because it was so crazy," said Wine.

Montreal finished with 71 wins, ten short of Mauch's goal of 81 and two less than the 73 wins the year before. Still, Montreal owner Charles Bronfman, John McHale, and Jim Fanning gave Gene Mauch a two-year contract extension. "If I was in your position," Mauch deadpanned to his bosses, "I would have done exactly the same thing."[13]

By now, Gene Mauch's winter predictions had become ritual. After "We're going for 70 in '70" and "We'll make a run at 81 in '71," Mauch's prediction was "What we didn't get done in '71-we'll do in '72."

On April 1, 1972, during spring training, major league players went on strike. During the work stoppage, Rusty Staub was sitting in his plush Montreal apartment at Three Westmount Square. Staub knew that Expos' President John McHale had just moved into the building. When he got a call asking him to come to McHale's apartment. Staub figured McHale wanted to talk about the strike, but when he saw not only McHale but General Manager Jim Fanning and Manager Gene Mauch, his stomach dropped.

They told Staub that he had been traded to the New York Mets for three young players: shortstop Tim Foli, 20; switch-hitting outfielder Ken Singleton, 24; and left-handed hitting first baseman Mike Jorgensen, 23.

"That was a tough day," recalled Staub. The first thing he did was call his mom and dad in New Orleans and told them, "This is going to be a great thing for me but it hurts me to leave Montreal. I'm going to miss Gene Mauch very much. He helped me to become a better man and a better player."

Although Mauch thought the trade helped his team, he would miss Staub. He respected how hard Staub played and the two had become friends.

Because of the players' strike, the Expos first two games with the Cubs were cancelled and they began the season in St. Louis. The new kids jumped right in. In his first Expos' at bat, Mike Jorgensen, hit a towering two-run homer and drove in another run with a sacrifice fly, driving in all the runs in a 3-2 win as Bill Stoneman pitched a complete game five-hitter.

In game two, the Expos rallied for two runs in the ninth to win again 3-2. The 20-year-old shortstop Tim Foli made two sensational plays to seal the win.

In their home opener, the Expos faced Rusty Staub and the New York Mets. An overflow crowd of 29,102 packed 28,000 seat Jarry Park. When Staub stepped onto the field, fans cheered. When he was introduced, he got a standing ovation. Fans cheered Staub in his first at bat but when he singled, there were a few scattered boos, which got louder with each at bat. Staub went one-for-four but Montreal won 7-2. After the game, he said, "I enjoyed every minute I played in Montreal and I appreciated the way they welcomed me. But once the game started, they were for their club and I'm a Met. They reacted as they should."

The Expos won their first five games and were 13-11 by mid-May. Then came what Mauch called, "one black week." On one road trip, they lost all eight games, four to the Mets and four to the Pirates.

The starting pitching fell apart. The Expos didn't have a single complete game during this stretch with Bill Stoneman, Carl Morton and Ernie McAnally each losing twice. After that, Montreal just couldn't generate momentum and didn't have any win streaks longer than three games.

"It was the toughest thing I've had to do as a manager," Gene Mauch said in July when the Expos released his longtime favorite Bobby Wine. With a younger shortstop Tim Foli playing so well, Wine was expendable. "Bobby Wine has been my shortstop for 11 years. He has probably given me as many thrills as anyone I have ever managed," said Mauch. Mauch offered Wine a coaching job with the team, but he returned to Philadelphia to accept a similar job with the Phillies.

Gene Mauch saw himself in the fiery shortstop, Tim Foli. The similarities were astonishing. Like Mauch, Foli was from Southern California and played basketball and football in high school. Physically, Mauch and Foli were about the same size with limited major league ability, and emotionally both were intense and combative.

"Gene was my father of baseball," said Foli. "He taught me the intricacies of the game, every aspect of it. Not just my position, but the whole game. I learned everybody's job and responsibility and what they had to do."

In the fourth inning of a game in Philadelphia, Ernie McAnally hit the Phils' Joe Lis. "It was intentional, "said Phillies' starter Steve Carlton. "That's Mauch's style of baseball."[14]

In the bottom of the fourth, Carlton retaliated, hitting Tim Foli in the back of the head, knocking him groggy. As Foli staggered toward Carlton, Mauch shot out of the dugout, charged Carlton and threw a roundhouse right that glanced off the pitcher's shoulder. Both benches emptied. Mauch wound up on the bottom of the pile. Phillies Jim Nash punched him in the back of the neck and Roger Freed and Don Money also landed some blows.

"Yes, I threw at him," admitted Carlton. "I didn't mean to hit him in the head. It's obvious that you have to retaliate in that situation and I did. I'm not ashamed of it."[15]

In the fifth inning, former Expo John Bateman homered off McAnally for the only run in the game. With Carlton up next, McAnally threw his second pitch behind Carlton and was ejected. Mauch, McAnally and Carlton were all fined although Carlton remained in the game and pitched a four-hitter, beating the Expos 1-0.

"When Gene Mauch tackled Steve Carlton, that was too much for me," recalled Mauch's boss, Jim Fanning. "I don't think I've ever told this story before, but after the game, Gene was hurting. We were leaving on a road trip and I told the traveling secretary, 'I gotta take Mauch to the hospital and I'll see you at the airport.' So, we whisked Mauch away from the clubhouse and had him looked at by doctors at our hospital. He got knocked around pretty good but the injuries weren't serious and I took him to the airport."

Bruised and so stiff he could hardly walk, Mauch spent most of the next day in the whirlpool.

"I got pounded on pretty good," Mauch said. "Probably a manager has no business going out there swinging at someone, but sometimes a switch goes off and you do something you shouldn't. When Carlton hit Foli, I just went blind. I know it wasn't the smartest thing in the world to do, but if I thought someone hit one of my players, I might get pounded on again."

In the first game of a doubleheader in Montreal, Tim Foli was ejected by umpire Bruce Froemming. Between games, Froemming told fellow ump Augie Donatelli, "Augie, you're the crew chief. You've got to control Foli."

When Gene Mauch came to home plate to present the lineup card, Donatelli told him, "Gene, if I see Foli move his lips, he's gone."

"Augie," Mauch said, "You don't understand. He's just a high strung competitor."

Donatelli replied, "I'm not a doctor, I'm an umpire." Mauch joined the umpires in a hearty laugh.[16]

Tim Foli was Gene Mauch's protégé and absorbed every word his mentor spoke. "In Montreal, we were all middle of the road players," explained Tim Foli. "We had to find the edge and that's what Gene was good at. Gene knew that in the long run, talent wins. You can't beat talent. It just surfaces and beats your brains out. But you can win a game sometimes because you are smarter. You find a way. It's not always the team with the best talent that wins."

Gene Mauch wanted to look and act like a tough guy. With his penetrating stare, terse speech and cigarette smoke billowing out of the dugout, Mauch was indeed the Little General. Even though he loved his players, he didn't want them to see any sign of weakness, no crack in the crusty exterior, no sincere smile. This was war, militaristic and Mauch *was* the General. There was only one goal: to win.

Not many people knew that Mauch was a softie at heart, a deeply caring man, who loved those around him and did everything he could to help them. As much as he wanted to hug a player, he held back. That approach wouldn't work. He had to be tough, authoritative, a father figure, and someone to fear.

The softer side of the Little General.

His family knew he was different. His sister Jolene and her husband Roy Smalley often spent time with Gene and Nina Lee. One night in Montreal, they all went out for dinner, had a few cocktails and were laughing and joking as they returned to the team hotel.

When Mauch saw some of his players sitting in the lobby, the smile disappeared from his face as he turned to his sister and said, "If you're not careful, you're going to ruin my image."

At Wrigley Field in Chicago, Cubs righthander Milt Pappas beat the Expos for his 200th career victory. When Gene Mauch and most of the Expos arrived at the Cubs' clubhouse door, Pappas must have thought they'd come to congratulate him. Hardly. Mauch was angry, claiming Cub outfielder José Cardenal had called him an obscene two-word name during the game. When Cubs' manager Whitey Lockman came to the door, Mauch yelled, "Nobody is going to call me that and walk away from me. The next time, I won't wait until the end of the game."[17]

On a frigid October night in Montreal, Bill Stoneman pitched his second no-hitter, blanking the New York Mets 7-0. Stoneman's teammates mobbed him, John McHale and Jim Fanning ran onto the field and Stoneman's wife Diane joined the celebration, giving her husband a kiss. Then, Stoneman took a victory lap in the buggy which takes relievers to the mound.

Ironically, this was the last complete game of Bill Stoneman's career. He is the only pitcher in major league history to throw no-hitters in his first and last career complete games.

Although the Expos lost the final game of the season at home to the Mets, 18,136 cheered when Mike Marshall was announced as the Expos Player of the Year. In 1972. Marshall won 14 games and saved 18, while pitching in 65 games and sporting an earned run average of 1.78.

O'Keefe's Brewery of Canada presented him with a $10,000 El Dorado Cadillac and Gene Mauch said, "I haven't been around as long as Casey Stengel but I've been around long enough to see maybe 15 or 20 of the best relief pitchers in baseball history. I truly believe that Marshall is the best that I have seen. I have never seen a pitcher excel in so many departments of the game. He is a truly deserving winner of this award."

With two games lost because of the players strike, with a disappointing 70-86 in 1972, the Expos fell short of Gene Mauch's prediction. Meeting with the media again in the winter, Mauch refused to make any predictions for 1973. "I'm not going to give you numbers this time. I know where our biggest weaknesses are and I'm going to fix them."

Mauch had been disappointed with the team's defense, saying, "There were too many parachutes dropping in front of our fielders." Mauch pinpointed center field and second base as positions the Expos needed to improve. "Our pitchers deserve to be given better defense."[18]

With better defense, Mauch felt Mike Torrez might win 20 games,

Bill Stoneman would have a comeback year and rookie Balor Moore would blow hitters away.

Carl Morton, who won 18 games and was named Rookie of the Year in 1970, went 10-8 and 7-13 the next two years and asked General Manager Jim Fanning to trade him. Fanning sent Morton back to Atlanta for 31-year-old Pat Jarvis, who could either start or relieve.

Carl Morton just didn't like Mauch. Neither did reliever Mickey Scott, who appeared in 22 games in 1973.

Gene Mauch told a reporter, "Mickey Scott doesn't have enough stuff to get my daughter out." A few days later, the lefthander and his manager had a heated talk and Scott found a reporter and told him, "It's absolutely ridiculous the way Gene Mauch handles his pitchers. Not only am I not in love with Gene, but I have reached the point where I hate his guts.[19]" Scott was eventually sold to the Baltimore Orioles.

There was no doubt about Mike Marshall's feelings. Mike Marshall who'd had a career year, signed a new contract for $50,000 and praised his manager. "Mayo Smith wouldn't let me use the screwball at Detroit, Barney Schultz and Sal Maglie wouldn't let me throw it in St. Louis and Harry Walker was against me using it in Houston. Without Gene Mauch," said Marshall, I don't have a major league career."

Although Mauch felt he needed a new second baseman, Ron Hunt the irrepressible vet was back. Midway through spring training Mauch predicted that Hunt might duplicate his great season in 1971. "When a man gets on base as much as he does," raved Mauch, "and fights for every extra base, you overlook a lack of range or a slightly slower arm. That man can play baseball."

After 34 games, Hunt was hitting nearly .300 with a .416 on base percentage, had been hit 12 times and walked 12 times. Hunt was the catalyst in a three-game weekend bludgeoning of the San Francisco Giants as the Expos won 17-3, 9-6 and 7-6.

Hunt set a record in the first game by reaching base five times and scoring every time. He had three singles, one walk and was hit by a pitch.

The Expos went on to win seven straight and on June 16, they were in second place with a 29-26 record, five games back of the Chicago Cubs.

"I want to improve this team right now," said Mauch, after pitchers Steve Rogers and Craig Caskey, and second baseman Jim Cox were recalled from Peninsula of the International League.

The two young pitchers were thrown right in the fire. Rogers started against the Astros in Houston. He worked eight innings, allowing two runs and four hits and Mike Marshall picked up the win 3-2 win in ten innings. Mauch immediately announced Rogers would be in the rotation.

The next day the struggling Bill Stoneman started against Cincinnati. He had nothing and Mauch yanked him after two-and-a-third innings. Craig Caskey relieved him, pitching four-and-one-third innings, giving up just a single and a walk in a 3-2 loss, charged to Stoneman.

As teams ahead of them struggled, the Expos remained close to the top for weeks. "We just have to stay close," said Mauch. "We just have to stay at .500-and then anything can happen."

In a game against San Francisco, Ron Hunt tried to score from second base on a single by Ron Woods. Rounding third, he saw Giants' catcher Dave Rader firmly holding the ball. Trying to knock the ball loose, Hunt's left knee met Rader's shin guard. He was carried off the field and taken to a hospital. X-rays showed that there was no ligament or cartilage damage, just a severely bruised knee. A few days later, when Hunt's knee filled with fluid and had to be drained, so he was placed on the disabled list.

The Expos had no idea how important Hunt was until he was gone. He could get on base either by a hit, walk, or being hit by a pitch. With Hunt in the lineup, the Expos averaged 4.2 runs per game. Without him, 3.3.

"When we had Hunt," said Gene Mauch, "we had continuous pressure on the pitcher because we could count on him getting on base at least three times in two games."

Hunt finally returned in September, but reinjured his knee trying to avoid Ron Woods as the two converged on a fly ball. He was again carried off the field and underwent surgery for torn cartilage in his knee.

Despite the loss of their catalyst, the Expos looked like a team of destiny. They had two six-game winning streaks in September and started the month 13-3. They won games they normally would have lost and there was a different hero every game. Steve Renko bounced back from a 1-10 season to enjoy his best year. Steve Rogers was 9-3 by mid-September, Ken Singleton was hitting over .300 and driving in runs and Bob Bailey was piling up game winning hits during a 16-game hitting streak.

If it wasn't them, it was Mike Jorgensen, Ron Woods, Ron Fairly, Hal Breeden, or Charles "Boots" Day.

Gene Mauch manipulated his roster, platooned, pinch hit, pinch ran, and made pitching changes that kept his team in contention. Even his coach Dave Bristol marveled at Mauch, "His concentration is unbelievable. He's able to shut off everything around him. He's fearless. He'll never go home saying, 'Damn, I should have tried this.' He won't have to because he will have tried it."

On September 15, 34,331, the largest crowd in Expos history, overflowed Jarry Park and saw their heroes beat Philadelphia 5-4 in 10 innings. Expos fans had caught their first dose of pennant fever. General Manger Jim Fanning said, "Going to Jarry Park every day was like going to the fair. It was a great time."

A 4-2 win over St. Louis the next day put the Expos in a virtual tie with Pittsburgh for first place with a 75-73 record, just four percentage points back of the Bucs.

Then, they lost 5-3 to the Cardinals in 12 innings, lost again to the Cards, were swept in a three game series in Chicago and returned home to lose two more to Pittsburgh, extending their losing streak to seven straight.

"Losing streaks are funny," said Mauch. "If you lose at the beginning, you got off to a bad start. If you lose in the middle of the season, you're in a slump. If you lose at the end, you're choking."

Mauch somehow kept the Expos into mathematical contention until the last day of the season. They wound up fourth in the National League East, with a 79-83 record, three-and-a-half games out of first place, the most successful season in franchise history.

"I think Gene even surprised himself," said Jim Fanning. "I used to tell people that in my opinion Gene Mauch is the best manager in baseball. Now I don't think there's any question about it."

After the season, Gene Mauch was voted National League Manager of the Year by both the media and the other managers.

Three of the best: Gene Mauch, Bill Virdon, Sparky Anderson.

Mike Marshall had a great year in 1973, with 14 wins and 31 saves. He also set major league records for appearances (92) and most innings by a reliever (179) and was runner-up to the Mets' Tom Seaver in voting for the Cy Young Award.

In the offseason, a stringer from UPI in East Lansing, Michigan interviewed Marshall and asked him to review the Expos' season. Thinking he was talking off the record, Marshall blasted some of his teammates, especially Bob Bailey and Ron Hunt. "Who the hell wants to go back and pitch for that defense anymore? Second base was terrible. There's no way we can play another year with Ron Hunt. Third base was terrible. With Bob Bailey, we have no defense. Zero. I can go back and look at my 11 losses and blame 8 of them on the defense."

Marshall said the interview was for the Michigan State alumni magazine and when he made the comments, he thought the interview was over and that he and the reporter were just chatting.

A few weeks earlier, Marshall had embarrassed the front office and their top radio and TV sponsor, O'Keefe Brewing Company, by refusing to accept the company's $5,000 Player of the Year award, because he felt players on the same team shouldn't compete for a cash prize and that the five writers who voted, were not qualified to judge players' abilities.

Jim Fanning said, "The players recognize that he's an unusual guy. We aren't about to run out and trade him on the strength of an outburst like this."

On December 5, Mike Marshall was traded to the Los Angeles Dodgers for centerfielder Willie Davis. Jim Fanning said that Gene Mauch came to him and pushed for a trade for Davis, even if the Expos had to part with Mike Marshall. Not everyone bought that story.

Columnist Dick Young wrote in *The Sporting News*: "The happy front put up by Mauch over the Mike Marshall-Willie Davis exchange hides his opposition to the deal. Marshall was Mauch's security blanket. A manager wants, more than anything, to be able to reach into the bullpen in the eighth or ninth inning of any game, knowing he has a sure wrap-up-especially with a staff of young starters."

When a reporter asked Mauch how he planned to replace Marshall's 31 saves, he said, "Davis will save 30 games himself with his defensive play. In the 15 years that I've managed, I've never had an outstanding centerfielder. Now I have the best."[20]

In their sixth year, the Expos season opener was scheduled for Jarry Park. Owner Charles Bronfman tried to convince major league baseball that the weather in Montreal was questionable at that time of the year but commissioner Bowie Kuhn insisted the Expos open at home against the Chicago Cubs.

Bronfman was right. The weather was brutal, with rain and a temperature of 30 degrees, followed by snow. The opener was postponed for two days, the games cancelled and Montreal opened the season in Pittsburgh.

While the team left for Pittsburgh, Gene Mauch flew to Los Angeles to be with his wife Nina Lee, who had undergone emergency abdominal surgery. In his absence, Coach Dave Bristol managed the club.

The foul weather followed the Expos to Pittsburgh. Snow and freezing temperatures forced a postponement in Pittsburgh. Finally on April 11, the Expos season began as Jimmy Cox doubled home a run in the 13th inning in a 12-8 victory.

The Expos had 14 hits prompting Ken Singleton to say, "This team can hit. If a pitcher doesn't have his best stuff, we'll score runs."

Then, with their bats blazing, Montreal won seven of their first eight and nine of eleven to start the season. The Expos were winning despite the fact that nine of their first 29 games were postponed because of weather.

Then, suddenly the clock struck midnight. The pitching remained decent but the defense collapsed and the team stopped hitting as the Expos lost six in a row and nine out of ten.

After that, the team hovered around the .500 mark for the rest of the year. It was a boring team with little personality.

Steve Rogers was selected for the National League All-Star team despite a 10-10 record but represented the strongest part of the Expos, starting pitching. "I sincerely believe you're going to see the best pitching you've ever seen an Expos team have in the second half, "said Mauch. Steve Renko, Mike Torrez, Ernie McAnally, and Dennis Blair were all pitching well. Veteran Bill Stoneman, the author of two no-hitters, started the season 1-8 and was sold to the California Angels.

Pitchers were getting little help from the Expos defense. Before the season started, Gene Mauch said, "I know one thing. We WILL be better defensively." They weren't, averaging one error per game.

Mauch said Willie Davis would save games with his defense but by early July, the three time Gold Glove winner, had seven errors. At first Mauch defended him, "Nobody else would have gotten to the ball." Ultimately, it was obvious at 34, Davis was past his prime.

Jimmy Cox was an improvement defensively at second but he went out with a broken hand. Mauch tried Larry Lintz and Pepe Frias there but they were inadequate and Ron Hunt, who spent the first three months at third, moved back to second base.

Bob Bailey spent the first half of the year in left field and was now back at third. "Bailey means wood," Gene Mauch had said. "Bailey doesn't mean leather."

At first, Ron Fairly, Mike Jorgensen and Hal Breeden had already passed the combined error total of previous year.

In Atlanta, in the first inning, after Expos starter Dennis Blair gave up a three-run homer to Dusty Baker and a solo by Davey Johnson, with an 0-2 pitch he hit the Braves' Craig Robinson in the jaw. Robinson was carried off on a stretcher, unconscious, taken to a hospital but X-rays were negative.

In the ninth, with two outs and a 6-1 Braves lead, Braves starter Carl Morton retaliated and drilled Tim Foli in the ribs. He was warned by the plate umpire, resulting in a $50 fine. Knowing Morton's dislike for Gene Mauch, the media crowded around the fiery pitcher's locker. "No comment," barked Morton. Then, he let it fly. "Ask Gene Mauch. Remember I played for this man for four years. I already know the answer. You look at Robby's head and ask yourself if that's the way baseball is supposed to be played.

I don't like anybody that throws at a man's head. That's bush baseball. It's got to be stopped. Foli can play tomorrow. Not so Craig. That's a bunch of crap. That's the end result of Mauch's teaching."

When told of Morton's comments, Mauch said, "In the first place, he only PLAYED for me for one season. To say that I ordered a 20-year-old kid to throw at a man's head-are you serious? It's ridiculous. I hate to even say that."

It was apparent this team was going nowhere. Steve Rogers had a poor second half and finished 15-22. Ken Singleton's average dropped from .302 to .276, his home runs, from 23 to 9, his RBI from 103-79. Mauch seemed to lose faith in his veterans and the housecleaning began. Ron Hunt was claimed on waivers by St. Louis. Ron Fairly was traded to the Cardinals and Ken Singleton and Mike Torrez were dealt to Baltimore.

Willie Davis put up numbers but at 34, greatness was slipping away. Toward the end of the season, Willie got wacky. He had words with Mauch a couple of times, over his omission from the lineup; he was 15 minutes late for a game; left another in the ninth inning, walking into the stands at Jarry Park to get his wife.

1974 was a disappointment. The Expos finished fourth at 79-82, eight-and-a-half games out of first place.

When the season was over, Gene Mauch met with G.M. Jim Fanning, President John McHale and Charles Bronfman to discuss rebuilding the aging team. Mauch explained that dumping veterans for young players, could be painful for a while but it was the only way to build a championship team.

In three days, G.M. Jim Fanning gutted the club.

He traded pitcher Tom Walker and catcher Terry Humphrey to Detroit for pitcher Woody Fryman.

He sent Willie Davis to Texas for pitcher Don Stanhouse and infielder Pete Mackanin. He swapped Ken Singleton and Mike Torrez to Baltimore for pitcher Dave McNally, outfielder Rich Coggins and a minor league pitcher.

And he sent Ron Fairly to St. Louis for two minor leaguers.

Sporting News columnist Bob Dunn wrote about the trades: "The initial feeling, within a 100-mile radius of Jarry Park, is that the Expos have been attacked, stripped, raped and left for dead."

The Expos began "Phase Two" of their rebuilding process, with emphasis on youth, speed, pitching, and defense.

The team had little power to begin with. The 1974 Expos hit 86 home runs, the second lowest figure in the league. Bob Bailey hit 20 of them. In an exhibition game Bailey was hit by a pitch, breaking his left hand and knocking him out for at least a month.

Still, Gene Mauch thought his team could be competitive if they had good starting pitching, played excellent defense, and stole bases.

They won the season opener, beating St. Louis 8-4, then dropped five straight. The starting pitching was decent but closer Dale Murray was ineffective. They made twelve errors in the first six games and stole only four bases in eight attempts. With speedsters Larry Lintz and Tony Scott the Expos wanted to run, but you can't steal if you can't get on base.

After having no lefthanders the year before, Mauch now had former Orioles' ace Dave McNally and Woody Fryman, who'd gone 10-2 for Mauch in Philadelphia. Fryman won his first five decisions.

McNally won his first two and then lost five in a row. He became frustrated, saying, "I was almost stealing money," and announced his retirement. He was 3-6 with a 5.24 earned run average.

Although the team didn't play well for most of the year, there were some fireworks.

In a game in St. Louis, the Cardinals' Reggie Smith slid hard into second base trying to break up a double play. Expos' shortstop Tim Foli accused him of sliding in too high. The two exchanged words, then Smith chased Foli, punching him twice in the back of the head. Both dugouts emptied and there was the usual pushing and shoving that takes place in a baseball fight. Expos Pitching Coach Cal McLish came away from the fracas with a black eye.

Smith felt that Expos' coach Dave Bristol had scratched him during the melee. The next day, Bristol took the Expos' lineup card to home plate. Cardinals' manager Red Schoendienst asked Ted Sizemore to present the Cards lineup, but when Smith saw Bristol, he took the lineup from Sizemore and went to home plate. Smith said to Bristol, "I owe you one from last night. You can't scratch me like a woman." The two started arguing and another fight broke out as both teams again spilled onto the field.

Gene Mauch said, "If I called a man a woman, I'd be ready to fight. If a man called me a woman, he'd better be ready to fight."

In August, a six-game losing streak buried the Expos in last place and Charles Bronfman, Chairman of the Expos' Board of Directors admitted the team had made mistakes by trading Ken Singleton, Mike Torrez, Mike Marshall, and Ron Fairly.

There were a few positives in 1975. Outfielder-catcher Gary Carter hit .270 with 17 homers and 68 RBI and was selected National League Rookie of the Year. Another rookie, third baseman Larry Parrish hit .274 with 10 homers and 65 RBI and would be a fixture for years.

The Expos finished 75-87, tied for last with the Chicago Cubs, seventeen-and-a-half games out of first place.

On October 1, the Montreal Expos fired Gene Mauch. "WATERLOO FOR THE LITTLE GENERAL," read the sports headline in the *Montreal Gazette*.

When a reporter reached Mauch in Palm Springs, he said, "I don't know how I feel yet. I was just brushing my teeth. I must have brushed them twelve times today trying to get rid of a funny taste in my mouth."

Mauch had been given complete control of the Expos. The front office did everything Mauch asked for in terms of making trades. Mauch could be stubborn and believed his way was the only way. Now his bosses felt that Mauch, according to one club official, had "become an island unto himself."

"Someday," Mauch said, "the man upstairs will call and take me away. Until that time, neither he nor anyone else will tell me what players I should put in my lineup."

Mauch's players were shocked and hurt by their manager's firing. "I'll play for the man anytime, anywhere," said Woody Fryman, "and I think nine out of every ten on our ball club will say the same thing."[21]

"I think he had to be a magician to win 75 games, "said Bob Bailey, "with that rinky-dink outfit we put out there all summer."[22]

"It was the worst thing they could do," said Steve Renko. "Gene is a super man and a super manager."[23]

"He's a hard man to play for, but when you win, he's a great man to play for," said Gary Carter[24].

Gene Mauch retreated to Palm Springs to rest, play golf, spend time with his beloved wife Nina Lee and think about his future.

Chapter Nineteen

Congratulations...
You've Got Twins

Unless Gene Mauch took another managing job, the Expos had to pay him for another year. He thought about taking time off or maybe he'd just retire, but his friends knew baseball was his religion and the fire still burned. Charley Finley, the A's owner called and the Dodgers and Padres were also interested in Mauch. So were the Minnesota Twins.

Twins' owner Calvin Griffith called repeatedly for a month, but Mauch never retuned his calls. Griffith put the other candidates on hold and kept calling Mauch. Mauch finally said that if Griffith called one more time he'd accept.

Griffith had never given a manager more than a one-year contract but Griffith admired how hard Mauch's teams played in spring training and wanted someone tough and experienced. Mauch signed the first three-year contract in Twins history at a reported $40,000 the first year.

Twins' outfielder Larry Hisle played for Mauch in Philadelphia. He knew Mauch was tough, but fair, didn't play favorites, and only asked that players give 100 percent. "He taught me everything I know about the game professionally," Hisle said. "He knows more about the game than anyone I had ever been associated with." Hisle told teammates to get in shape because Mauch would push them hard in spring training.

The Gene Mauch who arrived in Orlando, Florida had mellowed, well, just a bit. He still wasn't warm and fuzzy and rarely talked to players unless the subject was baseball, but on flights Mauch played bridge with veteran players and softened his stance about long hair and beards. With the Expos, he had rejects from other teams and felt players brought a diversity of those clubs' identities with them. He had enforced the rules to establish uniformity, but Mauch realized the times had changed. If you look at a Twins' team picture from that time, there are several players who look the same, each with a wispy moustache and a healthy head of hair.

While some Expos couldn't grasp Mauch's fundamentals or weren't good enough to execute them, most of the Twins had come up through their system, wanted to learn, and loved Mauch's lessons.

Mauch took the Minnesota job because he felt the Twins could really challenge the Oakland A's. This was the first time Mauch had taken over a talented team. The Phillies were a last place club when he took that job and the Expos were an expansion team. Mauch knew that previously successful Twins teams had relied on power, but that had fallen off in recent years. He wanted to increase the team's run production, improve the defense, and felt the team's biggest needs were at catcher and shortstop.

Glenn Borgmann was the incumbent catcher but in spring training, 20-year-old Butch Wynegar caught Mauch's eye. Despite the rookie's one-for-twenty hitting stretch, Mauch saw that he had a strong arm, quick release, and was a switch hitter. Wynegar had led the Appalachian League in hitting his first year with a .346 average and in 1975 in the Class A California League, he hit .314 with 19 homers and 112 RBI. When Wynegar made the club, he became the first Twins player to jump from Class A to the majors since Steve Braun in 1971.

In the 1960's the Twins had mashers like Harmon Killebrew, Bob Allison, Tony Oliva, Earl Battey, Don Mincher and Jimmy Hall. But those days were long gone and now the Twins won playing Gene Mauch's "Little Ball."

Mauch used the sacrifice bunt more than any manager in base-ball. He knew statistics showed that the team that scored first, won close to fifty percent of the time. So, he figured if his team scored first, his opponent would have to score two runs to take the lead.

So, the Twins used walks, bunts, hit-and-run plays, and took ad-vantage of opponents' mistakes to manufacture runs. "We don't care how we win," said Mauch, "as long as we win."

In a game in Detroit, the Twins leadoff batter reached base in three of the first four innings. The next batter laid down a sacri-fice bunt every time. In that game, they tied the club record with five sacrifice bunts.

Nine of the Twins first twenty-nine games were decided by one run with the Twins winning seven. Six of those went extra in-nings, with the Twins winning five.

Gene Mauch was a master psychologist. He loved his players and wanted them to succeed. He knew every player was unique and he'd have to take a different approach with each of them.

Although Rod Carew was a star, before Mauch arrived, he was perceived by some sportswriters as moody with a big ego. Mauch felt the Twins would be a better team if Carew moved from second base to first. He knew that he couldn't just tell Carew to change positions. So, during the offseason, Mauch called Carew and ap-pealed to his pride. "Rodney, you've never won a Gold Glove and I think that's a shame. With all your batting titles, you're going to be a Hall of Famer as a hitter, but the crowning glory would be for you to win a Gold Glove and I think you can do that at first base, in your sleep." When spring training arrived, Carew never said a word. He just went to first base.

Gene with Rod Carew. Credit: Minnesota Twins

Mauch also protected Carew from the media. "Rodney, I know the media sometimes skewers you for not playing against certain tough lefthanders," Mauch said. "I know you think it's unfair and I think it's unfair too, so I'm on your side. I would like you to trust me to handle that. What I'm going to do, I will pick the times when I'm going to rest you and for the most part, it will be against tough lefthanders. Whether you want to play against them or not, I'll be the one to decide and I'll tell the media that I'm the one that decides and they'll believe me, because they have to. I'd like you to trust me to take care of you during the season." The manager and his star player developed a close bond and Carew's best years were when Mauch was his manager.

The Twins were 21-22 when Calvin Griffith pulled off one of the biggest trades in Twins' history. Unable to reach contract agreement with ace pitcher, Bert Blyleven, he traded him and shortstop Danny Thompson to the Texas Rangers for pitcher Bill Singer, minor league pitching prospect Jim Gideon, infielders Roy Smalley and Mike Cubbage and a reported $100,000.

Smalley was Gene Mauch's nephew. Ray Smalley III, was the son of Roy Smalley Jr., who had married Mauch's sister, Jolene. An All-American shortstop at USC and the number one pick in the 1974 draft, Smalley had been moved to second base by Texas. Smalley's dream had been to play shortstop for his Uncle Gene. "No one in baseball knows him as I do," said Smalley. "If anyone did, he'd want to play for him, too."

Gene with Roy Smalley. Credit: Minnesota Twins

Smalley's old and new teams, Texas and Minnesota squared off in a bench-clearing brawl. With two outs in the first inning, Texas starter Jim Umbarger hit Dan Ford in the back. The pitcher was upset that Ford stole second base the night before with the Twins leading 8-0. Ford charged Umbarger and both dugouts emptied. Comic relief was provided by Gene Mauch. Wearing rubber-soled shoes, Mauch ran onto the field to get into the action but slipped and landed on his butt, to the delight of the crowd. The shadow-boxing stopped and no one was ejected.

Butch Wynegar, enjoying a great rookie year, and Rod Carew, represented the Twins in the All-Star game. After the break, the team lost three out of four but Mauch predicted that soon his team would start hitting and scoring runs. "When that happens," he said, "We'll beat anyone. I don't care who is pitching, we'll win."

Mauch was a prophet. During a two-week stretch, Minnesota went 14-3 including an eight-game winning streak to move into second place. The Twins went 21-8 in September and October to finish third in the A.L. West at 85-77. But what happened on the final day of the season was a baseball eyesore.

On October 15, when the Twins met the Royals in Kansas City, five-time batting champ Rod Carew was battling for another title with the Royals' George Brett and Hal McRae.

In the ninth inning, trailing McRae by four-tenths of a point in the batting race, Brett lifted a fly ball to left field. Twins' left-fielder Steve Brye, playing fairly deep, ran toward the ball but suddenly stopped. The ball hit the artificial turf in front of him and bounced over his head, rolling into the left field corner. Brett circled the bases for an inside-the-park home run. Later, Brye said he had just been playing too deep.

Up next, McRae, facing the Twins' Jim Hughes, grounded out to the shortstop. Brett won the batting title .33333 to McRae's .33270. Carew finished third at .33058. ˙

As McRae ran to first, he looked toward the Twins' dugout and gave a clenched fist obscene gesture, aimed at Gene Mauch. He pointed at the dugout and gestured two more times.

Mauch charged out of the dugout, but was stopped by Royals' players. He got away from them, as players poured onto the field and had to be held back by three umpires as he tried to get to McRae. McRae was held in check by his manager Whitey Herzog and two players.

After the Twins won the game 5-3, McRae sat on his stool in the clubhouse, cried into a towel and charged the Twins with deliberately letting Brett's ball drop safely to help him win the A.L. batting title. He implied that racism was behind the action and that Mauch had told his outfielders to let Brett's fly balls drop while catching McRae's, insuring that a white man would win the batting title.

"That's a bunch of crap," said Rod Carew, a black man. "Gene said he wanted me to win the championship."

Mauch was crushed by the accusations and said, "This is the worst thing that's happened to me in 35 years in baseball. I would never, never do anything to harm the integrity of baseball."

American League President Lee MacPhail said he could find no evidence of wrongdoing on the play. What a way to end the season.

Although they'd played Gene Mauch's small ball and hit only 81 home runs, the Twins led the league in runs, hits, batting average and of course, sacrifice hits with 93. Mauch's faith in Butch Wynegar was rewarded when he was named Rookie of the Year, in voting by his peers.

Gene Mauch knew Twins' owner Calvin Griffith was in deep financial trouble. The Twins were the last of the family-owned clubs who depended solely on their team's profits to exist. With the Twins, there were no profits. For five straight years, the team had drawn less than one million fans and Griffith reportedly lost two million dollars.

With the arrival of free agency in 1977, Griffith couldn't compete with owners like the Yankees' George Steinbrenner, the Padres' Ray Kroc or the Angels' Gene Autry. Griffith couldn't afford his best reliever Bill Campbell, who signed with the Red Sox.

Griffith gave Mauch freedom to trade for a pitcher, but for the third straight year, the Twins came home from the winter meetings empty-handed.

Mauch felt that his eight position players were as good as any in the American League, but pitching was a different story. As the Twins entered spring training in Orlando, Florida, Mauch held a casting call for pitchers.

He found one when Twins' infielder Jerry Terrell called Gene to say that he'd been working out at Cal State-Northridge with lefthander Geoff Zahn, who'd been released by the Cubs after injuring his arm. Mauch sent pitching coach Don McMahon to take a look at Zahn. McMahon told Mauch that Zahn was as good as any lefthander the Twins had.

Gene Mauch called Zahn and invited him to spring training. Knowing that Zahn was still recovering from arm surgery, Mauch told him, "I think it takes two years for a guy to come back at full strength." The manager said he couldn't promise the pitcher a job, but would give him a chance to make the club.

Zahn also found out early how tough the Little General could be. "The first time I ever pitched for him," said Zahn, "I got into the sixth or seventh inning and he came out to take me out. So, I turned my back to him and was facing the guy he'd called in. So I waited until Gene got to within fifteen feet and I flipped him the ball and walked off."

When Zahn arrived at the ballpark the next day, Don McMahon told him to go to Mauch's office. When Zahn walked in, Mauch said sternly, "Maybe I didn't make myself clear in spring training, but when I walk out to the mound, I'm going to put my fat little mitt out and you'll place the ball in it and then you are excused."

"As he was saying that," said Zahn, "I started to slink lower in my chair."

Mauch tried not to get too close to his players but inside the crusty exterior was a kind, caring man who loved to help his players succeed. His old manager Billy Southworth and others had told Gene never to fall in love with his players, but sometimes he couldn't help it.

The day after Zahn pitched, while the team was taking batting practice, Zahn would pick up balls and the put them in a bucket. Mauch would come out and join him. "We would go over the whole game," remembered Zahn, "it was fun and enlightening. He was such a strategist. He put a ton of thought into everything."

Zahn played for Mauch for four years in Minnesota and won 12 or more games each season.

Mauch knew he couldn't replace Bill Campbell, who pitched in 78 games, with a 17-5 record and 20 saves, but he hoped that righthander Tom Johnson and lefty Tom Burgmeier, who'd gone 8-1, could pick up the slack.

Righthanders Dave Goltz and Jim Hughes would most likely be in the rotation, but Mauch had to choose from a list of "who's he" candidates including 22-year-old Pete Redfern, the Twins' first draft pick in 1976, and Jim Gideon, a former University of Texas star, acquired from the Rangers. Righthanders Mark Wiley and Steve Luebber along with lefty Mike Pazik, had all pitched well in Tacoma. The 27-year-old Pazik, acquired from the Yankees, had gone 14-5 in the PCL. He impressed Mauch and made the club.

Pazik beat Oakland for his first major league win and through three starts was 1-0 with a 2.50 ERA.

In April, Pazik and righthander Don Carrithers were driving home from the airport when their van was hit head-on by a car driven by a woman who went the wrong way on a freeway entrance. Pazik suffered two broken legs and never pitched in the big leagues again. Carrithers fractured his right knee cap and broke his right wrist. It was Dennis Bennett all over again.

Gene Mauch realized that young men in the 1970's were different than when he first started managing. Not only did you have to tell a player what to do, you had to explain why and probably had to show them.

Under Gene Mauch, Rod Carew flourished, having the greatest season of his career. Through ten games, the Twins were 5-5 and Carew was hitting just .304. Suddenly, Carew and the team caught fire.

The Twins were the best hitting team in baseball, dubbed "The Lumber Company." Larry Hisle led the American League with 119 RBI and budding superstar Lyman Bostock hit .336 with 199 hits and 90 RBI.

But it was Carew who pulled the team together and put them in the spotlight. On Rod Carew T-shirt Night, 46,463 fans stuffed Metropolitan Stadium and saw one of the greatest games in Twins history. Both starters, the White Sox's Steve Stone and Twins' starter Bill Butler were knocked out early. The Twins' Glenn Adams hit a grand slam and drove in eight runs as the Twins won 19-12. But it was Rod Carew who sent Twins' fans home with memories they'd never forget.

Carew went 4-for-5, scored 5 runs and drove in 6 as the Twins-O Gram on the scoreboard flashed: ROD CAREW IS BATTING .403!!!

The Twins played classic Gene Mauch baseball. He changed his lineup more often than he changed his sanitary socks. He platooned at second, third, right field and the DH spot, fielded a different batting order almost every game and maneuvered his bullpen like Bobby Fischer playing chess.

The Twins moved into first place in early May and stayed in contention until late August, when they were just two-and-a-half games out of first place. Then, in one stretch, they lost 8 out of 10 and went 7-18 in September. The Twins finished the season in fourth place with an 84-77 record and drew over one million fans for the first time since 1970.

Although Gene Mauch transformed the Twins into a contender, Rod Carew was the story in 1977. He was named the Most Valuable Player in the American League. His .388 average was the highest since Ted Williams hit .406 in 1941. He had 239 hits, led the league with 128 runs scored and hit 14 home runs with 100 RBI.

Carew's season was so great that it overshadowed Dave Goltz's 20-11 record, Larry Hisle's 119 RBI, and Lyman Bostock's .336 year.

Instead of basking in the euphoria of a successful season, Twins' fans worried that tightwad Calvin Griffith wouldn't sign his six free agents. Lyman Bostock and Larry Hisle had become stars and Griffith would never match offers they would receive. Pitchers Tom Burgmeier and Ron Schuler along with infielders Jerry Terrell and Luis Gómez were also free agents.

Gene Mauch knew that without Bostock and Hisle, he'd have a tough time competing. During the World Series in Los Angeles, Mauch told California Angels' owner Gene Autry that he'd love to move back near his home in Rancho Mirage and manage the Angels.

At first, Calvin Griffith gave his blessings about Mauch's move. Then he changed his mind, seeking compensation in a pitcher and cash. When Griffith was unhappy with the list of pitchers offered by Angels' Vice-President Buzzie Bavasi, after meeting with his Board of Directors, he said no to Mauch's move to the Angels. He knew the players and fans liked Mauch and if their manager followed two star players out the door, Griffith said, "Our name in this area would be mud." Since Calvin Griffith had vetoed Mauch's attempt to leave, the skipper stayed for the final year of his contract at $80,000.

During his discussions with the Angels, Mauch told Gene Autry that Lyman Bostock was the second best hitter in baseball, behind Rod Carew. Bostock was young, incredibly talented and a great kid. He had played high school baseball at Manual Arts in Los Angeles and collegiately at Cal State-Northridge. Autry took Mauch's advice and signed him to a five-year contract worth a reported $2.5 million.

The Twins also lost Larry Hisle who signed a six-year, $3 million contract with the Milwaukee Brewers.

In 1977, the Twins scored a club record 867 runs but without Hisle and Bostock, they'd be hard pressed to match that number. When a reporter asked Mauch if he was looking for power hitters, he said, without smiling, that he had one in California and one in Milwaukee.

Mauch felt that it was pitching failure rather than any offensive breakdown that caused the team's collapse in September. "We're dead birds if we don't improve our pitching," Mauch said. So, Mauch and Griffith again went to the winter meetings, in Hawaii, looking for pitchers and again returned with only frequent flyer miles.

Despite losing Hisle, Bostock and 10 other free agents, Calvin Griffith felt his club could still be competitive by signing and developing their own players. The Twins' scouting staff was their life blood and over the years had provided a steady stream of outstanding prospects. And the club's financial picture had improved. With the success of 1977, the Twins cleared a profit of $800,000. But Griffith and Mauch had different goals. While the boss wanted to survive financially for 10 years, Mauch wanted to win a pennant in 1978.

At the start of every season, Gene Mauch was the eternal optimist. He knew that rookies Willie Norwood and Bob Gorinski couldn't replace Hisle and Bostock so he looked to veterans like Butch Wynegar, Dan Ford, Mike Cubbage and his nephew, Roy Smalley to supply firepower. "Smalley has been pumping iron every day during the off-season," said Uncle Gene. "He's put on thirty pounds and you wouldn't recognize him now." Mauch said Cubbage and Wynegar had also taken up weightlifting and hoped to provide more run production.

With poor pitching and a defense that committed 17 errors in the first 17 games, the Twins were buried early. Having lost six straight, they vented against the Angels with a bench-clearing brawl. In the fourth inning, the Angels led 4-1. With the count 2-1 on Bobby Grich, Twins' pitcher Roger Erickson fired a pitch behind Grich. Grich charged the mound and threw a left hand at Erickson that missed. Erickson threw a punch that hit Grich in the batting helmet. Then Rich Chiles charged Grich and hit him with a body block and the brawl was on. The Angels' Don Baylor scuffled with Camilo Pascual. Brian Downing wrestled Bombo Rivera to the ground and Rod Carew landed a couple of punches as Grich was falling down before being pulled away by Angels' manager Dave Garcia. After the game, Grich said he was more upset with Gene Mauch than Erickson because the pitcher was just carrying out his manager's orders. Grich said Mauch yelled, "Get him with the next one."

Mauch, of course, denied telling Erickson to throw at Grich and Erickson said he couldn't hear Mauch yelling at him anyway.

Mauch hoped the brawl would inspire his team. Instead, the Twins lost 5-3 on their way to a nine-game losing streak. And ace pitcher Dave Goltz was kicked in the ribs and missed four starts.

In early May, Gene Mauch spoke with Mike Marshall. Mauch thought his former pitcher had retired after two injury riddled seasons. But Marshall told Mauch that while he'd been pursuing a Ph.D. in exercise physiology at Michigan State, he'd been working out and felt he could still pitch.

Mauch invited him to Chicago to pitch batting practice. "He was unhittable," said Craig Kusick. "We had a pile of broken bats behind the cage that you could have started a bonfire with," said Rich Chiles. "I think he broke eight of them."

Mauch told Calvin Griffith the team should sign Marshall. "The guy's a weirdo and he's got all these weird ideas," said Griffith.

"I know Calvin," answered Mauch, "but he's a freak. He can pitch every day."

"That's why I don't want him," Griffith said.

Twins' players were angry and disappointed with Griffith's reaction. Rod Carew had been involved in frustrating contract negotiations with the Twins and the failure to sign Marshall pushed him over the edge. "The situation is ridiculous," said the MVP, "a joke. It's demoralizing for everyone."

Carew threatened to play out his option and become a free agent and if Griffith tried to trade him, he would veto the deal. "If he's going to stick it to us, I'm going to stick it to him," said Carew.

Griffith finally relented and signed Marshall. He turned out to be one of the few bright spots in a disappointing season. After Marshall signed, the Twins won seven of their next eight games, with Marshall picking up a win and four saves. Appearing in 54 games, he was 10-12 with a 2.45 ERA and 21 saves.

In two years in Minnesota, playing for his uncle, Gene Mauch, Roy Smalley had become the fans' scapegoat much like his father with the Cubs in the 1950's. If he made an error or struck out, fans booed him. They called him "nepot" as in nepotism and someone would yell, "You're only playing because your uncle is the manager."

On July 2, in an 8-5 loss to the Chicago White Sox, Smalley committed three errors, including two in one inning. When he fielded a ground ball and threw out the runner, the fans gave Smalley what he called "a standing Bronx cheer. I was really, really pissed," recalled Smalley, "So I took my hat off and doffed my cap to the fans."

The next day, with fans again booing him, Smalley hit a two-run homer to give the Twins a 7-2 victory. Gene Mauch arrived at the ballpark early, around noon for a night game. Wearing just his baseball underwear and shower shoes, Mauch sat in his chair down the right field line, working on his tan, but also watching opposing players, hoping they might tip off a weakness. In what Roy Smalley called, "the launching point in my career," the following day, Uncle Gene asked his nephew to join him.

Mauch began talking about the fans booing and said, "You are putting up with a lot. I like the way you're handling it for the most part, but I'm not real crazy about the tip of the hat bullshit. I will tell you, though, that what you did last night, hitting a game winning home run, no-talent cats can't do that." Mauch also told Smalley that "you are my shortstop and I wouldn't trade you for anyone."

From that point on, Smalley's career took off. He committed only two more errors and finished with a .273 average with 19 homers and 77 RBI.

In a game against Boston, Gene Mauch put on one of his better shows. When Red Sox catcher Bob Montgomery picked off Mike Cubbage at first base, Cubbage jumped up, got in umpire Bill Kunkel's face, threw his batting helmet and was ejected. Gene Mauch charged Kunkel, bumped the umpire, and also got tossed. Mauch then went into the dugout, grabbed armloads of bats and threw them onto the field as the crowd roared. After pacing back and forth in the dugout, Mauch ran his hand through his increasingly graying hair and left. He ended up getting fined $250.

The Twins got off to the worst start in team history, 10-20 and by June 11th, were 21-35, ten games out of first place. From then until July 13, they went 18-7 to move within 4 ½ games of the first place Angels. Streaky? They won six straight, lost nine in a row, won eight consecutive games, and then dropped eight straight. The Twins never recovered, finishing fourth, with a 73-89 record, 19 games behind first-place Kansas City.

Rod Carew hit .333 to win his seventh batting title and Dan Ford drove in 82 runs. Drawing just 787,878 fans, the Twins were again last in the American League in attendance.

As Gene Mauch studied newspaper box scores each day, he followed Lyman Bostock's 1978 season with the Angels. Mauch loved Bostock's talent and enthusiasm and was disappointed when the Twins couldn't hold on to him. His teammates nicknamed him "Abdul Jibber Jabber" because he talked as fast as he ran. After hitting .336 and finishing second to Rod Carew's .388 in the batting race, Bostock struggled as he began his first season with the Angels.

After hitting .150 in April, Bostock was so disappointed that he offered to give his salary back to the Angels. The team refused his offer, but he gave the money to charity. Eventually, Bostock found his stroke and raised his average to .296, the best on the ball club. After going 2-for-4 in a Saturday afternoon game against the White Sox in Chicago, Bostock left the team hotel and went to Gary, Indiana to visit friends and relatives.

After a meal at his Uncle Thomas Turner's house, the two went to visit Joan Hawkins, a woman Bostock had known as a teenager. After the visit Turner agreed to give Hawkins and her sister, Barbara Smith, a ride to their cousin's house. Turner drove with Hawkins in the passenger's seat and Bostock and Smith in the back seat.

Smith had been living with Hawkins while separated from her husband, Leonard Smith. As Turner stopped at a traffic signal, Smith's car pulled up beside them. Turner ran two red lights trying to get away from Smith, but was finally stopped by traffic congestion. Smith got out of the car and fired a shotgun into the back seat where his estranged wife and Bostock were sitting. Barbara Smith was wounded in the neck and the rest of the blast hit Bostock in the right temple. He died three hours later at a Gary hospital. Bostock was only 27.

When word of Bostock's death reached Gene Mauch, he said, "At first I was shocked. Then I was sad. Then I got very mad, thinking 'Why did this have to happen to him?' Then, I got downright sick. I've never known anyone in the game who wanted to be as good as Lyman Bostock wanted to be, who wanted to be more appreciated, and who wanted to be more respected."

On September 28, at a Lions' Club meeting in Waseca, Minnesota, Calvin Griffith, fortified by several cocktails, alienated his team, the Twin Cities and Twins' fans with a 40 minute tirade. Griffith was unaware that a *Minneapolis Tribune* reporter was in the audience. Griffith's comments were on the front page of the paper the next day.

Griffith said Rod Carew had been "a damned fool," for signing a three-year contract in 1976. He felt Carew would have made more money by signing a series of one-year contracts.

Griffith also said he decided to move his team from Washington D.C. to Minnesota in 1961 when, "I found out you only had 15,000 blacks here. Black people don't go to ball games."

When Rod Carew, already engaged in acrimonious contract negotiations with Griffith, heard his boss's comments, he said he'd never play for the Minnesota Twins and for a bigot.

Griffith was roasted by newspaper columnists, censured by baseball Commissioner Bowie Kuhn and *The Minneapolis Star* ran an editorial entitled, "Calvin Must Go." Griffith claimed he had been misinterpreted.

After being pursued by teams including the Giants, Yankees and Red Sox, Carew was traded to the California Angels for outfielder Ken Landreaux, catcher Dave Engle and pitchers Paul Hartzell and Brad Havens.

The Twins also sent disgruntled outfielder Dan Ford to the Angels for Danny Goodwin and Ron Jackson and dealt two minor leaguers to the Mets for left-handed pitcher Jerry Koosman. A 20-game winner in 1976, Koosman had gone 8-10 and 3-15 since. The Twins thought that at 36, a homecoming might rejuvenate the native Minnesotan.

With the player losses, the Twins were regarded as also-rans when they went to spring training in 1979 in Orlando. But Gene Mauch sensed a special chemistry on this club and felt his pitching staff might be the best he'd ever had. The five starters were so impressive in spring training, that when asked about the American League West race, Mauch said, "I feel like a man sitting in the weeds with a loaded twelve gauge shotgun."

The Twins shot out of the starting gate, sweeping a three-game series in Oakland and winning seven of their first nine. They matched the club record with thirteen wins in April and moved into first-place May 1, eventually opening up a four-and-a-half game lead.

The additions of third baseman John Castino, first baseman Ron Jackson and centerfielder Ken Landreaux, strengthened the defense. The Twins led the league in double plays and were getting great pitching. Jerry Koosman won his first five decisions en route to a 20-13 season. Geoff Zahn was 13-7 and Dave Goltz 14-13. Mike Marshall appeared in 90 games and led the league with 32 saves.

From opening day, Roy Smalley was a one man wrecking crew.

He became a team leader, belted home runs, led the league in hitting for several months, and played great shortstop. Fans voted Smalley in as the starting shortstop for the American League All-Star Team. He entered the All-Star break with the second highest batting average in the Major Leagues (.341). Though he tailed off in the second half, he finished the year hitting .271 with 24 home runs and 95 RBI, both career highs. The Twins stayed in contention until the last week of the season when their starting pitching collapsed. The Twins finished fourth with an 82-80 record, six games back of the first place Angels.

In 1980, despite the loss of pitcher Dave Goltz, who signed with the Los Angeles Dodgers, Gene Mauch said that if his young pitchers developed, his team could win 90 games. The young arms included Pete Redfern, Darrell Jackson, Roger Erickson and Terry Felton, all in their twenties.

"If one of those four pitches to his potential," said Mauch, "we have a chance. If two of them make it, we'll win it. If three of them make it, we'll win it easily."

Mauch liked the core of his team with Butch Wynegar, Ken Landreaux, John Castino, Rob Wilfong, Roy Smalley and Ron Jackson. He was also impressed by rookie centerfielder Rick Sofield and reliever Doug Corbett.

The Twins played up to Mauch's expectations, going 15-6 in spring training. Noted New York baseball columnists Dick Young and Phil Pepe picked Minnesota to win the American League West.

With negotiations over a new basic agreement stalled over free agent compensation, major league players walked out of spring training, forcing cancellation of the final eight games. Players said they would return to start the regular season but would strike if agreement wasn't reached before May 23.

The Twins began the 1980 season with an arduous twelve game road trip to Oakland, California and Seattle. In the season opener in Oakland, with the scored tied 7-7 in the twelfth inning, Roy Smalley led off with a homer off tiring starter Steve McCatty. Then, two batters later, rookie Rick Sofield homered off McCatty in a 9-7 Twins' win. Another newcomer, Doug Corbett pitched five scoreless innings for the win. But the Twins went just 5-7 on the trip, dropping the last five games. By the end of April they were a disappointing 10-10 but a disastrous 8-19 May buried them.

Mike Marshall returned to baseball because he respected Gene Mauch. Mauch had even given him leeway to train on his own and report to spring training later than other players. Mauch's preferential treatment for Marshall didn't sit well with several Twins players.

Mauch was also concerned about Marshall's role as player representative for the Twins and the American League. When Marshall joined the Twins in 1978, Mauch and Marshall agreed that the pitcher wouldn't become the rep. That changed when the player rep quit and the players asked Marshall to take over.

Marshall was one of the most militant players during negotiations. "It's time," he said, "to end the boss-boy relationship."

Mauch suggested that Marshall's poor start was due to pressure he felt from the negotiations. In the season opener in Oakland in just one-third of an inning, he allowed three earned runs, giving up a three-run homer to Rickey Henderson. His earned run average in April was 10.95. While Marshall struggled, minor league vet Doug Corbett made the most of his chance. Corbett, a sinkerball pitcher, drafted from the Cincinnati Reds organization, was 3-0 with a 2.16 ERA through his first 16 2/3 innings. More and more, Mauch turned to Corbett rather than Marshall in late inning relief.

Finally an agreement was reached between the players union and the owners, averting a strike. Gene Mauch was happy about the settlement but cautioned, "We can't put the fans through this too often. We can't put them through this strike talk again next season."

On June 6, the Minnesota Twins released Mike Marshall. Since Marshall still had the rest of 1980 and all of 1981 on his contract, the Twins would have to pay him $550,000. Marshall and Marvin Miller, executive director of the Major League Players Association, threatened legal action, claiming that Marshall was released because of his union activities rather than his poor performance. Marshall was 1-3 with a 6.19 ERA when he was released.

Marshall directed much of his rhetoric at Gene Mauch, saying that their relationship had begun to detiorate the previous September and that he had pitched poorly because Mauch hadn't used him enough.

The Twins denied Marshall's charges that union activities led to his release and Mauch added, "If I thought the man could pitch," said Mauch, "he'd still be here."

1980 was supposed to be the season the Twins finally became a contender. Instead, it was a nightmare.

Besides the distraction Mike Marshall created, several players regressed, including Butch Wynegar, Ron Jackson, and Rob Wilfong. Roy Smalley played on two bad legs all year and didn't match his previous numbers. Only one starting pitcher, Jerry Koosman had a winning record at 16-13. The outfield defense was awful, and at times the team seemed to sleepwalk through games.

There were only a few bright spots. John Castino played great defense, hit .302 and led the team in homers with a mere 13 and Doug Corbett replaced Marshall as closer.

Ken Landreaux had a 31-game hitting streak, the longest in the American League since Detroit's Ron Leflore had a 30-gamer in 1976. But when Landreaux wasn't hitting, his play was lackadaisical and Mauch benched him for a game.

The Twins sank further and further in the standings. Following a 3-2 loss to Detroit on August 24, the Twins were 54-71, 26 games back of first-place Kansas City. Gene Mauch told his nephew Roy Smalley that he couldn't take any more. Calvin Griffith kept losing players and couldn't pay the ones he had. It was a no-win situation. Mauch resigned, effective immediately.

"I kept waiting, waiting and waiting for something good to happen but it was never to be," Mauch said during a nine-game losing streak in August. "I've had some bad teams–teams that were bad enough to gag a maggot, but even those teams were able to steal some games with execution. This season we have lost because of a failure to execute."

"I'm disappointed that he didn't stay," said Rick Sofield. "He helped a kid tryin' to make it in the majors. I owe a lot to that man."

His nephew Roy Smalley wouldn't comment, except to say, "What I would have to say would be more than your editors could handle."

The 1980 collapse dropped Gene Mauch's lifetime record to 378-394, a .450 winning percentage. With the Twins, he had finished third once, and fourth three times. "His record may not show it," said Sparky Anderson, "but he may be the best manager who ever managed."

Third base coach John Goryl replaced Mauch and went 23-13 with a 12-game winning streak. Calvin Griffith gave Goryl a one-year contract to manage the Twins.

Chapter Twenty

Back to the Desert

Gene's Mauch's daughter Lee Anne said her dad's IQ was 160. If he hadn't solely dedicated his intellect to baseball, he could have been successful at anything, including financial matters. Whenever he signed a contract, Mauch had payments spread out over many years. Then, when he got the next job, he would have money from two sources. This practice has since been eliminated, but Mauch made the most of it.

Mauch said he turned down four offers to manage and one to be a general manager. Reportedly, the Giants, Padres, Cardinals and Yankees wanted him. But baseball was his passion, baseball was in his soul, baseball defined who he was and why he was here. He missed the players and no amount of pounding golf balls would fill the void.

In February of 1981, Mauch accepted a job as Director of Player Personnel for the California Angels. At a press conference, Angels' Executive V.P. Buzzie Bavasi and Mauch denied rumors that Mauch was hired to replace Jim Fregosi as manager. Rather than taking an office at Anaheim Stadium, Mauch worked from his home on the ninth hole at the Springs Country Club in Rancho Mirage.

You couldn't blame Fregosi for looking over his shoulder. He was surrounded by former major league managers. Besides Mauch, there was third base coach Preston Gómez and special assignment scouts Bill Rigney and Herman Franks.

Fregosi's team was losing, owner Gene Autry was getting increasingly impatient and the cowboy had previously tried to hire Mauch as manager. Fregosi was about to be fired when he got a stay of execution, Buzzie Bavasi talked Autry into giving Fregosi a little more time. When the team lost five out of six during a May home stand, Gene Autry fired Fregosi and replaced him with Gene Mauch.

Gene Mauch with Gene Autry. Credit: Los Angeles Angels of Anaheim

"John McGraw can't turn it around," said Mauch. "Connie Mack can't turn it around. Only the players can turn it around. If I didn't think they could, I wouldn't have taken the job."[1]

Gene Mauch was a master of the turnaround. He took a last place Philadelphia team and after four years, they went 92-70, just missing winning a pennant in 1964. He took an expansion team in Montreal from a 52-110 first year to 73-89. In Minnesota, he turned a 76-83 club into a winner at 85-77.

For years, Mauch's uniform number was four but Bobby Grich had that number so Mauch took uniform number 44. Mauch's first game as Angels' manager was May 30, 1981 at Chicago's Comiskey Park. Starter Geoff Zahn was knocked out in the third inning, the Angels committed four errors, and had just three hits in a 9-0 loss. "I'll forget about the loss," Mauch said, "probably in 1998 I'll forget about it."

Trade rumors involving the Angels and Mauch's old team, the Minnesota Twins, were rampant. Don Baylor was unhappy being a designated hitter and wanted to go somewhere he could play the outfield or first base. Gene Mauch wanted to acquire his nephew Roy Smalley and put him at third base.

Meanwhile, Mauch tried to motivate his players but how? "I think there are probably three parts," Mauch said. "One is remuneration. Number two is fear. Three is pride. They've got all the money they need. They're not afraid of losing their jobs. So you have to go after the third one, pride."

The next day, in the first game of a doubleheader, Mauch got his first win as Angel's skipper. Rookie Mike Witt pitched seven strong innings as the Angels beat the Chisox 7-4. "Gene was a father figure to me," said Witt. "I was 20, the youngest guy on the team and Gene let me know he was on my side." The 6'7" right-hander was a local product who'd starred at Anaheim's Servite High School.

After losing two out of three to Chicago, the Angels swept a three-game series in Toronto, winning the first two 3-0 behind the three-hit pitching of Ken Forsch followed by a combined shutout by Dave Frost and Andy Hassler. The Angels completed the three-game sweep, pounding out a season high 19 hits and hammering Toronto 17-6.

The Angels were 9-4 under Mauch and had won four in a row when on June 11, major league players went on strike.

"I'm amazed and sick that there's a strike," said Mauch. "You can't abuse the fans and expect their enthusiastic support," he said before retreating to Rancho Mirage.

After 49 days, the strike was settled on July 31. Because of the games lost, baseball divided the season into two parts. Every team would begin with a fresh slate in Season Two.

The Angels worked out at Fullerton College, lost an exhibition to Cincinnati at Anaheim Stadium and then opened the second season in Seattle.

14,527 turned out at the Kingdome to see Seattle win 5-4. The Mariners took the second game 4-1, but the Angels won the third, 4-1 in 11 innings as Bobby Grich hit two home runs and extended his hitting streak to 21 straight games. During the streak, Grich hit .440 with 12 home runs. Grich was making a contract run; he would be a free agent at the end of the season.

The Angels began the second half, losing six out of seven. In August, the Angels honored their owner with Gene Autry Day as the Angels met the Indians. The Angels won the first two games, led by Dan Ford's seven hits and seven RBI. In the third game, as Ford came up with two outs in the third inning, Cleveland pitcher John Denny drilled him in the back with a fastball. The benches emptied and during the melee, the Angels' Don Baylor punched Cleveland's Rick Waits in the face and was ejected. Waits said he had no idea why Baylor punched him and added, "He says he's a Christian, but I have to doubt it." Cleveland won the game 6-3.

Overall, it was a disappointing season. The Angels finished just 29-34 under Mauch. They finished fourth in the first half of the season, sixth in the second half, and overall were 51-59, leaving them fifth in the A.L. West.

Chapter Twenty-One

Last Chance for the Cowboy?

Angels' owner Gene Autry was almost 79. Time was running out. His horse was named Champion but a championship had eluded him. In December of 1981, relying on Gene Mauch's knowledge of players, Autry opened his saddlebags to build a winner.

Autry had long coveted Reggie Jackson for his star power as well as his home runs and signed Mr. October to a four-year contract worth $3 million with an attendance clause that could make him even richer.

A day after acquiring Jackson, the Angels sent Dan Ford to the Baltimore Orioles for third baseman Doug DeCinces and minor league pitcher Jeff Schneider.

The Angels also dealt minor league catcher Brian Harper to Pittsburgh for one of Gene Mauch's favorite players, 31-year-old Tim Foli, an emotional leader who could play any infield position.

In retrospect, the key acquisition though, was catcher Bob Boone. When Executive V.P. Buzzie Bavasi told Mauch the Phillies wanted to unload the veteran catcher, Mauch said, "Grab him." The Angels stole Boone for a mere $300,000, one of the best moves in Angels' history.

Boone had caught for the Phillies for ten years but was 34 and they felt he was over-the-hill, that all those innings behind the plate had taken their toll. Gene Mauch suspected otherwise and in spring training told Boone he would "check him out."

When the Angels played San Diego in a three-game series in Yuma, Arizona, Mauch put Boone behind the plate for a "B" game in the morning and then put him in for five innings in an "A" game that afternoon. "So, on my first day with the Angels, I played 14 innings," recalled Boone. "Then, I played every game, all spring. Gene was checking me out to see if I still had it. We had two other catchers, Ed Ott and Joe Ferguson but I played every day. I loved it."

As he often did, Mauch had an ulterior motive. With Boone catching every day, he learned the strengths and weaknesses of the Angels' pitching staff.

Mauch showed he meant business, with two-and-a-half-hour workouts emphasizing fundamentals. Reporters weren't allowed to talk to players during workouts or around the batting cage.

Mauch wanted to try an outfield of Don Baylor in left, Fred Lynn in center and Reggie Jackson in right, all three former MVP's. Baylor didn't want to DH so Mauch promised him a chance to play the outfield. The previous year, Baylor had played only one game in the outfield and had a weak arm.

With the acquisition of Bob Boone, catcher Brian Downing's initial reactions was, "I'm sick about it. The Angels can shove it. Apparently they're worried about my health. Well, some players can play hurt and some can't. I can."[1] Downing began his career as an outfielder before being moved behind the plate. When the Angels acquired catcher Ed Ott in 1981, Downing played the outfield. He knew his only chance to stay in the lineup was in the outfield.

In spring training both Baylor and Downing arrived early and stayed late, relearning their skills in the outfield. Juan Beníquez, a good hitter, had also entered the picture. As opening day approached, Gene Mauch hadn't decided on his starting left fielder.

Mauch felt that his infield of Rod Carew at first, Bobby Grich at second, Rick Burleson at short and Doug DeCinces at third, was the best in baseball.

While many questioned the talent of his pitching staff, Mauch said, "I'd like to think our pitching is okay the way it is." He figured that young Mike Witt and vet Geoff Zahn would improve and hoped that injured pitchers Ken Forsch, Bruce Kison, and Bill Travers were now healthy. "If every one of our people play to their potential," Mauch said, "I don't think there's anyone who can handle us."

In Minnesota, Geoff Zahn won 53 games in four years under Mauch but the lefthander was now 35. Mauch thought he needed a tune-up. At the end of the previous season, Mauch told Zahn, "You've been a decent pitcher for me but if you keep pitching the way you are, I might not be able to use you."

That got Zahn's attention and he listened as Mauch laid out his plan. "I've been up late thinking about this and I will tell you how I know you'll be effective. When you come to spring training, you're going to pitch backwards. Your changeup is going to be your best pitch and everything will come off the changeup."

Mauch told Zahn to spend the winter working on his changeup and changing speeds off the pitch. He also told him to find a pitch he could throw inside to right-handed hitters like a cut fastball.

When Zahn arrived in Orlando, he had a new catcher, Bob Boone, one of the best in baseball. When a catcher puts down one finger it usually means a fastball, but Mauch told Boone and Zahn, that one finger meant a changeup. "Even in the intrasquad games, Boonie would call one changeup after another," said Zahn.

Geoff Zahn's first start came in the second game of the season in Oakland. He pitched a four-hitter and Brian Downing homered, as the Angels won 7-0.

Following the series in Oakland, the Angels boarded the team bus for the airport. Zahn said goodbye to his wife Peggy and three-year old daughter Matti, who began to cry. "I could barely look at her because she was bawling her head off," remembered Zahn. Gene Mauch, sitting in the front row, got off the bus, picked Matti up and held her until she stopped crying.

Another time, Mauch was playing with Matti, tossing her up in the air and catching her. It was fun for awhile until she threw up on the Little General.

In Toronto, Mauch gave Matti a teddy bear, which she named "Mauchie."

Mauch respected Zahn, who was the club's chapel leader, loved his intensity and dedication. "Gene felt you had to have a plan," explained Zahn "and as long as you're trying to execute your plan, he didn't have any problem with you." Like Mauch, Zahn prepared by filling a notebook with his personal scouting report on hitters.

Zahn went 4-0 with a 1.05 ERA in April and was named American League Pitcher of the Month. He had a career year, going 18-8 with a 3.73 ERA and made the All-Star team.

Concerned with the work load of reliever Don Aase, the Angels traded promising outfielder Tom Brunansky to Minnesota for two more Mauch favorites, reliever Doug Corbett and second baseman Rob Wilfong. Corbett had pitched well for Mauch in Minnesota and said, "Gene treated me like a king and I'll play like a king for him." The Corbett trade was the only mistake the team made in acquiring players. With the Angels, he went 1-7 and watched his sinkers sink over the outfield wall.

The Angels also acquired 37-year-old Steve Renko, who'd pitched for Mauch in Montreal. Starting and relieving, through his first nine appearances, Renko was 5-1, with two complete games and a 1.70 ERA.

The newcomers blended with an Angel team that was playing vintage Gene Mauch baseball. Although Rod Carew had an injured wrist and Reggie Jackson was struggling, the team was winning with pitching, speed, and defense–Mauch's formula for success.

When shortstop Rick Burleson tore his rotator cuff and was lost for the year, Tim Foli took over. Foli had played for Mauch in Montreal and loved his manager. "Gene was always so brilliant on the field, in the management of the game," said Foli. "He knew what was going to happen before it did and if he could get his guys to execute, we'd win."

Nobody beat Gene Mauch to the ballpark. For a 7:30 p.m. game, he sometimes arrived by 10 a.m. and never later than noon. Sitting around in his baseball underwear, he spent hours putting together different batting orders, thinking about the game's possible scenarios and trying to find a winner. "Ninety percent of a manager's responsibility is completed before the game starts," said Mauch. "It's in the preparation during the spring and in the two or three hours before the first pitch."[2] His wife Nina Lee said that if Gene wasn't married, he'd probably live in the clubhouse year around.

The Little General talks strategy.
Credit: Los Angeles Angels of Anaheim

Bob Boone and Tim Foli usually arrived shortly after Mauch and they spent hours talking baseball. Boone and Mauch discussed opposing hitters and designed pitch sequences to get them out.

"I'd take my early hitting and then come out on the bench and sit with Gene," said Boone, "and watch the other team hit. He really taught me what to look for and how to do it; he was tremendous in helping me call games." In Philadelphia, Boone had played on a World Series winner, been an All-Star and won Gold Gloves but said, "With Gene, that's when I really started learning about baseball."

Philadelphia thought Boone couldn't throw out runners any more but Mauch changed that. "Gene was really the initiator of controlling the running game," Boone said. "He would call for throw overs, step offs and pitch-outs."

The Phils were playing the Cubs and Boone figured a hit-and-run was on, so he called for a pitch-out. When the runner didn't go, he heard the metallic sound of a folding chair being thrown down the dugout tunnel.

"What was that?" asked the umpire.

"I suspect Gene is somewhat mad at me for pitching out."

Boone said Mauch was the first manager who worked on pitchers getting the ball to home plate quickly. Mauch showed them how and almost every pitcher could get the ball to the plate in 1.0 seconds. With the pitchers holding runners and being quick to the plate, Boone never had to rush throws and got into a groove with his throwing.

"The Phillies didn't think I could throw any more but the first year in Anaheim, I threw out 63% of the runners. I know because it was the year of the Erasermate Award, given by the pen company, so they kept track and I won."

"Not many people know this," Gene Mauch told Bob Boone, "I call it page 38. I don't know why it works but it works every time. When you have an opposite pitcher vs hitter, right-handed pitcher vs left-handed hitter or vice versa and you are in a battle with him and you've got two strikes and he fouls some pitches off, so you throw a breaking ball in and they rip it foul. Then, come back with a fastball in and it will freeze the hitter, every time. I don't know why it happens but it's on page 38 of my book."

"So I would do it and look over at Gene with a big-shit-eating grin on my face," said Boone, "and I'd call a fastball in, the batter would freeze, strike three, inning over."

"One day we're in Minnesota and we get into that situation and Roy Smalley is hitting. I call for a breaking ball in and he rips it foul. OK, here we go, page 38. I call a fastball in and Wham! He hits it out down the line."

"Son of a bitch, that's the first time that ever happened," Boone said. "When I got back to the dugout, Gene says, 'I forgot to tell you, Smalley knows about page 38.'"

Gene Mauch was the master of "Little Ball," but with the Angels, he played two different games. With a wealth of power hitters, he let the big boys swing away but when he got to the bottom of the order with Tim Foli batting eighth and Bob Boone ninth, Mauch could advance runners, have them bunt and play hit-and-run.

"We've got Reggie Jackson, Rod Carew, and Don Baylor; we've got some studs," Mauch told Foli. "Tim, you've got to make sure you take care of Reggie and Rodney when they get down. You've got to pick them back up when they get down."

"Gene, who picks me up?" Foli asked.

"Tim, we don't need you as bad as we need them," answered Mauch, with a wry smile.

In Baltimore, the Orioles beat the streaking Angels 9-4. After the O's Gary Roenicke hit a three-run homer, reliever Luis Sánchez hit former Angel Dan Ford. Ford started toward the mound but was restrained by umpire Jim McKean.

Ford felt that Mauch had ordered the hit. When Ford played for Mauch, they just didn't mix and Mauch traded him. "It might be Gene Mauch," said Ford, "I know how Gene manages. When somebody hits the long ball....well."

"If Ford was that smart, I would never have traded him," said Mauch. How'd I order Sánchez? After the home run did I raise my arms and yell 'drill him'?"

With Rick Burleson sidelined for the year after undergoing surgery for a torn rotator cuff, Tim Foli was a godsend. "He's an old-fashioned ballplayer," said Gene Mauch. "He comes to the ballpark to win the game."

In a 10-2 win in Boston, Foli drove in four runs four different ways: with a single, a sac fly, a squeeze bunt and a home run.

In late May and early June, the Angels lost seven straight and fell out of first place. Shortly after that, on a 13-game home stand, the Angels went 9-4.

Brian Downing was an atypical leadoff hitter. When a writer asked Gene Mauch how Downing felt about leading off, he said, "Brian would rather eat green flies than leadoff."

Downing's teammates called him "The Incredible Hulk, "after he built a gym in his garage and bulked up. How many leadoff hitters could bench press 475 pounds? Downing got the Angels started with six leadoff home runs to begin games. Through hard work, he became a solid outfielder, who didn't commit an error the entire year.

Another player Mauch loved was Rod Carew, who'd played for him in both Minnesota and California. "At the All-Star break, Carew was hitting about .500," remembered Tim Foli. "Gene came up to me and said, 'Carew is really special, he can really hit.'"

"Wait a minute," said Foli. "He's hitting .500 and has a perfect swing. How about taking my swing and playing 16 years in the big leagues. I think that's talent."

Mauch laughed and said, "You're right."

While the 1981 Angels had underachieved and were a listless

team that went through the motions, with Tim Foli and Reggie Jackson, this team had attitude and emotion.

Gene talks hitting with Reggie Jackson.
Credit: Los Angeles Angels of Anaheim

Not only was Reggie Jackson a drawing card, he hustled, became a team leader, and brought pennant-race experience to the team. He passed 2,000 hits and hit 39 home runs to tie Milwaukee's Gorman Thomas for the league lead.

Another huge acquisition was third baseman Doug DeCinces. In Baltimore he'd been under tremendous pressure as heir apparent to Brooks Robinson, but back home in Southern California, DeCinces was relaxed and confident. In August, he became only the second American Leaguer to have two three-home run games in the same season. DeCinces homered three times against the Minnesota Twins in Anaheim and repeated the feat in Seattle, five days later. DeCinces had 11 home runs in ten games. "I've never seen anything like this," said Gene Mauch. "The way DeCinces is swinging the bat, it doesn't matter who's pitching."[3]

Writer Joe Goddard of *The Sporting News* wondered how the Angels could stay in contention with a pitching staff that "looked like the drummer, flutist, and flag-bearer from the Revolutionary War." Veterans Geoff Zahn, Ken Forsch, Steve Renko and young Mike Witt were the usual starters. Bruce Kison overcame injuries, pitched as a starter and reliever, and went 10-5. Tommy John was signed late in the season and added four wins.

The bullpen was a season-long tryout camp. Closer Don Aase spent much of the year on the disabled list with a bad elbow and Mauch used 15 different pitchers in relief.

The Angels moved into first place in late April and stayed there until early May. For the next four months, the Angels and Kansas City Royals fought like angry dogs, snarling and snapping at each other for the lead.

Geoff Zahn put the finishing touches on a career year, tossing a five-hit shutout and beating Texas 4-0 to cut the Angels magic number for clinching the A.L. West to one. "You put the radar gun on Geoff Zahn's fastball and it doesn't register," said Mauch. "Put the gun on his heart and it will blow the lid off."[4]

Finally, on October 2, the next to last day of the season, at home, the Angels clinched the A.L. West Title with a 6-4 win over Texas. Reggie Jackson, Bobby Grich, and Fred Lynn all homered. Luis Sánchez pitched three near-perfect innings in relief.

Fans mobbed and kissed the players as they headed to the clubhouse to celebrate. Geoff Zahn and Doug DeCinces poured champagne on Gene Mauch's head. Hugging Mauch, Reggie said, "I hope God gives me the strength to be Mr. October just one more time for this guy, because he deserves it."[5]

On the final day of the season 62,020 showed up on Fan Appreciation Day as the Angels beat Texas 7-6 to finish with a team record 93 wins. That lifted the season attendance to 2,807,360, an American League record. With a clause that paid Reggie Jackson 50 cents for each admission over 2.4 million, Mr. October picked up a $203,680 bonus.

The Angels and Milwaukee Brewers began the American League Championship series in Anaheim before a record crowd of 64,406. Don Baylor tied a Major League Championship record with five RBI and Tommy John pitched a complete game five-hitter in the 8-3 win.

In Game Two, 64,179 packed the Big A to see Bruce Kison throw a five-hitter and Reggie Jackson hit a 430-foot home run in a 4-2 win as the Angels took a 2-0 lead in the best-of-five series.

History was on the Angels side. No team had ever won a League Championship Series after losing the first two games. One more win would send the Angels and Gene Mauch to the World Series for the first time.

In Milwaukee, the Brewers stayed alive behind the pitching of Don Sutton, who shutout the Angels for seven innings in a 5-3 Brewers win. Still, the Angels led the series 2-1. One more win and they could pack for the World Series. Milwaukee would have to win two.

Gene Mauch scratched Ken Forsch as the Game Four starter and handed the ball to Tommy John, pitching on three days' rest. Sportswriters immediately banged on their word processors comparing Mauch's decision to the 1964 Phillies, when the Little General used Jim Bunning and Chris Short on two days' rest and had blown the Phillies chances of winning a pennant.

Although John said he preferred pitching on three days' rest, the man with the bionic arm lasted 3 1/3 innings, allowed six runs on four hits, walked five and threw three wild pitches as the Brewers won 9-5 to even the series at two games apiece. "Pitching on three days' rest had absolutely no effect on the way I threw," said Tommy John.

"I'm satisfied that he (John) had as good of stuff as I've seen him go out there with," added Mauch.

Gene Autry had gone 21 seasons without a pennant, Gene Mauch

22. Bruce Kison, also with three days' rest, started the deciding Game Five.

Through the first five innings, the Angels had 12 baserunners, but scored only three runs. The Angels had 11 hits, including three by Fred Lynn, who set an LCS record with 11 hits and was named the series' MVP.

In the seventh, with one out and Luis Sánchez pitching, a freak infield hit by Charlie Moore over the pitcher's mound began the Angels' downfall. Jim Gantner singled, putting runners at first and second. After Paul Molitor fouled out to the left fielder, Robin Yount walked, loading the bases. Left-handed hitting Cecil Cooper, a .318 hitter, was up next. Decision time for Gene Mauch. Should he stay with Sanchez, who'd been effective in the late innings or bring in the lefthander Andy Hassler to face Cooper?

Cooper hesitated before going to the plate. He'd had little success against Hassler and was sure Mauch would bring him in. "To this day I don't know why Mauch didn't bring Hassler in," said Cooper.[6]

Cecil Cooper was just 2-19 in the playoffs and had committed some costly errors. It was redemption time.

Cooper settled into the batters' box, a gold chain swinging from his neck, with an open stance as he leaned over the plate. A cobra in a basket, coiled and ready to strike. Sánchez got two quick strikes, threw a ball and Cooper fouled off a pitch. Brewers' fans chanted "Coop....Coop." As Cooper watched Sánchez's fastball coming in high and tailing away, he took a controlled swing and lined a base hit to left. As he left the batter's box and saw his drive land in front of left fielder Brian Downing, Cooper shook his fists twice and ran to first. Charley Moore and Jim Gantner both scored to give the Brewers the lead. Irate Angel's owner Gene Autry rose from his seat and walked away.

Relievers Bob McClure and Pete Ladd held the Angels scoreless, the rest of the way, Milwaukee won 4-3 to win the American League Championship. The Brewers became the first team in history to lose the first two games in a series and come back to win.

"When we lost to Milwaukee," said Tim Foli, "it hurt because I wanted that so bad for Gene. I wanted that more than anything. I had won a World Series with the Pirates in '79 but I wanted Gene to have that World Series and put a stamp on his career."

As the Brewers celebrated in their clubhouse, the Angels seethed. Gene Mauch explained to reporters why he'd left Sánchez in, rather than going to lefty Andy Hassler to face Cooper.

Mauch said the walk to Robin Yount "trapped us." If Yount gets a hit and ties the game, then Andy has a little more room to work with. Then, I have no problem bringing him in to face Cooper."

Mauch said that he was worried that Hassler might walk home the go-ahead run. "Ninety percent of his (Hassler) outs come on balls."

When told of his manager's comments, Hassler vented. "If he (Mauch) isn't man enough to admit his mistakes," Hassler said, "then I'm going to admit it for him. He's not going to put the monkey on my back."[7] Hassler reportedly asked to be traded.

The depth of Gene Mauch's baseball knowledge was beyond that of the average fan, sabermatricians and most baseball managers. His nephew, Roy Smalley III, was in the stands at County Stadium and witnessed Cooper's game-winning hit. Mauch explained to Smalley why he left Sanchez in and didn't bring in Hassler.

"The Sánchez deal was the most Gene-like decision making process that I could possibly tell you," said Smalley. "Gene told me, 'If we'd had first base open when Cecil Cooper came to the plate, it would have been Andy Hassler, lefthander against lefthander but we didn't. Hassler's best stuff is below the strike zone. When he throws above the knees, his stuff straightens out, he doesn't have that nasty sinker and nasty slider. If he has to throw a strike, his stuff is not as good. So, now I'm looking at Cecil Cooper and he doesn't swing at bad pitches. He's hitting three million and hits lefthanders pretty well. If you throw him a strike, he's right on it. So I don't have the luxury of telling Hassler to just pound his hard sinker and slider below the knees and make Cooper get himself out because we don't have first base open. Hassler doesn't have nearly the chance he would have if he could pitch and not be afraid of walking him. Sánchez, on the other hand, has great movement in the strike zone. So, I don't think it matters to Cecil Cooper whether the guy is right-handed or left-handed. He's hitting well against both righthanders and lefthanders. What I need is a ground ball, what I need is a guy who can throw a ground ball sinker in the strike zone because Cecil Cooper is going to walk if I don't. So, I went with the guy that I thought had the best chance of getting a ground ball by throwing a strike.'"

Although little was said publicly, Buzzie Bavasi and the Autry's didn't agree with some of Mauch's moves in the playoffs. Bavasi and Mauch met for ninety minutes expressing their concerns. During the discussions, Mauch reportedly asked for a 2 or 3-year contract, but the Angels offered one.

On October 23, sports headline in *The Register,* screamed: "Going, going, gone: Mauch resigns." Although it was unclear whether Mauch was fired or resigned, he was finished as Angels' manager.

As Mauch was leaving the Angels, Harvey Kuenn, the Brewers' manager was named American League Manager of the Year by the Associated Press. Baltimore's Earl Weaver was second and Mauch was third in the voting.

Chapter Twenty-Two

The Toughest Game of All

Gene Mauch headed to the Rancho Mirage home and his beloved wife Nina Lee. After all those years on the road, Mauch looked forward to playing golf and bridge and spending time with the woman he'd been married to for 35 years.

In April of 1983, Nina Lee was diagnosed with melanoma, an often fatal form of cancer. Three months later, on July 15, 1983, she died.

Gene Mauch was devastated. His sister Jolene said, "Gene viewed himself as the manager of all things but he couldn't manage that one."

"He struggled and struggled and I was worried about him," said Jolene. "Roy and I were with him a lot and so was his daughter, Lee Anne. It was as bad as it gets for him. They had been together since junior high school. She was the one with whom he talked and she passed no judgment on Gene and she was his best friend. She was a very lovely lady, my best friend."

Geoff Zahn had played for Gene Mauch for nine years and they had developed a bond. Zahn conducted the Angels' Chapel and was honored when Gene Mauch asked him to conduct his wife's funeral. "There's only one guy I want to do the funeral," Mauch told him, "and that's you."

Mauch felt like he'd never manage again. He lost interest in baseball and everything else. "I was so indifferent that I was indifferent about being indifferent," Mauch said.

Shortly after Mauch left the Angels, the team signed John McNamara to a one-year contract as manager. The 50-year-old McNamara had previously managed the Oakland A's, San Diego Padres and Oakland A's.

Three months after his wife's death, Mauch accepted a job as player personnel director for the Angels. Mauch had held the job in 1981, and when Jim Fregosi was fired as manager, Mauch replaced him. Despite media speculation, Mauch again said he had no desire to manage again.

Although Mauch had been away from the club, he hadn't lost touch with baseball. He watched games on television and loved to study box scores. By looking at the outs, at bats, pitching changes and other information, Mauch could recreate a game. One of his favorite tricks was to tell you who made the last out in a game.

Since Mauch left the club, the Angels had hired Mike Port as chief administrative officer. Port and Mauch would make player personnel decisions with Buzzie Bavasi overseeing the operation.

1983 was a disaster. Decimated by injuries and aging players, the Angels dropped to 5th, 70-92, 29 games out of first place. Despite the abysmal season, the Angels offered McNamara a one-year contract extension

The 1984 Angels were an older version of the 1983 team and with the club locked into multiyear deals with aging players, there was little flexibility to get McNamara the help he needed. The Angels led the division for 52 days in the first half of the season and were in contention at the end, but lost eight of their last twelve to finish 81-81, 2nd in the A.L. West.

One of the few highlights came on the last day of the season, in a game between the Angels and Texas Rangers. 24-year-old right-hander Mike Witt, who had a 15-11 season, pitched a perfect game in Arlington, Texas.

Witt gave a lot of credit for the gem to his catcher Bob Boone.

"In the perfect game, I never shook him off," Witt said. "I never thought about shaking him off. There were plenty of games where I didn't shake him off one time."

Witt said Boone was a master at knowing what certain hitters were looking for in certain situations. "Guys like Wade Boggs, Don Mattingly and Eddie Murray-they knew they weren't hitting off the pitcher, they were hitting off Bob Boone."

Boone was the complete catcher. "He was a great pitch stealer," said Witt. "He could steal balls off the corner of the plate and turn them into strikes. Umpires loved him because he gave a good target and made himself as small as possible so the ump would have a full view of the strike zone."

The only Angels' telecast Bob Boone has ever watched was Mike Witt's perfect game. Years later, Boone, working for the Washington Nationals, was in Norwich, Connecticut to scout a player. That night, at his hotel, he couldn't sleep so he turned on MLB Classic and there was the perfect game. "I watched the whole thing," remembered Boone, "and I was thinking–look at that guy catching, he's really good."

Witt had a great curveball and Boone noticed that in that game, he had called for it more than usual. The next day he flew to California to play in an Angels' charity golf tournament. With his golf bag flung over his shoulder, Boone saw Mike Witt on the putting green.

"Hi Mike....I want to apologize, I'm so sorry," said Boone.

"What are you talking about Bob?"

"Well, I watched your perfect game and I had no idea I'd called that many curveballs. Your elbow must be killing you."

As his former catcher walked away, Witt just stared at Boone with a puzzled look on his face.

Chapter Twenty-Three

I've Got That Feeling Again

As the season ended, Buzzie Bavasi resigned as Executive Vice-President of the Angels and was replaced by Mike Port. Bavasi remained with the organization as an adviser.

John McNamara's contract as Angel's manager had expired and he was mentioned in rumors about job changes. When Ralph Houk retired as Red Sox manager, McNamara was considered the favorite because of his friendship with Boston co-owner Haywood Sullivan.

McNamara told Mike Port that he would not return as Angel's manager and shortly after was hired by the Red Sox. Speculation was that McNamara felt the Angels' would do little to field a winning team.

Mike Port's hand was held to the fire. He compiled a list of candidates to replace McNamara. Likely prospects were Joe Torre, Del Crandall, Don Zimmer and Earl Weaver. But the odds on favorite was the Little General, Gene Mauch.

When asked if he'd return as manager, Mauch said, "It's delicate. If you had asked me a month ago, I would have said 'no way.'"[1]

Port said Mauch was not a candidate but when they met to discuss possible candidates and the traits the team was looking for in a manager, Port finally said, "Gene, that sounds like you."

Mauch laughed and said, "Well, I've got that feeling in my stomach again. I can feel the fire." Port consulted the Autrys who agreed with the hiring. Mauch was again manager of the California Angels.

Gene Mauch with Mike Port. Credit: Los Angeles Angels of Anaheim

Explaining his return, Mauch said, "Bumming around is all right until you start feeling like a bum. I had a plan for 40 years–all baseball and a little golf. I tried it the other way the last two years and I didn't like it at all."

In 1985, Gene Mauch took over an old team. Doug DeCinces and Brian Downing were 34, Bobby Grich 36, Bob Boone 37, Reggie Jackson 38 and Rod Carew 39. The starting pitchers included Geoff Zahn and Ken Forsch, both 38 and Tommy John 41. In the bullpen, Donnie Moore and Luis Sánchez were 31, Doug Corbett 32 and Jim Slaton 34.

Marcel Lachemann had been the Angels' pitching coach under John McNamara and when McNamara took the Red Sox job he asked Lach to come with him, offering a multi-year contract and double his salary.

But Gene Mauch had been impressed by Lachemann and wanted to keep him. "I knew Gene had the reputation of being a control freak," said Lachemann, "but I met with him." Lach told Gene he'd had free reign to run the pitching staff under McNamara and told Mauch, "I hear you like to control everything."

"Listen, I promise you," said Mauch, "I give you my word. Just do what you did last year. That's all I'm asking you to do." So, Lach got a two-year contract extention and remained as Mauch's pitching coach.

This was a difficult time for Mauch. His beloved wife was gone and he felt a void. "He didn't mingle," said Lachemann, "He never really let anybody else in but in 1985, he was as wide open as you could be. The passing of Nina Lee gave him a different perspective. He was more open and friendly and helpful to everybody. He was without a doubt one of the most caring guys I've ever known."

In spring training in Arizona, the Angels' coaching staff including Lachemann, Bobby Knoop, Preston Gómez, and Bob Clear lived in a place called the Rodeway. "It wasn't very fancy," said Lachemann "but Knoop was a great cook, so we'd go to Bobby's place and barbecue almost every night."

Gene Mauch, Jimmy Reese, Moose Stubing and Frank Sims, the traveling secretary would play bridge and the others would talk baseball. "We became an unbelievably tight group," said Lach.

Mauch and Lachemann became close friends. "I'm entering my 53rd year in baseball," said Lachemann, "and I've been around a lot of managers but Gene is the smartest of all. He became a close and a dear friend. Other than my brother (Renee Lachemann, former manager) I've never had a closer relationship."

Gene and pitching coach Marcel Lacheman.
Credit: Los Angeles Angels of Anaheim

Mauch was true to his word, allowing Lach more power than he'd ever allowed a pitching coach. He also let Lach make pitching changes during a game.

Mike Port knew, that for the Angels to compete, he would have to mix young talent with the old timers but he had one hand tied behind his back. Increasingly, Gene Autry's wife Jackie had become involved in the operation of the team and urged her husband to stop wasting millions. The team's philosophy changed. Rather than buying high-priced free agents, the Angels would build from within, through the farm system.

Centerfielder Gary Pettis and shortstop Dick Schofield had come out of the farm system in 1984, but both had struggled offensively. Another rookie, pitcher Ron Romanick showed promise with a 12-12 record.

The only moves Port made were to sign outfielder Ruppert Jones and when Fred Lynn, a free agent, signed with Baltimore, he took pitcher Donnie Moore from Atlanta in the compensation draft. The vets didn't take kindly to the front office moves, particularly with Lynn and pitcher Don Aase going to Baltimore.

Hours after the players reported to spring training, Mauch summoned Bob Boone, Rod Carew, Brian Downing, Bobby Grich, Reggie Jackson, and Rob Wilfong to meet with him. Mauch told these proud vets that the 1984 team had been a lackluster club that just went through the motions. Mauch told his team they would have to be focused and motivated if they had any chance of competing. The players, especially Jackson, seemed to buy into the pep talk.

Sports Illustrated picked the Angels to finish 25th out of 26 teams but they underrated the Little General.

With an old team, Mauch knew he would have to rest his players and he used 155 different lineups. With the worst hitting team in the league at .251, he played Gene Mauch "Little Ball" with 99 sacrifice bunts. Get 'em on, get 'em over and get 'em in. Somehow, the Angels overachieved, spending 142 days in first place at various points of the season.

In his final season, Rod Carew hit just .280 but got his 3,000[th] career hit, only the 16th player in history to do so. On August 4 at Anaheim Stadium, against his former club, the Minnesota Twins, Carew singled to left field off of the Twins' Frank Viola in a 6-5

Angel's win. The crowd of 41,630 gave him a standing ovation and Carew tipped his batting helmet to the fans. His teammates rushed out of the dugout to congratulate him. Gene Mauch and Carew hugged and then Mauch uprooted first base and gave it to Carew.

The Angels were battling Kansas City for a divisional title. Although the Angels couldn't hit, their pitching, led by three home-grown products was fantastic. Mike Witt was 15-9, Ron Romanick 14-9 and Kirk McCaskill 12-12. Donny Moore had become a dominant closer with 31 saves, and Stew Cliburn was 9-3 out of the pen.

The Angels released Tommy John in June and in August, traded outfielder Mike Brown and pitchers Bob Kipper and Pat Clements to Pittsburgh for pitchers John Candelaria and Al Holland and outfielder George Hendrick. Then, Port sent two minor leaguers to Oakland for Don Sutton, who had 293 career wins.

"Mike Port has done everything he can, and now it's up to us to do everything we can," Gene Mauch said.

With a week left in the season the Angels went to Kansas City, but stopped hitting, lost three out of four to the Royals, and finished second at 90-72, one game back of the Royals.

In February of 1986, Geoff Zahn retired. A shoulder injury had limited the lefthander to just seven appearances during the season. At an Anaheim Stadium press conference, accompanied by his wife and daughter, the pitcher thanked Mauch for reviving his career and for his friendship.

With his voice cracking and tears in his eyes, the normally stoic Mauch said, "I was told a long time ago not to fall in love with any of my players. Most will tell you that I've handled that pretty well. This is different. I'm going to miss him."

Gene Mauch didn't allow himself to get close to many players but Zahn was one of the few who saw the flip side of the Little General.

After retiring, Geoff Zahn became baseball coach at his alma mater, Michigan, where he met another strong personality, football coach Bo Schembechler. Zahn was in Palm Springs for a fund raiser with Schembechler and another Michigan alum, former president Gerald Ford. Zahn called Gene Mauch and invited him to meet the coach, because he thought they were similar. "I wish I'd taped that conversation," said Zahn. "That was two guys probably the most intense men I've been around and yet, two of the softest hearts."

Chapter Twenty-Four

The Last Hurrah Gang

Someone named them "The Last Hurrah Gang." If they were old in 1985, they were ancient now. With 8 players approaching free agency at the end of the 1986 season, the old-timers knew it was now or never. The Angels also didn't resign their two best hitters, future Hall of Famer Rod Carew and Juan Beníquez.

Mike Port made a veiled threat, suggesting that if the team didn't do well in 1986, he would break up the old gang. Port said, "If the season is a complete disaster and I pray it isn't, then a 'worst-case' scenario could mean that-overnight-we could go from being the oldest team in baseball to the youngest team in baseball."

The Angels opened the season in Seattle and lost 8-4 in ten innings, although in his first at bat of the season, Reggie Jackson hit his 531st home run off Mike Moore. Jim Presley hit a two-run homer off Donnie Moore in the 9th to tie the game at 4-4 and then belted a two-out, grand slam of Ken Forsch in the tenth to win it.

In the second game, John Candelaria left after two innings with a bad elbow. Jim Slaton finished up with 7 strong innings. Rookie Wally Joyner hit his first home run and Brian Downing hit 2 in a 9-5 victory.

The Angels finished April with a 12-11 record, but by mid-May, Wally World had opened. 23-year-old rookie first baseman Wally Joyner put the team on his back and carried them. During a six-game spree, he had five homers and 12 RBI, homered twice in two games, and hit the first grand slam of his pro career.

The Little General at work. Credit: Los Angeles Angels of Anaheim

Fans demanded curtain calls and Joyner was mobbed by the press and Anaheim Stadium, just down the street from Disneyland, was dubbed Wally's World. Joyner, who played at BYU, had never hit more than 12 home runs in any of his three pro seasons. But he had started lifting weights, won the Triple Crown in the Puerto Rican winter league and taken the American League by surprise.

Joyner carried the club through the first months and capped an amazing first half of the season when fans voted him into the starting lineup at first base on the American League All-Star Team. It was the first time a rookie had ever made the starting lineup by a fan vote. Pitcher Mike Witt was also selected.

The Angels had a 60-year-old manager, Gene Mauch, and an 80-year-old coach, Jimmy Reese, who had once roomed with Babe Ruth. Don Sutton was 42, Reggie Jackson 40, Ken Forsch 39, Bob Boone 38, Bobby Grich 37, George Hendrick 36, and Doug DeCinces, Brian Downing, and Rick Burleson 35.

After three weeks, the geriatric Angels were in first place and Reggie Jackson was leading the league in hitting. After hitting home run number 537 to move past Mickey Mantle for sixth on the all-time list, Jackson met with Gene Mauch. Mauch knew that Jackson's trying to hit home runs was counterproductive. "You don't know how many rallies you've helped by getting base hits," Mauch told him. "Keep thinking that way. There's nothing wrong with hitting .300."

Later, when Jackson found out Mike Port had no plans to resign him for the next year, he went back to whaling away. His batting average dropped, but he did hit some tape measure home runs.

Besides the old boys, 23-year-old Dick Schofield was making a name for himself at shortstop. As a rookie in 1984, Schofield led American League shortstops in fielding. The son of former major leaguer Dick "Ducky" Schofield, he anchored the league's best defense.

Mike Witt, Don Sutton, Kirk McCaskill, and John Candelaria, back from elbow surgery, comprised the best rotation in the league.

In the bullpen, while Donnie Moore, who had 31 saves in 1984, was hurt, Doug Corbett and Terry Forster were effective.

There were 17 players older than 30, including nine over 35. They had a combined total of 222 *years* of major league experience.

The Angels were winning with exceptional pitching, air-tight defense, clutch hitting, and the "smarts" of a Gene Mauch team.

When Joyner cooled off in June, other heroes surfaced. Brian Downing drove in 17 runs in July, Doug DeCinces 24 in August and Reggie Jackson had 7 homers and 18 RBI in September. Playing just .500 ball at 31-31 in mid-June, the Angels and Texas Rangers were battling for first place and met in one of the most memorable series in team history.

In the first game, the Angels won 2-1 although they had just one hit. With Texas ahead 1-0 and knuckleballer Charlie Hough pitching a no-hitter into the ninth, left-fielder George Wright muffed a line drive by Angels' pinch hitter Jack Howell for a three-base error. Wally Joyner singled him home to tie the game at 1-1. Joyner moved to second on a passed ball by catcher Orlando Mercado, who couldn't handle a knuckler. After Reggie Jackson was walked intentionally, with George Hendrick up, Mercado committed another passed ball and Joyner scored from second for a 2-1 victory.

In the second game, Mike Witt pitched a shutout for his eighth victory as the Angels won 4-0.

Don Sutton completed the three-game sweep with his 300th career win, a masterful, 3-hit, 85 pitch complete game as the Angels took a 5-1 victory.

During this stretch, the club won five in a row and eight out of ten to move into first place in the A.L. West. After that, there was no catching them.

In late August Mike Witt shutout the Yankees 2-0 on four hits to complete a two-game sweep. As he and Wally Joyner were walked off the field at Yankee Stadium, a metal object flew out of the stands and hit Joyner on the right forearm. It was a big folding knife and it was open.

The two players may have been scared but were uninjured. Gene Mauch picked up the foot long knife and said, "You wouldn't have too much trouble killing a bear with it."[1] Mauch gave the knife to a security guard. Despite flying objects, the Angels increased their lead to four games over the Rangers.

On September 26 at Anaheim Stadium, the Angels blew out runner-up Texas 8-3 to clinch the A.L. West. John Candelaria pitched seven innings and held the Rangers to five hits to get the win. Brian Downing hit two of the Angels four home runs. In his 23rd year of big league managing, Gene Mauch finally had his first title of any kind.

"I won't consider the season a success unless we get to the World Series," said Bobby Grich. First, they had to get past the A.L. East Champion Boston Red Sox.

The 1986 ALCS began at Boston's Fenway Park with a matchup of the Red Sox' Cy Young favorite, Roger Clemens facing Mike Witt. Clemens was 24-4 during the season including a 3-0 record against the Angels. Witt was 18-8.

In his first post-season start, Witt was brilliant, pitching a complete game five-hitter as the Angels won 8-1 to take the lead in the best of seven series. Witt mixed his blazing fastball, biting curveball, and changeup with impeccable control. He took a no-hitter into the sixth before giving up a two-out single to Wade Boggs. Brian Downing provided much of the offense, driving in four runs, with a two-run double in the fourth and a two-run single in the eighth.

The Angels defense had the highest fielding percentage in club history but you wouldn't know it by the way they played in Game Two.

To accommodate network television, the game was played at noon with a blinding sun, menacing shadows and swirling winds. With Boston leading 1-0, in the second inning, Angels' starter Kirk McCaskill lost Boggs' high bouncer in the sun, fumbling the ball to load the bases. Then Marty Barrett's single made it 2-0.

The Angels tied the game at 2-2 in the fifth on a Wally Joyner home run, the first by a rookie in LCS history. But second baseman Bobby Grich and shortstop Dick Schofield lost sight of a Dwight Evans pop-up, a run-scoring double that proved to be the winning hit.

In the sixth, a base-running mix-up cost the Angels dearly. Bobby Grich rounded third base and headed for home on California's third straight hit. Instead of using hand signals to stop Grich at third, third base coach Moose Stubing yelled at Grich to stop. Grich didn't hear him and was easily thrown out. Grich slammed down his batting helmet, screamed at Stubing and stalked off the field.

In the seventh, the normally reliable infield came unglued. With one out, Bill Buckner reached on an error by second baseman

Bobby Grich. A Jim Rice single and a walk to Don Baylor loaded the bases. Dwight Evans hit a ground ball to third, which Doug DeCinces booted for an error, allowing another run to score. The third error was a bad throw by shortstop Dick Schofield. The Red Sox scored three runs on only one hit, taking advantage of the three Angels errors in a 9-2 Boston rout.

Tied 1-1, the series moved back to Anaheim Stadium. Game 3 was a pitcher's duel between the Angels' John Candelaria and Boston's "Oil Can" Boyd. In the seventh Dick Schofield and Gary Pettis both homered as the Angels won 5-3.

Before Game Four as the Angels completed batting practice and were picking up baseballs, reliever Doug Corbett said to Gene Mauch, "I'm going to get it done tonight Skip, if you need me."

Mauch did need Corbett, who pitched three-and-two-thirds innings of hitless, scoreless relief to get the victory. Bobby Grich's single won it 4-3 in eleven innings. The Angels played without Wally Joyner, who'd been sent to the hospital with a bacterial infection in his leg. Joyner hit .455 through the first three games of the ALCS, with two doubles, a homer and two RBI, while playing flawlessly at first base.

Leading 3-1, the Angels needed just one more victory to win the ALCS and go to the World Series.

64,223 fans packed Anaheim Stadium on Sunday, October 12 for game five. The often laid back Southern California crowd was raucous from the beginning, shaking the Big A, knowing the Angels were one win away from the World Series. Gene Autry, who had owned the team since 1961, was on the verge of reaching baseball's summit for the first time and beleaguered manager Gene Mauch, who had come so close twice before, now had a chance to win his first World Championship.

Game One winner Mike Witt faced Boston lefthander Bruce Hurst.

Jim Rice led off the Boston second with a single to right field. Then Witt struck out Don Baylor swinging and Dwight Evans looking. Left-handed hitting catcher Rich Gedman powered a 2-2 pitch from Witt over the fence in deep right field as Boston took a 2-0 lead, momentarily muffling the crowd.

In the bottom of the third, leadoff hitter Bob Boone worked the count in his favor to 3-1 and then homered to deep left field off Bruce Hurst. Red Sox 2 Angels 1.

In the Angels' sixth, with two outs, Doug DeCinces doubled to right and first baseman Bobby Grich, playing in place of Joyner, sent a drive to deep center field. Centerfielder Dave Henderson leaped, collided with the wall as the ball hit the heel of his glove and fell over the fence for a home run giving the Angels a 3-2 lead.

Bob Stanley relieved Bruce Hurst and in the bottom of the seventh, pinch hitter Rob Wilfong's RBI double drove in a run and Brian Downing's sacrifice fly added another, for a 5-2 Angels lead.

The crowd was delirious as Mike Witt took a three-run lead to the ninth. Bill Buckner, who could barely walk because of a bad ankle, singled to center field and hobbled off the field, replaced by pinch runner Dave Stapleton. The crowd grew louder as Jim Rice took a called third strike. Two more outs to go.

Then Don Baylor stepped in to face Witt. The former Angel still harbored anger at his old team for letting him go. Witt missed with a curve. Baylor fouled off two fast balls. In the dugout, Gene Mauch stood, arms folded, expressionless. Witt overthrew a fastball and put it in the dirt. A curveball just missed and the count was 3-2. Then, Witt made a good pitch, a curve ball, down and away, about two inches outside. But Baylor, one of the strongest men in the game, reached out and pulled it to left-center, a high fly ball just over the glove of the leaping Gary Pettis for a home run to make it 5-4 Angels.

In the Angels' bullpen, lefthander Gary Lucas and right-handed closer Donnie Moore, warmed up.

By now, there were more riot helmets than batting helmets in the dugouts as California State policemen readied for the game's end. Then, Witt threw a hanging curveball that Evans popped up. Third baseman Doug DeCinces spread his arms wide, indicating he would make the catch. As the ball disappeared into his glove, he shook it before returning it to Witt. One more out to go.

As DeCinces returned the ball to Witt, catcher Bob Boone came to the mound and then, Pitching Coach Marcel Lacheman, who made pitching changes.

"I didn't know he came to take me out," said Witt. "I was ready to discuss strategy with Boone and see if Lach had anything to add to the conversation."

Instead, Lacheman tapped his left arm indicating he wanted lefthander Gary Lucas to come in and face Rich Gedman, who was 3-for-3 with a home run off Witt in the game.

Many fans booed, thinking Witt could get one more out. Boone and DeCinces looked at each other, agreeing with the crowd. As Witt walked toward the dugout, he received a thunderous ovation and nodded his head to the crowd.

"Gene had made the decision to take Mike out in the fifth or sixth inning," said Lachemann. "After Rich Gedman had hit three rockets off Witt, Gene looked at me and said, 'if this guy comes up with the game on the line in the 8th or 9th inning, Mike's not going to pitch to him.'"

While the crowd looked at the manager's move with their hearts, Gene Mauch had to look at the situation logically. Gedman had hit three bullets of Witt with a home run, double, and single. Gedman had always hit Witt. Witt had thrown 121 pitches and given up two home runs in the game. Gary Lucas was a lefthander and had struck out Gedman the day before and once earlier in the year. Lucas had outstanding control and hadn't hit a batter in over four years.

So, what happened? With his first pitch, Lucas hung a forkball that came in shoulder high and hit Gedman, putting the tying run on.

Again, Lacheman walked to the mound, this time, tapping his right arm, indicating he wanted closer Donnie Moore. Although Moore had a bad shoulder and had gotten a cortisone shot the day before, he'd told Gene Mauch he could pitch.

"Donnie was our best alternative," said Marcel Lachemann. "We wouldn't have been in the ALCS without Donnie. After saving 31 games in 1985 and making the All-Star Team, Moore had 21 saves in 1986 and had been instrumental in helping the Angels win the A.L. West.

On the mound, Moore tugged the bill of his cap, pulled up his belt, then bent over and juggled the resin bag with his right hand. Then, he stood up, took a deep breath and stared in at the right handed hitting Dave Henderson.

"Hendu" as he was known, was hitless in the series and had nearly worn the goat's horns in the sixth, when a fly ball hit the heel of his glove and fell over the fence for a home run.

Donnie Moore's first pitch was a fastball, low, as the crowd quieted. Then, a fastball for a strike as the fans roared. Henderson swung and missed at a fastball. One ball. Two strikes. The Angels were one strike away. Moore missed with a fastball in the dirt and then Henderson fouled off another. Two balls. Two strikes. Moore then walked around on the mound and catcher Boone came out and said something to him. Henderson took a healthy rip at another fastball, fouling it straight back, He turned and walked around, collecting his thoughts, then spit and stepped back in. Bob Boone then called for a forkball. "That was his best pitch," said Boone, "he was automatic but that year he had a bad back and some arm problems. He actually threw a decent one, it was down, but it tumbled and it was the time of day when the ball was really carrying."

With a quick flip of his wrists, Henderson connected, sending the ball over the left field fence as outfielder Brian Downing looked on helplessly. Gene Mauch stood impassively in the dugout, not showing one ounce of emotion. As Henderson watched the ball sail over the fence, as he ran to first, he jumped three feet in the air and nearly fell down. After a few more steps, he planted both feet, jumped even higher, doing a pirouette and then began a home run trot that will never be forgotten in Boston.

"I've looked at the tape so many times," said Marcel Lachemann, "the ball that Hendu hit wasn't a bad pitch, it was below the strike zone. He just went down and got it."

Donnie Moore took the hit. He became the fall guy. One strike away. But time has blurred the facts. Many think the game ended there. "A lot of people forget different situations throughout that game," said Mike Witt. "We had chances to win it."

Donnie Moore stayed in and retired Ed Romero on a fly ball to right. In the bottom of the ninth, Rob Wilfong singled in Ruppert Jones to tie the score at 6-6. With rookie righthander Steve Crawford in to pitch, Dick Schofield singled and Brian Downing was walked intentionally, loading the bases.

Doug DeCinces already had two doubles. A rookie on the mound, in the biggest game of his life, Crawford was nervous. "Crawford was literally shaking and Doug probably could have gone up there with the *Sporting News* in his hand, not swung the bat, and he wouldn't have thrown a strike," said Marcel Lachemann.

Most figured DeCinces would take a strike but knowing Crawford's best pitch was a sinker, he didn't want to hit the ball on the ground. A deep fly ball could win it. So, when Crawford threw a first pitch fastball, DeCinces swung, sending a fly ball to shallow right, not deep enough to score a run. Bobby Grich then lined out to end the inning. Dave Henderson's sacrifice fly in the eleventh won it for Boston 7-6.

"After the game," remembered Mike Witt, "Gene came up to me by my locker and told me, 'I didn't want him (Gedman) to beat you. I'd rather have him beat somebody else than you."

Although Witt didn't want to come out of the game, he had no problem with Gene Mauch's decision. "I had been used really well that year," said Witt. "98% of the time, every move was right on the money as far as my stuff and my pitch count. I had 16 complete games. They let me finish games and sometimes they took me out."

Many consider Game Five to be one of the most exciting games in baseball history. After the game, Marcel Lachemann said, "I've never been as drained, I was wrung out. Gene turned to me and said, 'This is the greatest game I've ever been involved in.'"

The Angels still had a 3-2 series lead going to Boston but the loss had ripped the Angels' hearts out, destroying their emotional resolve. "In retrospect, it took the life out of the team," said Witt, "going coast to coast and trying to muster a second wind after a loss like that, we would never recover."

Wally Joyner never returned and Donnie Moore's arm was still hurting. The Red Sox beat the sleep-walking Angels twice 10-4 and 8-1 to win the American League pennant and a berth in the World Series.

Minutes after the game ended, Bobby Grich announced his retirement from baseball. Grich had hinted at retirement before but his frustrating performance in the ALCS may have pushed him over the edge.

After Mauch went to his office to corral his emotions, the door opened. "I don't have a hell of a lot to say," Mauch told the media. "I hurt like hell for the players. I hurt like hell for Gene Autry. We laid our hearts out there and got stepped on."[2]

Baseball is the greatest second guessing game in the world. Several people including Gene Mauch thought Bob Boone should've called for a fastball rather than a forkball when Dave Henderson broke the Angels' hearts in Game Five.

Instead of playing in the World Series, Boone was at home watching the Red Sox and Mets on television. "I remembered Gene saying, 'Henderson can't hit a fastball.' So, in Game 2 of the World Series, Dwight Gooden threw him a fastball and Henderson hit it out. So I called Gene and said, Gene are you watching the game?"

"Yeah."

"Did you see the ball Henderson hit?"

"Yeah, he hit it pretty good," said Mauch.

"Well, there's that fucking fastball he couldn't hit, I said as I slammed the phone down."

Chapter Twenty-Five

Let's Run For It

In 1987 the Angels attempted to make a transition from power to speed. Two rookies, 22-year-old Mark McLemore, a switch-hitting, base-stealing, second baseman and 24-year-old outfielder Devon White, another racehorse, moved into the starting lineup. They joined centerfielder Gary Pettis, a Gold Glove winner and premier base thief and shortstop Dick Schofield, capable of swiping 25 bags.

Gene Mauch had never managed a team with this kind of speed. Not only would the running Angels be dangerous on the bases, but he felt they would improve defensively, particularly in the outfield.

Mauch knew it would take his team awhile to mold its personality, so he was patient as the Angels won only six of their first 21 spring training games. But Devon White and Mark McLemore had great springs and the team caught fire, winning nine straight, including a three game sweep of the Los Angeles Dodgers in the Freeway Series, to finish 15-15.

There were some question marks about the pitching. Closer Donnie Moore, who'd pitched hurt in 1986, was trying to overcome shoulder problems, starter John Candelaria lost feeling in his leg, and reliever Gary Lucas had a bad shoulder.

Gone were Reggie Jackson, who returned to the Oakland A's and Bobby Grich, who retired. Still unsigned as the season began was 39-year-old catcher Bob Boone.

With the team's speed and versatility, Mauch began to tinker. Mauch recalled 1982, when he moved Brian Downing into the leadoff spot and he had the best all-around season of his career. Downing hit .282 with 28 home runs, 84 RBI, 86 walks, and 109 runs scored. Downing had also hit six leadoff home runs. So, five years later, Mauch put the now designated hitter back in the top spot in the order. Then, he put two speedsters, Gary Pettis and Mark McLemore in the eight and nine holes. Mauch reasoned that since a leadoff hitter gets more at bats in a season than anyone else, Downing would often follow Pettis and McLemore and would have a chance to drive in runs.

Mauch's formula worked to perfection in the season opener, a 7-1 victory over Seattle at Anaheim Stadium. Downing drove in three runs with two doubles, Pettis had three hits and scored three runs and McLemore had the game winning RBI with his first major league hit. Mike Witt pitched a complete game five-hitter for his first win.

Brian Downing hit five home runs in the Angels first nine games as they went 6-3.

Before the Angels game in Boston on May 9, Gene Mauch got a phone call from Wally Joyner's mother Karma. She told Mauch that Joyner's 31-year-old brother had died of a heart attack earlier in the day and asked Mauch to wait until after the game to tell Wally. Crandon Neil Joyner died after being hospitalized with pneumonia and coronary complications earlier in the week. He died in a Sacramento hospital, leaving his wife and six children.

"They thought it would be a good idea to let Wally enjoy the day before telling him,"[1] Mauch said. In the game, Joyner's three-run homer in the first gave the Angels a 3-0 lead en route to an 8-1 victory.

With his photographic memory of every word in the rule book, Mauch could occasionally steal a game with his smarts. In Detroit, after a pitch in the dirt, Tigers' catcher Mike Heath scooped up the loose ball with his mask. Mauch immediately came out of the dugout to remind umpire Durwood Merrill about Rule 7.05, which calls for an automatic two-base error whenever a player stops the ball with a piece of equipment other than his glove.

Mauch was right and the umpire told Angel baserunners Mark McLemore and Brian Downing to advance 180 feet.

Tigers' manager Sparky Anderson shook his head in amazement and said, "No one knows the rules better than Gene Mauch. He could teach a seminar on it." Detroit won the game 15-2.

Then, opponents started to pound Angels' pitching, particularly Urbano Lugo. After pitching well in the season opener, Mike Witt began a strange pattern of a good game followed by a bad game and in four of his first eleven starts, failed to go more than four innings. Don Sutton was getting shelled and went 2-5 through the first two months. After pitching a shutout, Kirk McCaskill had surgery to remove bone chips on his elbow. Another starter John Candelaria was arrested twice within a month on charges of driving while intoxicated. The Angels, then placed him on the 15-day disabled list for personal reasons.

Gary Pettis had a terrible year. After losing his arbitration case, he hit just .232 in spring training and was striking out in bunches. Plagued by trade rumors that had Pettis going to the Dodgers, he slumped even more. After Pettis' average dropped to .211, Gene Mauch benched him and after a 5-for-54 stretch, Pettis was sent to AAA Edmonton.

Mark McLemore didn't live up to expectations and after veteran Johnny Ray was acquired from Pittsburgh, McLemore was demoted to the California League.

In late May, the Angels lost nine in a row and suffered through a 3-7 home stand to fall into sixth place with a 21-28 record. They won eight in a row in late June, but a poor August and 7-19 September buried them.

By late September, Gene Mauch was stressed to the max. In Cleveland, young lefthander Chuck Finley was scheduled to make just his second major league start. Bob Boone and Pitching Coach Marcel Lacheman knew Finley could get wild, so they told Mauch,

"Let us take care of it. You just sit back and enjoy the game."

The Angels scored twice in the first inning to give Finley a 2-0 cushion. In the bottom of the first, Finley walked the leadoff batter as Mauch seethed in the dugout. Finley walked five batters in the inning, walked in a run, and the Indians tied it 2-2. Both Boone and Lacheman made trips to the mound to settle Finley down. The Angels scored twice in the second to take a 4-2 lead and Finley pitched two scoreless innings.

The Angels scored twice in the fourth to take a 6-2 lead. But in the bottom of the fourth, Finley walked the leadoff batter as Mauch's blood pressure began to climb. Boone went to the mound. After Finley gave up a single and another walk, to load the bases, Mauch couldn't stand any more. He stood up on the top step of the dugout and screamed at Finley, "Throw a fucking strike." After Finley gave up another bases loaded walk, he was replaced by Don Sutton. Finley wound up walking eight in three-and-two-thirds innings.

The Angels wound up winning 11-8. Almost thirty years later, Boone said, "Lach and I still laugh about that day."

A once-promising season had become a disaster. In winning two of their last three games, the Angels finished at 75-82, tied for sixth place with Texas. They had become only the second team in major league history to finish first one year and last the next.

Right after the final game, 61-year-old Gene Mauch confirmed that he would return for his 27th season as a manager in 1988.

Gene Mauch felt that a manager's first job was to pick the right players for his team and then establish the proper atmosphere. That was Mauch's task as he began spring training in Mesa, Arizona.

Mauch announced that Mike Witt would be the opening day starter in 1988, but after him were a lot of question marks. Pitcher Kirk McCaskill was coming back from arm surgery. Dan Petry's arm had recovered from injury but he'd suffered a herniated disc in his back. Mauch would have to decide on a fifth starter with the leading candidate rookie Chuck Finley. Mauch was encouraged by Donnie Moore, who appeared to be in good shape, after undergoing a back operation in October.

Gene Mauch's big experiment was converting veteran second baseman Johnny Ray into an outfielder. The 31-year-old, acquired from Pittsburgh, had hit .318 in 1987. Mauch loved the thought of having Ray in the outfield and Mark McLemore at second base. Lee Walls, who had played for Mauch in Philadelphia, was brought in to tutor Ray. Walls had been the outfield coach who'd helped Oakland's Rickey Henderson, Dwayne Murphy and Tony Armas become the best outfield in baseball.

Mauch was enjoying spring training and looking forward to Opening Day. Then on March 11, he shot a bolt of lightning through the Angels. Mauch announced he was stepping down as manager, at least temporarily, because of health problems. Angels' advance scout Cookie Rojas was named interim manager.

Mauch became concerned about his health in August, when he was tired and couldn't shake a chest cough. He said when he'd felt tired before, he always bounced back but about a month ago he'd gotten sick. "Maybe when you get to be 62 years old," he said, "this is how you're supposed to feel, but I don't think so."

Mauch checked into St. Joseph Hospital in Orange and after two days of testing, he was diagnosed with chronic bronchitis, was given medication and sent home to the desert to rest. The Angels' organization heaved a sigh of relief, having feared that Mauch, a heavy smoker, might have had cancer. A doctor gave Mauch a clean bill of health but told him to cut down on his smoking.

During his time at home, Mauch realized that the strain of being a big league manager, especially the losing, was taking its toll. Mauch met with Gene and Jackie Autry and told them he had decided to retire. He recommended Cookie Rojas as his replacement.

"The losses got so hard for him," said Bob Boone. "You expect the wins, but the losses really get to you. The losses were getting to him more and more at the end. When his wife died, everything went out of him."

Gene Mauch managed in the big leagues for 26 years with a record of 1902-2037. He is twelfth on the all-time win list and fourth among the losingest managers.

He managed for more years than any skipper without winning a league pennant or appearing in a World Series.

Chapter Twenty-Six

Losses of a Lifetime

"1986 had really taken its toll on my Dad," said Gene Mauch's daughter Lee Anne. "He knew in his heart of hearts that he'd had one last chance to win a World Series and it didn't happen. That was a horrific time for him but he didn't want to show it."

Lee Anne said her dad saved many garbage bags full of unopened newspapers from 1986, thinking perhaps that someday he'd get around to reading about that season. He never did.

On the surface, it appeared Mauch had settled into a familiar routine. He hit the links early, played 18, then to the clubhouse for bridge and cocktails. After dinner, back home to watch baseball.

Aside from baseball, golf and bridge, Mauch had no real outside interests. Although he was brilliant, he rarely read a book. When asked what he read, he said, "box scores."

Mauch religiously studied box scores of the previous day's games and could cull more information from a box score than any man who ever lived. Mauch could tell you who made the final out of a game by looking at the box score. He could tell which pitchers and hitters were hot and which were not. He could discern managerial trends and tendencies.

Mauch felt he was staying close to the game he loved by staying informed, but he missed the nine inning involvement of the game and most of all, missed most of his players.

In the fall of 1988, Gene Autry decided to replace Cookie Rojas as the Angels' manager and asked Gene Mauch if he'd like to return. When Mauch expressed uncertainty about taking the job, Autry hired Doug Rader.

Physically, Mauch felt great, saying he could finally get a good night's sleep. After the cancer scare, his doctor told him to stop smoking. Mauch said, at one time, he smoked as many as 75 cigarettes in a day. He said that there were times when he'd have one cigarette in the ashtray, one in his left hand, then put one in his right hand and start to light it. More relaxed, Mauch might go two hours after a meal before smoking a cigarette. But, when he wanted one, he'd have it.

In July of 1989, Mauch and the entire Angels' family was saddened by the news that his former pitcher Donnie Moore had shot his wife three times before turning the gun on himself. Like his manager, Moore was unfairly blamed for the Angels' 1986 collapse. Mauch knew that Moore's gopher ball to Dave Henderson in the 1986 World Series was a contributing factor to his death. Out of the public eye, Mauch had little to say except that Moore "had a lot of demons."

Occasionally, old baseball friends showed up. Geoff Zahn took his wife and daughter to Rancho Mirage to see Gene. Reggie Jackson, Rod Carew, and Tim Foli stopped by to play golf and talk baseball. And as often as he could, Mauch played golf and shared cocktails with his best friend Don Drysdale.

Gene with best friend Don Drysdale.

Mauch had always admired Drysdale as a competitor and later as a broadcaster, and said, "He talks very well for a guy who's had two fingers in his mouth all his life."

Drysdale had joined Mauch in Montreal as a TV commentator and pitching instructor. Later, they played golf, drank, talked baseball and life, and deepened their friendship.

On July 3, 1993, while Mauch was sinking putts in Rancho Mirage, Drysdale was broadcasting for the Dodgers. In Seattle, when Drysdale didn't appear at the usual time, Dodgers' personnel became concerned and contacted the team hotel.

Hotel employees broke into Drysdale's room and found his body on the floor near his still-made bed. Drysdale had died of a heart attack. Drysdale had a history of heart problems. In 1989, he undergone angioplasty to clear blocked arteries.

Gene Mauch had lost his beloved wife, a profession he loved, and now, his best friend.

More than 1,000 friends and family members attended the memorial service for Don Drysdale. Mauch was one of five asked to eulogize the Hall of Fame pitcher.

"The big guy was a giant of a man who walked among giants," Mauch said, "and if Don could hear me say that, he'd say, 'Gene, either start over or sit down. I never had anything to do with the Giants in my life."

Mauch had been out of baseball for six years. His closest friends and family knew he'd built a moat around his feelings. You can only play so much golf, drink so many cocktails, and eat so many steaks. Inside, Mauch felt a void.

Chapter Twenty-Seven

The Pupil Calls

The Little General returns to battle in Kansas City.

In 1995, Bob Boone became manager of the Kansas City Royals. With the Angels, Gene Mauch and Bob Boone had become mentor and student and great friends. They spent countless hours talking baseball and plotting strategy. Boone said Gene Mauch was "the finest baseball man I've ever met and certainly the smartest."

So, Boone knew he wanted the 69-year-old Mauch to be his bench coach in Kansas City. He drove to Rancho Mirage several times to test Mauch's interest and finally the Little General said yes.

Mauch told Boone, "I'll only do it for you." Mauch spelled out his salary and per diem demands and Boone told Royals' G.M. Herk Robinson to hire Mauch.

"Tremendous" is how Boone described his time with Mauch in K.C. "Gene and I argued all the time," recalled Boone, with a laugh. "I spent so much time with him. I love him."

And Mauch loved being back with the boys. Before a spring training game between Kansas City and the New York Mets, the Royals had moved inside to a batting cage because it was raining. Mauch was leaning against the cage when four of his former players approached: Dallas Green, Bobby Wine, Mike Cubbage and Rusty Staub. "We stayed there for 45 minutes," remembered Staub, "telling Gene Mauch stories. Mauch laughed at most of them but finally said, 'Geez guys, I must have really been an asshole.' And we all reacted at the same time, "You really were."

Boone's players also loved Gene. The Royals had taken a 23-year-old outfielder, Jonathan Nunnally, in the Rule 5 draft from Cleveland and Boone put him in the hands of the Little General. Mauch spent hours working with Nunnally and before each at bat, told the rookie what to expect, "OK, Jonathan, here's what this pitcher is going to do to you this time." Nunnally became the Royals' starting right fielder, hit .244 and was second on the club with 14 home runs.

Third baseman Gary Gaetti was 38 and Boone said, "Most people thought he was washed up, but he hit 35 home runs for me. I credit Gene for most of that. He got him to relax and be a leader."

One of the toughest decisions for a manager is knowing when to make a pitching change. When a Royals' starter was struggling, Bob Boone turned to Mauch and asked, "What do you think? Do you think he's about done?"

"Look," Mauch said, "don't ask me what I think about this. This is your game. If you want to ask me what I would do, I will tell you, but don't ask me what I think should be done."

The Royals finished second in the A.L Central with a 70-74 record and just missed landing a wild card spot. Boone loved having Gene Mauch with him and was disappointed when the short-sighted G.M. Herk Robinson, didn't bring him back. "We had a great year," Boone said, "and then Herk wouldn't hire him the next year. Gene was completely under-used."

Chapter Twenty-Eight

TV Star

Now 70, Mauch returned to Rancho Mirage, knowing he was probably done with baseball. He settled back into his routine: an early tee time, a round or two of golf, cocktails, dinner, and baseball on television.

Mauch had played golf since he was a kid and was damned good. At one time he had a two handicap and even in his 70's, he was a five handicapper.

In 1987 when Nick Faldo won the British Open by making 18 straight pars in the final round, Mauch said, "I only did that once." He and Raymond Floyd became friends and Floyd would occasionally send Mauch new equipment to try.

Playing golf in Palm Springs, he met many celebrities including former presidents Richard Nixon, Gerald Ford, Dwight D. Eisenhower and Ronald Reagan.

When he was active in baseball, he played in offseason tournaments for baseball players, it was usually Mauch or his friend and long-time coach Peanuts Lowery who won. He also played in numerous celebrity tournaments, including those televised nationally by NBC. After a round of golf, Mauch liked to play bridge. He felt that you could learn a lot about people by the way they played cards.

*To Gene Mauch
With best wishes*

Gerald R. Ford

Gene with Gerald Ford at an All-Star Game.

Gene on the golf course with Ike.

Harmonizing with Ronald Reagan. Mauch on far left,
Reagan-second from right.

In 2002, after leaving the San Diego Padres, I accepted a job as a sportscaster for KPSP-TV, Channel 2 in Palm Springs, a startup CBS station that needed viewers.

The California Angels were headed for the World Series and I remembered that former Angels' manager Gene Mauch lived in Palm Springs. I thought it might be fun to have him on as a commentator before and after World Series games.

Gene had experienced three of the biggest failures in baseball history with the 1964 Phillies and the Angels in 1982 and 1986, so I figured he might be a bitter old man.

I called Gene, told him what I had in mind and he invited me to his house, minutes from the station.

As I drove, I remembered when I'd first met Gene Mauch. In 1981, I was a young announcer for the Texas Rangers who were in Minneapolis to play Mauch's Minnesota Twins. It was a cold, rainy Saturday at Metropolitan Stadium. Nearing the end of a long season, I needed some fresh broadcast material. Walking into the

Twins' dugout, I saw Mauch, sitting on the ledge atop the dugout bench, smoking a cigarette and holding court with two writers.

When they finished, I introduced myself and said I'd like to ask a few questions about his club. With piercing blue eyes, all white hair, and a lined face, Gene Mauch was intimidating.

As I recall, I asked a question about the Twins' pitching staff. I'll never forget Mauch's reaction. He took a long drag on his cigarette and blew the smoke into the frigid Minnesota air as the writers snickered. As I waited for Mauch's answer, he stared toward the outfield and took another drag. I figured he hadn't heard my question and just as I started to repeat it, he held up his hand and said, "Wait, I'm trying to think of a good answer."

Mauch began talking and gave me a long, thoughtful answer which provided me with information for several telecasts. Then he flicked his cigarette aside and headed down into the Twins' clubhouse. The writers looked at me and shrugged, as if to say, "That's Gene."

Gene's house was on the ninth hole of the Springs Golf Club in Rancho Mirage. When Gene opened his front door, he guided me toward the driveway. "Let's go out here," he said, lighting a cigarette. "My wife won't let me smoke in the house." As we talked about the Angels and the World Series, I found out that he wasn't a bitter old man. His face lit up and his eyes sparkled as he said, "It's great. I'm so happy for Jackie Autry and Mike Scioscia."

He agreed to become my pre and post-game analyst on World Series games. When I told him that we couldn't pay him because Channel 2 was brand new with no advertising revenue, I figured he'd turn me down.

Instead, he said, "Fuck it. Just get me a gross of blue dot golf balls." He invited me inside for a cocktail. As we watched an Angels' game, he explained how his old team would win the series. I was astounded by his knowledge. I had my man.

Gene admitted that the Angels had invited him to throw out the first pitch when the series began, but he said no because he thought he might jinx them.

Looking back at the video from 2002, I recalled how handsome and athletic Gene looked. At 79, he still had it. Gene wore a red golf shirt with a white knit short sleeved sweater that matched his head of all white hair. He was lean and bronzed from all the golf he played.

Mel Proctor and Gene Mauch talking baseball.
Credit: Mel Proctor

On one of the pregame segments, I asked Gene to evaluate Barry Bonds, who was hitting .350 with seven home runs in postseason.

"Prior to this year," said Mauch, "I didn't put him in the same class with Stan Musial or Ted Williams, but he's emerged now and he can flat do it."

Then, I asked Gene how he would try to get Bonds out. "If I had pitchers that can throw a lot of slop up there, slow stuff," he said, "I'd kind of play with his mind. If you recall the one time Francisco Rodriguez struck him out, he got him with four sliders in a row. Try to change his eye level but I wouldn't give into him with strikes."

The Angels took game six and won it in seven. Gene was overjoyed at the Angels' success. We maintained our friendship after the World Series. He invited me to his house for cocktails and we talked baseball. I treasured every moment I spent with this fascinating man.

Guarded at first, Gene opened up as our friendship developed. I had no idea I would write a book about Gene, so I didn't pepper him with questions. But one time, I asked, "Do you miss baseball?"

Following his trademark pause, he said, "I don't miss the travel or being away from home for weeks at a time, but God I miss the two or three hours I spent in the dugout managing a game. I've never found a way to replace that."

There was a sad and lonely side to this man. One night, standing in the driveway as he smoked a cigarette, Gene told me, "After my wife Nina Lee died, I was single for many years. I was so damned lonely." I could feel the hurt. Then he told me he'd met his second wife Jody, whom he'd married in the early 1990's.

Gene had a dry wit and was a master of one-liners. After a celebrity golf outing, I asked Gene if I could buy him a drink.

"I don't drink anymore," he said.

"Oh."

"But I don't drink any less. Let's go."

Over cocktails the conversation shifted to golf. I knew he was an avid golfer but wondered how good he was. "Gene, are you a scratch golfer?" I asked.

"No, but I'm a scratch drinker."

Shortly after that, I landed a job doing radio play-by-play for the Los Angeles Clippers. I went to Gene's house to say goodbye. As I got ready to leave, we shook hands and Gene said, "Stay in touch." I walked to the car with tears in my eyes.

In 2003, I was in Palm Springs with the Clippers who held part of their training camp there. I called Gene who said he really admired the team's coach Mike Dunleavy.

"Why don't I come pick you up," I suggested. "You can watch practice and I'll introduce you to Mike."

"I wish I could come," he said, "but my doctors won't let me."

Gene explained that he had just had part of a lung removed. Lung cancer. The cigarettes had taken their toll. He tried to be optimistic, "The doc says if I take care of myself, I should make it to 80." I hung up the phone, wondering if I would see this wonderful man again.

Knowing their old skipper was ill, many baseball friends stopped by including Preston Gómez, Reggie Jackson, Rod Carew and Geoff Zahn. Every week, the ultra-religious Alvin Dark wrote, encouraging Gene to find God.

His close friend Marcel Lachemann and his wife visited Gene and Jody in Rancho Mirage. "Gene was still sharp and alert," said Lach. "We talked baseball and he asked how his old players were doing. He missed them." After about an hour, Gene was tiring and Jody gave the high sign indicating it was time for his friends to go.

"When he got sick that was hard on me," said Zahn. "We talked a lot and he said at one point he was either going into the ministry or was staying in baseball." At first, that notion seems ludicrous since Mauch was the master of the four-letter word. But Zahn, who'd been involved in the ministry said, "He would have been a great pastor because he cared so much about everything he did and took ownership for it."

Often, Mauch and his daughter Lee Anne sat on the patio and talked about life. "One of his great regrets," said Lee Anne, "was that his dad hadn't seen what he'd accomplished in baseball. He regretted that he hadn't made the Hall of Fame. He felt the greatest gift he could have given him was to show George what he did for him by leaving Kansas for California."

In 2005 I became the TV announcer for the Washington Nationals. It was exciting to be back in the game and occasionally I called Gene to share the experience. In the first half of the season, the Nationals were in first place and were 24-8 in one run games. When I told Gene, he repeated one of his famous sayings, "Most one-run games are lost." As usual, Gene was right. In the second half of the season the Nationals went 5-23 in one run games and fell from first place to last.

The next time I called, Gene's voice was weak and faded in and out. He didn't sound good and said he had to go. He had a doctor's appointment. That was the last time I talked to Gene. He died of lung cancer on August 8, 2005 at the Eisenhower Medical Center in Rancho Mirage. Gene Mauch was 79.

End Notes

Chapter One

1. *Los Angeles Times,* interview with Al Wolf, 1954
2. *Sports Illustrated,* October 31, 1981, "A Man Has to Care," Ron Fimrite
3. Ibid
4. *Los Angeles Times,* August 9, 1992, 1
5. Ibid
6. Ibid
7. *Los Angeles Times,* August 9, 1992, 1

Chapter Two

1. Barney, Rex and Macht, Norman L., *Rex Barney's Thank Youuuu,* Centreville, Md., Tidewater Publishing, 1993, 28
2. Ibid
3. Ibid, 30.
4. *Sports Illustrated,* June, 1935, 17
5. *Sports Illustrated,* June 3, 1957
6. *The Sporting News,* May 4, 1944, 777
7. *Ludington Daily News,* Aprill 7, 1971, 148
8. Ibid
9. Ibid
10. *Dunkirk* (NY) *Evening Observer,* April 10, 1944, 12

Chapter Three

1. *Tucson Daily Citizen,* June 7, 1945, 122
2. *Tucson Daily Citizen,* February 7, 1945, 12

Chapter Four

1. *Brooklyn Daily Eagle*, May 8, 1948, 6
2. Vitti, Jim, *Cubs on Catalina*, New York, Settefrati Publishing, 147

Chapter Five

1. *The Sporting News*, April 4, 1962, 16.2
2. Vitti, Jim, *Cubs on Catalina*, New York, Settefrati Publishing, 2003, 32.
3. Ibid

Chapter Six

1. *The Charleston (SC) Daily Mail*, August 11, 1959, 92
2. Ibid
3. Ibid
4. *The Sporting News*, April 26, 1950, 15
5. Ibid
6. *Sports Illustrated*, October 7, 1985
7. *The Times Herald Record*, August 1, 1972, 57
8. Ibid

Chapter Seven

1. *The Sporting News*, December 5, 1951, 34
2. *Baseball Digest*, April 1965, 72

Chapter Eight

1. *The Sporting News*, August 9, 1956,
2. Ibid
3. *The Sporting News*, March 18, 1953, 2
4. Ibid
5. *The Sporting News*, March 18, 1953, 28
6. *The Sporting News*, June 3, 1953, 35
7. Ibid

8. Ibid
9. *The Sporting News*, June 3, 1953, 35
10. Ibid
11. *The Sporting News*, April 22, 1953, 26
12. Ibid
13. *The Sporting News*, July 6, 1955, 3
14. *Baseball Digest*, April 1965, 72
15. Ibid
16. *The Sporting News*, March 5, 1958, 23
17. *The Sporting News*, October 7, 1953, 29
18. *Long Beach Press Telegram*, May 19, 1955, A 20

Chapter Nine

1. *Philadelphia Bulletin*, March 29, 1961, 14
2. www.thisgreatgame.com/stevens
3. Ibid
4. *Los Angeles Times*, June 9, 2005, 1
5. *The Sporting News*, July 7, 1954, 25
6. *Long Beach Press Telegram*, June 8, 1954, A 12
7. *The Sporting News*, June 13, 1954, 30
8. *Long Beach Press Telegram*, June 8, 1954, A 12
9. *Long Beach Independent*, May 12, 1955, 21
10. Ibid
11. Ibid
12. Ibid
13. *The Sporting News*, April 6, 1955, 29
14. *Long Beach Press Telegram*, April 28, 1953, 25
15. Vitti, Jim, *Cubs on Catalina*, New York, Settefrati Publishing, 2003, 33

Chapter Ten

1. *The Sporting News*, June 27, 1956, 25
2. *The Bakersfield Californian*, March 24, 1956, 42
3.White, Gaylon H., *The Bilko Athletic Club*, New York, Rowman & Littlefield, 2014, 74
4. *Long Beach Press Telegram*, June 6, 1954, A 12
5. *Sports Hollywood*, July 4, 2013
6. *The Sporting News*, May 2, 1956, 26

7. White, Gaylon H. *The Bilko Athletic Club,* New York, Rowman & Littlefield, 2014, xxi.
8. *The Sporting News,* June 6, 1956, 15
9. *The Sporting News,* August 1, 1956, 26
10. *Sports Hollywood,* July 4, 2013
11. White, Gaylon, H. *The Bilko Athletic Club,* New York, Rowman & Littlefield, 2014, 63.
12. Ibid
13. *The Sporting News,* August 1, 1956, 26
14. *The Sporting News,* June 27, 1956, 25
15. *Long Beach Independent,* July 13, 1956, 19
16. *Long Beach Press Telegram,* August 12, 1956, A 12
17. Ibid
18. Klima, John, *Willie's Boys,* Hoboken, N.J., John Wiley & Sons, 266
19. *Long Beach Press Telegram,* August 3, 1956, 12

Chapter Eleven

1. *The Sporting News,* April 10, 1957, 6
2. Magee, David and Shirley, Phillip, *Sweet Spot: 125 Years with Baseball and Louisville Slugger,* Chicago, Triumph, 2009, 75.
3. Ibid
4. Ibid
5. *The Sporting News,* April 10, 1957, 6
6. *The Sporting News,* April 10, 1957, 6
7. *Lubbock* (TX) *Morning Avalanche,* April 30, 1957, D 1
8. *The Lowell* (MA) *Sun,* March 14, 1957, 24
9. *The Lowell* (MA) *Sun,* April 9, 1957, 14
10. *The Sporting News,* April 10, 1957, 6
11. *The Sporting News,* May 1, 1957, 19
12. Ibid
13. White, Gaylon H., *The Bilko Athletic Club,* New York, Rowman & Littlefield, 116
14. *The Sporting News,* December 18, 1957, 18
15. *Sports Illustrated,* April 29, 1963, 8
16. *The Sporting News,* December 4, 1957, 14
17. Ibid
18. Ibid
19. *The Sporting News,* December 4, 1957, 14

Chapter Twelve

1. *The Sporting News*, April 27, 1960, 8
2. Ibid
3. Ibid
4. *The Sporting News*, June 1, 1956
5. Ibid
6. *The Sporting News*, December 18, 1957, 187
7. *The Sporting News*, December 4, 1957, 14
8. Ibid
9. *The Sporting News*, June 11, 1958, 53
10. *Morgantown* (W. Va) *Post*, June 15, 1958, 56
11. Thornely, Stew, *On to Nicollet: The Glory and Fame of the Minneapolis Millers*, Minneapolis, Nodin Press, 1988
12. *The Sporting News*, October 8, 1958, 27
13. *The Sporting News*, December 18, 1959, 15
14. *The Sporting News*, April 22, 1959, 17
15. Ibid
16. Ibid
17. Thornely, Stew, *On to Nicollet: The Glory and Fame of the Minneapolis Millers*, Minneapolis, Nodin Press, 1988
18. Ibid
19. Ibid
20. Yasztrzemski, Carl and Hirshberg, Al, *Yaz*, New York, Viking Press, 1968, 96
21. Ibid
22. Ibid
23. Thornely, Stew, *On to Nicollet: The Glory and Fame of the Minneapolis Millers*, Minneapolis, Nodin Press, 1988, 5

Chapter Thirteen

1. *The Sporting News*, December 16, 1959, 2
2. *The Sporting News*, December 18, 1959, 18
3. Ibid
4. *The Sporting News*, April 20, 1960, 26
5. *Delaware County Daily Times*, April 15, 1960, 14
6. *The Sporting News*, April 20, 1960, 26
7. *The Sporting News*, May 25, 1960, 17
8. *The Sporting News*, June 14, 1961, 33

9. *The Lima* (Ohio) *News*, May 16, 1960, 17
10. Ibid
11. Ibid
12. *The Sporting News*, July 6, 1960, 27
13. *The Sporting News*, August 31, 1960, 20
14. *The Sporting News*, August 9, 1961, 14
15. *Daily Illini*, December 16, 1960, 1
16. Ibid
17. *Delaware County* (PA) *Daily Times*, March 16, 1965, 16
18. *The Sporting News*, April 5, 1961, 8
19. Ibid
20. Ibid
21. *The Sporting News*, May 3, 1961, 12
22. *The Sporting News*, August 30, 1961, 28
23. Ibid
24. *The Sporting News*, August 30, 1961, 28
25. Ibid
26. Ibid
27. *The Sporting News*, August 30, 1961, 8
28. *Sports Illustrated*, April 29, 1963
29. *The Sporting News*, August 30, 1961, 8
30. Ibid

Chapter Fourteen

1. *The Sporting News*, August 18, 1962, 15
2. *The Sporting News*, June 30, 1962, 7
3. *The Sporting News*, August 18, 1962, 15
4. *The Sporting News*, June 30, 1962, 7
5. *The Sporting News*, June 30, 1962, 25
6. *The Sporting News*, October 10, 1962, 29
7. Ibid
8. *The Sporting News*, August 18, 1962, 15
9. *The Sporting News*, January 4, 1964, 36
10. *The Sporting News*, August 18, 1962, 15.
11. *The Sporting News*, July 2, 1963, 7

Chapter Fifteen

1. *The Sporting News*, May 23, 1964, 3
2. *Daily Times*, April 9, 1964, 1
3. *The Sporting News*, May 23, 1964, 3
4. Ibid
5. *The Sporting News*, June 20, 1964, 6
6. *The Sporting News*, July 2, 1966, 6
7. *The Sporting News*, September 5, 1964, 6
8. *The Sporting News*, October 3, 1964, 32
9. Ibid
10. Ibid
11. *The Sporting News*, October 3, 1964, 32
12. Ibid
13. *The Sporting News*, May 2, 1964, 21
14. Ibid
15. Ibid

Chapter Sixteen

1. *The Sporting News*, 31 February 26, 1966
2. Ibid
3. *The Sporting News*, May 8, 1965,
4. Ibid
5. *The Sporting News*, May 8, 1965, 17
6. Ibid
7. Delaware County (PA) Daily Times, May 26, 1965, 27
8. Ibid
9. *The Sporting News*, October 3, 1964, 32
10. Ibid
11. Ibid
12. *The Sporting News*, July 2, 1966, 6
13. Thomas, Frank, *Kiss it Goodbye: The Frank Thomas Story*, Dunkirk, Md., 2005, 462
14. Ibid
15. Jenkins, Fergie, and Freedman, Lew, *Fergie: From the Cubs to Cooperstown*, Chicago, Triumph Books, 2009, 32
16. *The Sporting News*, February 26, 1966, 31
17. *The Sporting News*, July 2, 1966, 6
18. *The Sporting News*, May 7, 1966, 8

19. *The Sporting News,* July 2, 1966, 6

Chapter Seventeen

1. *The Sporting News,* February 18, 1967, 29
2. Ibid
3. *Sports Illustrated,* August 7, 1967, 14
4. Ibid
5. Ibid
6. Ibid
7. Ibid
8. *The Sporting News,* May 3, 1969, 20

Chapter Eighteen

1. *The Sporting News* May 3, 1969, 20
2. Ibid
3. *Delaware County* (PA) *Daily Times,* April 15, 1969, 18
4. *The Lethbridge Herald,* May 26, 1969, 10
5. *The Lethbridge Herald,* June 4, 1969, 12
6. *The Sporting News,* May 2, 1970, 21
7. *The Sporting News,* July 19, 1969, 19
8. Ibid
9. *The Sporting News,* March 7, 1970, 19
10. *The Sporting News,* January 8, 1972, 40
11. Ibid
12. Ibid
13. *The Sporting News,* October 2, 1971, 18
14. *Evening Observer* (NY), June 26, 1972, 18
15.
16. *Chicago Tribune,* May 5, 2007, 2
17. *Camden* (NJ) *News,* September 21, 1972, 11
18. *The Sporting News,* February 17, 1973, 44
19. *The Sporting News,* September 8, 1973, 36
20. *The Sporting News,* December 22, 1973, 43
21. *The Sporting News,* October 25, 1975, 19
22. Ibid
23. Ibid
24. Ibid

Chapter Twenty

1. *The Sporting News*, June 13, 1981, 27
2. *The Sporting News*, August 1, 1982, 27
3. *The Sporting News*, December 26, 1981, 39

Chapter Twenty-One

1. *The Sporting News*, February 10, 1973, 51
2. *The Sporting News*, August 1, 1982, 27
3. *Los Angeles Times*, February 13, 1986,1
4. *The Sporting News*, October 11, 1982, 37
5. *Baseball Digest*, March-April, 2008, 70
6. *The Orange County Register*, October 11, 1982, D 1

Chapter Twenty-Three

1. *The Orange County Register*, October 10, 1984, D 6
2. *The Sporting News*, May 12, 1986, 12

Chapter Twenty-Four

1. *The Sporting News*, May 12, 1986, 12
2. *The Sporting News*, March 6, 1982, 19
3. *Los Angeles Times*, August 27, 1986, 1
4. *The Orange County Register*, October 16, 1986, 1

Chapter Twenty-Five

1. *Los Angeles Daily News*, May 10, 1987, 1

Bibliography

Anderson, Dave, *Pennant Races*, New York, Doubleday, 1994

Barney, Rex and Macht, Norman L., *Rex Barney's Thank Youuuu*, Centreville, Md., Tidewater Publishing, 1993.

Beverage, Richard, *The Los Angeles Angels of the Pacific Coast League*, Jefferson, NC, McFarland and Company, 2011

Brosnan, Jim, *Pennant Race*, New York, Harper & Brothers, 1962,
.

Carew, Rod with Berkow, Ira, *Carew*, New York, Simon and Schuster, 1979

Conlin, Bill, *Batting Cleanup*, Philadelphia, Temple University Press, 1997

Cook, William A., *The Summer of '64, A Pennant Lost*, Jefferson, NC., McFarland, 2002.

Dickson, Paul, *The Hidden Language of Baseball*, New York Walker and Company, 2003.

Dobbins, Dick, *The Grand Minor League: An Oral History of the Pacific Coast League*, Emeryville, CA., Woodford Press, 1999

Dolson, Frank, *Jim Bunning: Baseball and Beyond*, Philadelphia, Temple University Press, 1998.

Drysdale, Don with Verdi, Bob, *Once a Bum, Always a Dodger*, New York, St. Martin's Press 1990.

Grow, David, *We're Going to Win Twins*, Minneapolis, University of Minnesota Press, 1976.

Halberstam, David, *October 1964*, New York, Villard Books, 1994.

Jenkins, Fergie with Freedman, Lew, *My Life From the Cubs to Coopers-*

town, Chicago, Triumph Books, 2009.

Koppett, Leonard, *The Man in the Dugout,Baseball's Top Managers and How They Got That Way*, Philadelphia, Temple University Press, 2000.

Luciano, Ron and Fisher, David, *Remembrance of Swings Past*, New York, Bantam Books, 1988.

Nemec, David, *The Official Rules of Baseball*, New York, Barnes and Noble 1994.

Newhan, Ross, *The Anaheim Angels: A Complete History*, New York, Hyperion, 2000.

Richter, Ed, *View from the Dugout, A Season With Baseball's Amazing Gene Mauch*, Philadelphia, Chilton, 1964.

Sowell, Mike, *One Pitch Away, The Players' Stories of the 1986 League Championships and World Series*, New York, Macmillan, 1995.

Swaine, Rick, *The Integration of Major League Baseball*, Jefferson, N.C., McFarland and Company Inc, 2009

Thornley, Stew, *The Glory and Fame of the Minneapolis Millers*, Minneapolis, Nodin Press, 1988.

Turner, Dan, *The Expos, Inside Out*, Toronto, McClelland and Stewart Limited, 1983.

Turbow, Jason with Duca, Michael, *The Baseball Codes*, Pantheon Books, 2010.

Vitti, Jim, *The Cubs on Catalina*, Settefrati Press, 2003.

White, Gaylon H., The Bilko Athletic Club, The Story of the 1956 Los Angeles Angels, New York, Rowan & Littlefield, 2014.

Will, George F., *Men at Work*, New York, Macmillan Publishing Co, 1990.

Yastrzemski, Carl and Hirshberg, Al, *Yaz*, New York, Viking Press, 1968.

Quotes

Gene Mauch was certainly one of the most quotable managers in baseball history. Here is a sample.

"If it's true you learn from adversity, I must be the smartest guy in the world."

"Baseball and malaria keep coming back."

"I'm not the manager because I'm always right, but I'm always right because I'm the manager."

"Losing streaks are funny. If you lose at the beginning you got off to a bad start. If you lose in the middle of the season, you're in a slump. If you lose at the end, you're choking."

"Most one run games are lost, not won."

"The worst thing is the day you realize you want to win more than the players do."

"You can't lead anyone else further than you have."

"He (Gaylord Perry) should be in the Hall of Fame with a tube of KY jelly attached to the plaque."

"He (Don Drysdale) talks very well for a guy who's had two fingers in his mouth all his life."

"He (Sandy Koufax) throws a 'radio ball,' a pitch you hear but you don't see."

"Play him (Dick Allen), fine him, and play him again."

"You have to bear in mind that Mr. Autry's favorite horse was named Champion. He ain't ever had one called Runner UP."

"If it's true you learn from adversity, I must be the smartest SOB in the world."

"Close only counts in dancing and grenades."

"I don't know everything there is to know about baseball but there isn't anyone who knows more."

"He (Jim Cox) majored in micro-biology and minored in hanging sliders."

"A man feels pressure only when he doesn't know what he is doing."

"Brian Downing would rather eat green flies than lead off."

"I don't believe in curses. I believe in a good bullpen."

Gene Mauch's Manager Records

RK	Year	Age	Team	League		W	L	WP%	G	Finish
1	1960	34	Philadelphia	NL	3rd of 3	58	94	.382	152	8
2	1961	35	Philadelphia	NL		47	107	.305	155	8
3	1962	36	Philadelphia	NL		81	80	.503	161	7
4	1963	37	Philadelphia	NL		87	75	.537	162	4
5	1964	38	Philadelphia	NL		92	70	.568	162	2
6	1965	39	Philadelphia	NL		85	76	.528	162	6
7	1966	40	Philadelphia	NL		87	75	.537	162	4
8	1967	41	Philadelphia	NL		82	80	.506	162	5
9	1968	42	Philadelphia	NL	1st of 3	27	27	.500	54	7
10	1969	43	Montreal	NL		52	101	.321	162	6
11	1970	44	Montreal	NL		73	89	.451	162	6
12	1971	45	Montreal	NL		71	90	.441	162	5
13	1972	46	Montreal	NL		70	86	.449	156	5
14	1973	47	Montreal	NL		79	83	.488	162	4
15	1974	48	Montreal	NL		79	82	.491	161	4
16	1975	49	Montreal	NL		75	87	.463	162	5
17	1976	50	Minnesota	AL		85	77	.525	162	3
18	1977	51	Minnesota	AL		84	77	.522	161	4
19	1978	52	Minnesota	AL		73	89	.451	162	4
20	1979	53	Minnesota	AL		82	80	.506	162	4
21	1980	54	Minnesota	AL	1st of 2	54	71	.432	125	3
22	1981	55	California	AL	2nd of 2	9	4 First Half	.692	13	4
23	1981	55	California	AL	2nd of 2	20	30 Second Half	.400	50	7
24	1982	56	California	AL		93	69	.574	162	1
25	1985	59	California	AL		90	72	.556	162	2
26	1986	60	California	AL		92	70	.568	162	1
27	1987	61	California	AL		75	87	.463	162	7
26 Years						1902	2037	.483	3942	

Gene Mauch's Major League Managerial Stats

Gene Mauch's Player Records

Year	Team	Level	G	AB	R	H	2B	3B	HR	RBI	BB	SO	SB	BA
1943	Durham	B	32	115		37	5	1	0					.322
1943	Montreal	AA	31	77	5	13	1	0	0	4	11	5	1	.169
1944	Montreal	AA	14	53	12	15	0	0	0	2	7	2	1	.283
1946	St. Paul	AAA	149	536	74	133	19	3	6	55	91	68	9	.248
1947	Indianapolis	AAA	58	217	37	65	13	4	0	16	39	14	1	.300
1951	Milwaukee	AAA	37	109	30	33	2	0	1	16	26	10	2	.303
1952	Milwaukee	AAA	102	327	58	106	24	3	4	60	58	19	7	.324
1953	Atlanta	AA	111	340	65	91	23	3	9	51	71	19	3	.268
1954	Los Angeles	Open	153	565	81	162	26	2	11	58	65	55	12	.287
1955	Los Angeles	Open	155	584	93	173	37	4	8	49	59	38	22	.296
1956	Los Angeles	Open	146	566	123	197	29	3	20	84	70	43	2	.348
1958	Minneapolis	AAA	65	210	25	51	12	2	3	29	26	19	5	.243
1959	Minneapolis	AAA	8	8	1	4	0	0	0	0				.500

Gene Mauch's Minor League Player Stats

Year	Team	League	G	AB	R	H	2B	3B	HR	RBI	BB	SO	SB	BA
1944	Brooklyn	NL	5	15	2	2	1	0	0	2	2	3	0	.133
1947	Pittsburgh	NL	16	30	8	9	0	0	0	1	7	6	0	.300
1948	Chicago	NL	53	138	18	28	3	2	1	7	26	10	1	.203
1949	Chicago	NL	72	150	15	37	6	2	1	7	21	15	3	.247
1950	Boston	NL	48	121	17	28	5	0	1	15	14	9	1	.231
1951	Boston	NL	19	20	5	2	0	0	0	1	7	4	0	.100
1952	St. Louis	NL	7	3	0	0	0	0	0	0	1	2	0	.000
1956	Boston	AL	7	25	4	8	0	0	0	1	3	3	0	.320
1957	Boston	AL	65	222	23	60	10	3	2	28	22	26	1	.270
9 Years			**304**	**737**	**93**	**176**	**25**	**7**	**5**	**62**	**104**	**82**	**6**	**.239**

Gene Mauch's Major League Player Stats